1004501654

D0116237

ADDRESSING CULTURAL COMPLEXITIES IN PRACTICE

A FRAMEWORK FOR CLINICIANS AND COUNSELORS

PAMELA A. HAYS, PhD

AMERICAN PSYCHOLOGICAL ASSOCIATION
WASHINGTON, DC

ADDRESSING CULTURAL COMPLEXITIES IN PRACTICE

LIBRARY
GRANT MacEWAN
COLLEGE

Copyright © 2001 by the American Psychological Association. All rights reserved. Except as permitted under the United States Copyright Act of 1976, no part of this publication may be reproduced or distributed in any form or by any means, or stored in a database or retrieval system, without the prior written permission of the publisher.

First printing April 2001
Second printing November 2001
Third printing October 2002
Fourth printing June 2004
Fifth printing November 2004
Sixth printing October 2005

Published by
American Psychological Association
750 First Street, NE
Washington, DC 20002
www.apa.org

To order
APA Order Department
P.O. Box 92984
Washington, DC 20090-2984
Tel: (800) 374-2721, Direct: (202) 336-5510
Fax: (202) 336-5502, TDD/TTY: (202) 336-6123
Online: www.apa.org/books/
Email: order@apa.org

In the U.K., Europe, Africa, and the Middle East, copies may be ordered from
American Psychological Association
3 Henrietta Street
Covent Garden, London
WC2E 8LU England

Typeset in Meridian by Innovation Publication Services

Printer: Automated Graphic Systems, White Plains, MD
Cover Designer: Nini Sarmiento, NiDesign, Baltimore, MD
Technical/Production Editor: Innovation Publication Services, Philadelphia, PA

The opinions and statements published are the responsibility of the authors, and such opinions and statements do not necessarily represent the policies of the American Psychological Association.

Library of Congress Cataloging-in-Publication Data
Hays, Pamela A.
    Addressing cultural complexities in practice: a framework for clinicians and counselors /Pamela A. Hays—1st ed.
      p. cm.
    Includes bibliographical references and index.
    ISBN 1-55798-768-8
    1. Cross-cultural counseling. 2. Psychotherapy. I. Title.

    BF637.C6 H367 2001
    158'.3—dc21   2001022341

British Library Cataloguing-in-Publication Data
A CIP record is available from the British Library.

Printed in the United States of America

For Marjorie J. Hays and Hugh R. Hays

Contents

Acknowledgments

The first person I must thank is Margery Ginsberg, who pulled the word ADDRESSING out of the earlier (and easily forgettable) acronym I had been using. Next, I want to thank Peg LeVine for her contribution of "I" in reference to Indigenous people, which allows for an individual's diversity within this group's identity across nations. I am also grateful for the stimulating discussions Peg and I had early on regarding this new approach to multicultural counseling.

I am equally grateful to the following friends and colleagues for their suggestions and encouragement: Mary Ann Boyle, Richard Dana, Ned Farley, Janice Hoshino, Gwen Jones, Kamuela Ka'Ahanui, Carolyn Bereznak Kenny, Lina LePage, Anthony J. Marsella, Bob McCard, John Moritsugu, Jan Santora, Isadora Arévalo Wong, Lisa Zaidi, and Jawed Zouari. I would also like to thank the staff of the American Psychological Association books Department, particularly Susan Reynolds, Acquisitions Editor and Ed Meidenbauer, Development Editor; Peg Markow, Managing Editor of Innovation Publishing Services; and the outside reviewers.

Finally, none of the case examples in this book are of real people—all are composites. I deliberately chose to use names rather than initials for these examples, because familiarity with names from diverse cultures is an important part of one's cross-cultural knowledge base.

INTRODUCTION

Seeing the Forest and the Trees: The Complexities of Culture in Practice

1

In the mid-1970s, I graduated from high school and left my family home in Soldotna, Alaska, to attend college at New Mexico State University (NMSU). I had chosen NMSU because it met my three criteria: (a) it had a late admissions deadline, (b) it was someplace far away that I'd never been before, and (c) the climate was hot. (It also turned out to have some very good professors, but that was not on my mind at the time.)

A large proportion of the students at NMSU were Latino, and in those days, in New Mexico, people of Latino heritage referred to themselves as "Spanish." I was not Spanish, nor did I speak Spanish, but I wanted to learn. I remember one day talking with some friends about Spanish surnames. I was impressed that they all seemed to know which surnames were Spanish and which were not, and I wanted to know how they knew. "Take the name García," I said in all sincerity, glancing at the sign over García Hall. "Is that a Spanish name?" When the laughter died down, my friend Anita said, "Yes, it is." "But how do you know?" I replied, a bit frustrated. She patiently answered, "I don't know how I know; I just know."

During the past couple of decades, as North Americans have moved from an assimilationist orientation regarding cultures to one that recognizes and (at some levels of society) values differences, therapists are being expected to "just know" increasingly more about the cultural influences relevant to a growing number of minority groups. This expectation may feel frustrating and, at times, even overwhelming. Fortunately, in response to the need for more information, multicultural research has expanded rapidly since the 1970s, with whole fields of research being developed with specific populations (Fukuyama, 1990; Hays, 1996a).

At this point, the most common approach among U.S.-oriented multicultural counseling texts is to provide one chapter on African Americans, one on Asian Americans, one on Native Americans, and one on Latino Americans. Separate books exist for working with gay and lesbian clients, older people, people who have disabilities, and women (see reference list). I have found this focus on ethnicity to be helpful for certain aspects of multicultural education; however, the one-chapter-per-group approach has its limitations, namely that most people do not think of themselves in such unidimensional terms. Rather, there are Latino and Latina elders, lesbian and gay people who have disabilities, Jewish and Christian people who have immigrated and speak English as a second language, poor Euroamerican women who are homeless—and the list goes on of people whose identities are complex, multidimensional, and frequently changing depending on the context (Myers et al., 1991; Pedersen, 1990; Root, 1996).

A related limitation of the one-chapter-per-group approach is that the groups commonly chosen (i.e., African, Asian, Latino, and Native American) are not necessarily relevant to therapists practicing outside the United States. Hogan (1995) estimated that less than 40% of psychologists now live in the United States. As political changes have led to increasing numbers of immigrants and refugees internationally (Marsella, Bornemann, Ekblad, & Orley, 1994), and Indigenous people have become more politically active and visible (Adams, 1995; Adelson, 2000; Kidd, 1997; Young, 1995), cross-cultural issues in counseling, social work, and clinical psychology are gaining recognition in many countries and regions, including Canada (Waxler-Morrison, Anderson, & Richardson, 1990), Australia (Adams & Gilbert, 1998; Cox, 1989), New Zealand (Greenwood, 2000), Hong Kong (Spinks & Kao, 1995), South Africa (Louw, 1995), China (Lee & Gong, 1996), Indonesia (Sarwono, 1996), and sub-Saharan Africa (Ebigbo, Oluka, Ezenwa, Obidigbo, & Okwaraji, 1996). Increasingly, practitioners are recognizing the need for information that addresses the complexity of clients' and therapists' lives beyond as well as within U.S. borders (D'Andrea, 1999; Sleek, 1998; Sunar, 1996).

In this book, I present a practitioner-oriented framework that I have found helpful in training therapists of diverse identities and origins to work effectively with clients of complex and multidimensional identities. This framework outlines specific principles and guidelines for working with people of minority, dominant, and mixed cultural groups, and it makes use of case examples, anecdotes, and the research literature to describe and illustrate this work. I call it the ADDRESSING framework.

The ADDRESSING Framework

In an effort to focus practitioners' attention on those groups that have traditionally been neglected, professional organizations in the United States and Canada have issued a number of publications aimed at educating clinicians. "Guidelines for Providers of Psychological Services to Ethnic, Linguistic, and Culturally Diverse Populations" have been endorsed by the American Psychological Association (APA, 1993), as has "Multicultural Counseling Competencies and Standards" by the American Counseling Association (Sue,

Arrendondo, & McDavis, 1992, further operationalized by Arrendondo et al., 1996). Both the APA (1992) and the Canadian Psychological Association (1991) have revised their ethical guidelines to attend to cultural issues. Together, these guidelines call attention to the following cultural influences (with related minority groups noted in parentheses):

■ age and generational influences (e.g., children, adolescents, elders)
■ disability (e.g., people who have developmental or acquired physical, cognitive, psychological disabilities)
■ religion and spiritual orientation (e.g., people of Muslim, Jewish, Buddhist, Hindu, other minority religions and faiths)
■ ethnicity (e.g., people of Asian, South Asian, Pacific Islander, Latino, African, African American, Arab, Middle Eastern heritage)
■ socioeconomic status (e.g., people of lower status by occupation, education, income, rural or urban habitat, family name)
■ sexual orientation (e.g., people who are gay, lesbian, bisexual)
■ Indigenous heritage (e.g., in North America—American Indians, Alaska Natives, Inuit, Métis, Pacific Americans, including Native Hawaiians, Samoans, and the Chamorro people of Guam)
■ national origin (e.g., immigrants, refugees, international students); and
■ gender (e.g., women, transgender people)

Given the impossibility of any one therapist holding insider-level expertise with all of the influences and groups included in this list, what is needed as a first step toward culturally responsive therapy is a system of organization. The ADDRESSING framework offers a system for organizing and addressing these cultural influences and groups in the form of an acronym: **A**ge and generational influences, **D**evelopmental and acquired **D**isabilities, **R**eligion and spiritual orientation, **E**thnicity, **S**ocioeconomic status, **S**exual orientation, **I**ndigenous heritage, **N**ational origin, and **G**ender (Hays, 1996a).

The ADDRESSING framework conceptualizes cross-cultural work as involving two broad categories of effort by the therapist. The first category concerns the therapist's personal self-exploration and growth; key to this process is a growing understanding of the influence of culture on one's own belief system and worldview. The second category consists of the therapist's self-education about clients' cultures, which usually leads to a deeper understanding of clients. These two "paths" have been described by Aponte (1994) as "reaching within to understand" and "reaching out to understand" (pp. 188–189). In clinical work, the two areas frequently overlap.

THE THERAPIST'S PERSONAL WORK

The ADDRESSING approach begins with an emphasis on understanding the impact on therapists' worldviews of diverse cultural influences (e.g., of therapists' age and generational experiences, experience or inexperience with disability, religious or spiritual upbringing, ethnicity, and so on). Through a series of exercises, therapists can explore their own identities in relation to each of the ADDRESSING influences. By recognizing the areas in which they are members of dominant groups, therapists will become more aware of the ways in which such identities can limit their knowledge base and experience, particularly regarding minority cultures of which they are not members.

Therapists are encouraged to pay special attention to the role of privilege, defined as the advantages one holds as a result of membership in a dominant group (see McIntosh, 1998). The areas in which a therapist holds privilege vary depending on the particular therapist's identity. In general, one's knowledge base and experience are greater in those areas in which one is a member of a nondominant group. For example, as a result of her membership in a sexual minority group, a middle-class Euroamerican lesbian therapist is more likely to be aware of the subtle sexist and heterosexist biases against lesbian, gay, and bisexual clients. However, this does not mean that she will automatically hold greater awareness with regard to people of color, people who have disabilities, or people of lower socioeconomic status; the privileges she holds in relation to her ethnicity, education, and professional status will generally work to separate her from people who do not hold such privileges. Furthermore, if her friends and family are relatively homogeneous with regard to ethnicity, social class, and disability, she will have to work hard to find sources of information that challenge her assumptions, biases, and ways of seeing the world.

LEARNING ABOUT CLIENTS' CULTURES

Research suggests that at the level of the individual, prejudice is lower when one holds the "knowledge structures" to categorize others as having multiple group memberships (Hamilton, 1981; Sun, 1993). By calling attention to these multiple memberships and identities, the ADDRESSING framework helps therapists avoid making inaccurate generalizations on the basis of a client's physical appearance, language abilities, and/or family name.

For example, using the ADDRESSING acronym as a guide, a therapist attempting to understand an older man of East Indian heritage would not consider as sufficient a general understanding of values, beliefs, and behaviors considered common among East Indian people. Rather, the therapist would want answers to the following questions:

- What are the **A**ge-related issues and generational influences on this client, particularly given his status as a second-generation immigrant?
- What is this man's experience with **D**isability? That is, might he have a disability that is not immediately apparent or have experienced the impact of disability as a caregiver for a partner, parent, or child?
- What was his **R**eligious upbringing, and what are his current beliefs and practices? (Reasonable hypotheses would be that he is Hindu or Muslim or Sikh, but any one of these cannot be assumed; see Almeida, 1996.)
- What is the meaning of his **E**thnic identity in an urban area where he is often mistaken by non-Indians to be Pakistani or Arab?
- What is his current **S**ocioeconomic status as defined by his occupation, income, education, marital status, gender, ethnicity, community, and family name, and might this status be different from that of his parents before their immigration?
- What is the client's **S**exual orientation, not assuming heterosexuality simply because he has been married?

▪ Might he hold **I**ndigenous heritage in his premigration history?

▪ What is his **N**ational identity (Indian, that of his country of residence, both, or neither?) and primary language (Hindi, English, or other language?)?

▪ Finally, what **G**ender-related information (e.g., regarding roles, expectations, and relationships) is significant given the client's cultural heritage and identity as a whole? (See Assanand, Dias, Richardson, & Waxler-Morrison, 1990, and Almeida, 1996, regarding the diversity of South Asians.)

Around the world, it is now common to find individuals who hold more than one cultural identity simultaneously. Biethnic and multiethnic people may identify strongly with the differing minority and majority identities of their parents and grandparents (Root, 1996). People of Indigenous cultures frequently identify simultaneously with a particular band or community, a larger Indigenous culture, and a national and non-Indigenous society (e.g., see Allen, 1998, regarding the assessment of cultural identity among American Indians and Alaska Natives). For example, in Hawaii, the same individual may identify as Native Hawaiian, as an Indigenous or Aboriginal person, and as an American (K. Ka'Ahanui, personal communication, July 1, 2000).

Similarly, many individuals hold a combination of ethnic and nonethnic identities (Comas-Díaz & Greene, 1994a; Hays, 1996c; Hermans & Kempen, 1998; Marsella, 1998; Robinson & Howard-Hamilton, 2000). For instance, a gay man of Filipino heritage may identify with a predominantly heterosexual Filipino community but also be involved in a politically active, mostly Euroamerican gay community; the salience of these identities may vary depending on the particular environment in which he finds himself (Chan, 1992).

Although therapists will not necessarily ask clients all of the questions raised by the ADDRESSING framework, they would certainly want to consider the relevance of each category and gather more information about the influences and identities that seem important to the client. With a focus on one identity at a time, many excellent books have been written on working with members of the four largest ethnic and racial minority groups in the United States, including African Americans (Bass, Wyatt, & Powell, 1982; Boyd-Franklin, 1989); Asian Americans (E. Lee, 1997; Uba, 1994); American Indians and Alaska Natives (Herring, 1999; Swan Reimer, 1999; Swinomish Tribal Community, 1991); Latinos and Latinas (Falicov, 1998; Geisinger, 1992; LeVine & Padilla, 1980); English-speaking West Indians (Gopaul-McNicol, 1993); and on the first four of these groups (Aponte, Rivers, & Wohl; 1995; Atkinson, Morten, & Sue, 1993; Baruth & Manning, 1991; Dana, 1993; Ho, 1987; C. Lee, 1997, who also adds Arab Americans; Paniagua, 1998; Ponterotto & Casas, 1991; Sue, Ivey, & Pedersen, 1996; Sue & Sue, 1999).

A variety of U.S. ethnic groups were addressed by McAdoo (1999), an even greater number by McGoldrick, Giordano, and Pearce (1996), and with regard to children of color by Canino and Spurlock (1994), Johnson-Powell and Yamamoto (1997), and Gibbs, Huang, and Associates (1989). Canadian and Australian ethnic minority cultures have been well-covered by Waxler-Morrison, Anderson, and Richardson (1990) and Pauwels (1985), respectively, although neither fully addresses Aboriginal peoples' concerns.

There are also feminist therapy books that focus on women of diverse identities (Brown & Root, 1990; Comaz-Díaz & Greene, 1994b). And there are texts on assessment and counseling with diverse gay, lesbian, and bisexual people (Dworkin & Gutiérrez, 1992); people of religious and spiritual faiths (Burke & Miranti, 1995; Fukuyama & Sevig, 1999; Kelly, 1995; Lovinger, 1984; Miller, 1999; Shafranske, 1996); elders (Brink, 1986; Burlingame, 1999; Duffy, 1999; Nordhus, VandenBos, Berg, & Fromholt, 1998; Storandt &VandenBos, 1994; Zarit & Knight, 1996); refugees (Marsella, Bornemann, Ekblad, & Orley, 1994); and people with disabilities (Krueger, 1984; Maki & Riggar, 1997a; Olkin, 1999).

Why This Book?

Given the impressive list above, you're probably wondering, why write a whole new book? The primary reason is that in teaching and supervising therapists in the United States and abroad, I have been unable to find a practitioner-oriented book that pulls together practical suggestions for assessment, diagnosis, and therapy and that also addresses issues relevant to people of all these overlapping groups. My solution has been to develop a framework that I believe does this. Furthermore, by focusing on individual and family cases, rather than on cultural groups, I have tried to minimize the problems of overgeneralization.

Unfortunately, it proved too difficult to include cases placed outside the United States or Canada, because what constitutes a minority group in one country may be a dominant culture in another. However, I do include examples and cases involving clients and therapists of diverse ethnic and national cultures that are not commonly found in U.S. texts—for example, Indonesian, Tunisian Arab, French Canadian, Haitian, East Indian, Cuban, Kenyan, Chinese Vietnamese, Guatemalan, Filipino, Costa Rican, Korean, Greek, and Alaska Native cultures. And of course these examples involve people of different ages, sexual orientations, religions, physical abilities, and socioeconomic statuses. I do include some cases set in Canada, because the histories of Canada and the United States are parallel in many ways, and their inclusion helps to highlight U.S. assumptions. (See Elliott & Fleras, 1992, regarding multiculturalism in Canada; Takaki, 1993, regarding the United States; and Dobson & Dobson, 1993, for an overview of professional psychology in Canada.)

In the multicultural counseling literature, I have also seen the need for guidelines in specific areas such as cross-cultural testing and diagnosis. Unfortunately, much of the cross-cultural testing literature seems stuck on discussions of the need for better norms (for exceptions see Allen, 2000c; Cuéllar, 1998; Dana, 1993, 2000; Okazaki, 1998; and several others reviewed in chapter 7). Similarly, with regard to diagnosis, there is very little discussion in the multicultural counseling literature of the 4th edition of the *Diagnostic and Statistical Manual of Mental Disorders* (*DSM-IV;* American Psychiatric Association, 1994) and how to use it in a culturally responsive way; such work is found mainly in the psychiatric literature (an exception is Smart & Smart, 1997). For these reasons, I add many practical suggestions regarding assessment, diagnosis, testing, and psychotherapy. These suggestions, along with specific guidelines, are organized in Key Ideas lists following each chapter and may be useful for instructors teaching multicultural counseling courses as well as clinicians.

Another element I've found missing in multicultural texts, especially journal articles, is information about the author's own experiences and perspectives. Sue (1993) and Kiselica (1998) have noted the need for more humanness in the literature, that is, more sharing of personal mistakes and challenges encountered by people doing cross-cultural work. Toward this end, I weave vignettes about my experiences throughout the book in the hope that these examples will give you a feeling for who I am as a person, as well as my areas of expertise and weakness (which, in turn, should help you in assessing the value to you of the information provided). Because I also consider humor to be an under-utilized resource in learning, I include information on humor and occasionally some humorous anecdotes.

Organization of This Book

Chapters 2 and 3 describe specific steps and exercises for facilitating your own cultural self-assessment. Chapter 2 addresses the first and most essential part of cross-cultural work: the therapist's personal self-exploration, including information on values, biases, and the necessity of humility and critical thinking skills in maintaining compassion and preventing defensive behaviors. Chapter 3 provides an example of this self-assessment process with a particular therapist. Specific exercises are offered to help you understand the role of privilege and of your own cultural identity and sociocultural context in your work. Beginning from the assumption that the therapist is engaged in and committed to the self-assessment process, chapter 4 explains in detail how therapists can use the ADDRESSING framework to facilitate their understanding of clients' identities through the formulation of hypotheses and questions that are closer to clients' experiences.

The remaining chapters discuss the use of the ADDRESSING framework in relation to the specific tasks and processes of assessment, diagnosis, and therapy. Chapter 5 outlines considerations in establishing rapport and demonstrating respect with clients of diverse identities. Chapter 6 provides specific suggestions for conducting culturally responsive assessments, including guidelines for working with interpreters. Chapter 7 focuses on standardized testing, including mental status, intellectual, neuropsychological, and personality assessments. Chapter 8 addresses cross-cultural issues in the diagnostic process, particularly with regard to the *DSM-IV*. Chapter 9 describes a range of therapeutic approaches, including culturally related therapies and strategies; the adaptation of some mainstream approaches (e.g., cognitive-behavioral, psychodynamic) with clients of minority groups; nonverbal expressive or creative therapies; and systems-level therapies, including family, couple, group, and sociocultural interventions. Finally, chapter 10 illustrates the use of most of the suggestions in the preceding chapters via the case example of an older African American woman who has a disability and her family, who see an African American male psychologist. Chapter 11 adds some concluding observations.

Concepts and Categories in Multicultural Research

Although the topic of terminology may not sound very interesting, understanding commonly used concepts and categories is an essential aspect of cross-cultural work. A therapist's assumptions, knowledge base, experience, and reference points are all communicated to clients through the use of language (Henley, 1995). Currently, the vast majority of therapists in the United States are Euroamerican (95% of U.S. psychologists—Hammond & Yung, 1993; figures for master's-level therapists and Canadians are not available). In addition, therapists often hold higher social status in relation to clients by virtue of their professional position (e.g., Acosta, Yamamoto, Evans, & Wilcox, 1982). Research indicates that Euroamericans commonly do not think of themselves as having a culture (Pack-Brown, 1999), suggesting that therapists' judgments may be affected by influences of which they are unaware.

Learning why terms have different meanings for different cultures and even different individuals can help to bring some of these assumptions and biases into awareness. In addition, the perspectives of diverse groups are communicated by different concepts, categories, and terms. Four of the most frequently used (and confused) terms in the multicultural literature are *culture, race, ethnicity*, and *minority*.

CULTURE

Culture is the most inclusive term but also the most general. Definitions of culture abound (see Kroeber & Kluckhohn, 1952), but common to most is the idea that culture consists of the "shared elements" involved in "perceiving, believing, evaluating, communicating, and acting" that are passed down from generation to generation with modifications (Triandis, 1996, p. 408). Shared elements include language, history, and geographic location.

Although culture is often equated with race and ethnicity, the most commonly accepted definitions of culture say nothing about biological links (which the concept of race implies), and as such are broad enough to include people of nonethnic groups as well (Pope, 1995). For example, Muslim religious communities within many cities in North America include people of African, Arab, African American, Pakistani, East Indian, Indonesian, and Middle Eastern descent (Abudabbeh, 1996; Bernstein, 1993). For many Muslims, the mosque functions as a cultural center, providing social, financial, and spiritual support for its members. And in North America, prejudiced attitudes emanating from the dominant Judeo-Christian society tend to reinforce a sense of separateness among many Muslims, which in turn increases the latter's sense of themselves as a culture.

RACE

The concept of race was originally used by European scientists to classify people on the basis of geography and physical characteristics (such as skin color, hair texture, or facial features) into groups of genetically related peoples (Spickard, 1992). Over the years, researchers made up differing classification schemes that emphasized a wide range of factors from skin tone to tribal affiliations, nationalities, language families, or simply minority status (Thomas & Sillen, 1972). Underlying many of these schemes was the assumption that races were organized hierarchically, with light-skinned, Christian Europeans at the top. Politics and beliefs of the time often determined the choice of a scheme, which in turn reinforced racist beliefs and laws. For example, the illegality of interracial marriage in many U.S. states until 1967 reflected the common belief that "White blood" could be tainted by "Black blood." Hence, in nine states at the turn of the century, a child of predominantly European ancestry and even one great-grandparent of African heritage was for legal purposes considered a "Negro" (Spickard, 1992).

In addition, racial classifications are problematic in that they fail to account for the enormous variation in physical characteristics within the so-called racial groups. For example, many people who self-identify as "White" have skin that is visibly darker than many people who identify themselves as "Black." Most social scientists now recognize that there are no pure gene pools; human beings of dominant and minority cultures are quite mixed, genetically speaking (Betancourt & López, 1993).

Recognizing the danger in presenting race as a biological fact, the United Nations Educational, Scientific, and Cultural Organization (UNESCO) (1979, in Yee, Fairchild, Weizmann, & Wyatt, 1993, p. 1132) passed a statement recommending that the concept of ethnic group replace that of race. However, within the field of psychology, there is still a wide range of opinions on the subject. For research purposes, Johnson (1990) suggested reserving the use of the term for work aimed at demonstrating the effects of racism and progress to eradicate it. However, many researchers continue to conceptualize race as an independent variable synonymous with culture—for example, by comparing Black and White people on test scores or on their responses to particular treatments. Recognizing the controversy, Yee and colleagues recommended that the American Psychological Association establish an interdisciplinary committee to develop "a comprehensive scientific policy on race" that may be used to guide research (p. 1138).

But in clinical practice, use of the term may be necessary because race is an essential aspect of many individuals' self-identification (Glass & Wallace, 1996; Thornton, 1996). As Cornel West (1993) put it, race matters. Currently, in the United States the most commonly used term for people of African ancestry is *African American* (e.g., Moore Hines & Boyd-Franklin, 1996), which communicates an identification based on ethnic and social heritage rather than on racial or physical characteristics. However, since the 1960s, when "Black Pride" led to increased interest among many African Americans in family history and cultural heritage (Boyd-Franklin, 1989), the term *Black* has also acquired a positive connotation. However, language is continually changing, and therapists need to keep in mind that even these two terms may be offensive to some older people, because *Black* and *African* were used derogatorily by White Euroamericans before younger generations reclaimed the terms.

Whether or not a person uses a racial identification, it is helpful to remember that a racial identity in itself provides little information about an individual; it says nothing about a person's educational level, cultural context, religious upbringing, or current environment (Jones, 1987). What is most important with regard to racial identity is an understanding of its meaning—for the individual (if the person conceptualizes her or his identity in this way), for the dominant and minority cultures, and for the therapist.

ETHNICITY

For the purpose of understanding the beliefs, values, and behaviors of both clients and therapists, the concept of ethnicity is usually much more informative than that of race. McGoldrick and Giordano (1996) defined the term as the "common ancestry through which individuals have evolved shared values and customs" (p. 1). Although ethnicity is generally understood to involve some shared biological heritage, its most important aspects in terms of individual and group identity are those which are socially constructed (e.g., beliefs, norms, behaviors, and institutions).

But the concept of ethnicity also includes complications. For one, the term holds different meanings in different countries. In the United States, where American Indians joined together early on with African, Asian, and Latino Americans to call for equal rights, the term *ethnic minority* is assumed to include people of Indigenous or Aboriginal heritage. (The term *Indigenous* is often used interchangeably with *Aboriginal*, as in Indigenous or Aboriginal people—Adelson, 2000; Maracle, 1994.) However, in Canada and Australia, where Aboriginal people see their situations as separate from all subsequent immigrant groups, the term *ethnic minority* is used to describe only cultures with a history of immigration. Because Aboriginal Canadians emphasize their originality in these lands, they do not conceive of themselves as ethnic minority cultures (Elliott & Fleras, 1992); Aboriginal Australians are similar in this regard (see Young, 1995).

Aboriginal people of Canada are often referred to as Canada's First Nations, in contrast with the Second Nations (i.e., the French and English, who came as colonizers) and the Third Nations (all subsequent immigrant groups to Canada; Elliot & Fleras, 1992). However, the term *First Nations* is perceived by some people to be exclusive because it originates with the dominant cultural assumption that some nations are second or lesser (Adams, 1995). The more inclusive term is Aboriginal peoples, which legally includes the following four groups:

1. status Indians—those admitted to a central registry, affiliated with one of 592 bands, and defined as Indian by the Indian Act of 1876
2. non-status Indians—those who are not governed by the Indian Act but are recognized as Aboriginal peoples by the Canadian Constitution of 1982
3. the Métis, people of mixed Aboriginal and European (primarily French) heritage
4. the Inuit, people of the Canadian Arctic, who never signed treaties with the Canadian government and recently formed a federally recognized territory known as Nunuvut (summarized from Elliott & Fleras, 1992).

Another problem with the description of people by ethnicity is that ethnic groups are currently labeled very broadly, as in the use of the term *Asian* for people of Japanese, Korean, Chinese, Vietnamese, Cambodian, Thai, and even East Indian and Pakistani heritage (Uba, 1994). Similarly, the term *Hispanic* combines into one ethnicity the diverse cultures of Central American Indians, South Americans of African and Spanish heritage,

Mexican Americans, Cuban Americans, Puerto Ricans, and Dominicans (Novas, 1994). This is not to say that the broader, politically recognized ethnic groupings are always offensive or meaningless (because they are not always), but rather that there are dangers in assuming an ethnic identity and a specific meaning for an individual in a particular context.

Recognizing these complications, Phinney (1996) suggested that misunderstandings persist because ethnicity is commonly conceptualized as a discrete categorical variable. That is, one is considered either Latino or not Latino, despite the fact that there are other possibilities (e.g., a person may be bicultural, or the salience of this ethnic identity may shift depending on the context and on developmental changes). Phinney suggested that ethnicity needs to be broken down into its component parts—that is, norms and values; the strength, salience, and meaning of one's ethnic identity; and minority status—which are then more accurately conceptualized as dimensions along which an individual may vary. Thus, "two individuals who belong to the same group may differ widely on their identification with the group and their commitment to it" (p. 923). Moreover, even one individual may vary in his or her identification with a particular ethnic group depending on the time and context.

MINORITY

The term *minority* has traditionally been used in reference to groups whose access to power is limited by the dominant culture. In North America, the term may apply to ethnic, religious, national, and sexual minorities; elders; people who are poor, less formally educated, or of rural or Indigenous heritage; people who have a disability; and women and children. All of these populations fit the broad definition of a culture (Fukuyama, 1990) and have consistently been excluded, marginalized, or misrepresented by mainstream psychology; in this sense they may be considered cultural minorities. (Euroamerican children and adolescents are somewhat of an exception in that, although they may be considered minorities in relation to the larger society, they have been the focus of much attention in psychology beginning with Freud's developmental interests; this is certainly not true for children and adolescents of ethnic minority cultures.)

Of course, there is more to being a member of a minority culture than the experience of oppression. Identification with a minority culture or group may lead to the development of "traits and qualities" that may not develop in people whose lives are buffered by privilege (McIntosh, 1998, p. 101). Minority status may bring with it unique forms of knowledge, awareness, emotional and tangible support, a sense of community, and an opportunity to contribute to others in ways that are deeply meaningful (Newman & Newman, 1999). It should be noted that describing a group of people as a minority culture is different from referring to a person as a minority. The latter may be perceived as disempowering because it places a label on the individual.

CHOOSING TERMS FOR DIVERSE GROUPS

One's choice of terms is equally important with regard to older people; people who have disabilities; gay, lesbian, and bisexual people; and women. For example, consider the differences in connotation between the set of descriptors "elderly, old, old man, old maid" and a second set of "elder, older person, senior." Although the two sets are quite similar, the first may be perceived as patronizing, while the second set is more respectful.

With regard to *sexual orientation*, the term sexual preference is offensive because it suggests that one has chosen to be gay or lesbian and thus can "change back." The term *homosexual* is also problematic because of its historical equation with sin and sickness; more affirmative expressions are *gay, lesbian,* and *bisexual* (Dworkin & Gutiérrez, 1992). Also off-putting are questions that reflect an assumption that heterosexuality is normal and other orientations are not (e.g., asking a client why he thinks he became gay; therapists generally do not ask heterosexual clients why they became heterosexual; Martin, 1982).

With regard to people who have disabilities, preferred identifications are those that reference the person first, then the disability. Thus, describing someone as a "person with a disability" is more respectful than calling her or him a "disabled person." In addition, emotionally neutral terms are preferable to those with negative connotations (e.g., victim, afflicted, crippled, suffering; Maki & Riggar, 1997b).

Saying that someone "uses" a wheelchair or other assistive device avoids the assumptions embedded in "confined to" or "wheelchair bound," which imply that the person and chair are inseparable. The terms *visually impaired* and *hearing impaired* (or *hard of hearing*) are more accurate then *blind* or *deaf* because the latter do not recognize the range of impairments that people may hold. In addition, people who identify with Deaf culture do not consider themselves to have a disability; rather, it is the hearing world's ignorance of their language that creates the disability (Olkin, 1999). (Note that not all people who are hearing impaired identify with Deaf culture.) Also, using the term *blind* as a synonym for ignorant, unaware, or unknowing is offensive (e.g., "He was blind to the impact that his actions had on others" or "They robbed him blind").

Caveats and Reassurances

As the preceding discussion indicates, therapists of dominant cultural backgrounds will need to be extra careful not to assume that commonly used terms (i.e., terms commonly used in the therapist's milieu) are acceptable, because they may not be for everyone. In general, the more specific term is usually preferable because it shows a greater level of awareness of the uniqueness of groups, although this is not always the case. For example, the term *Alaska Native* is commonly used and accepted among the Indigenous peoples of Alaska and includes three broad cultural groups: Indians, Aleuts, and "Eskimos" (Morgan, 1979). More specifically, Alaska Natives belong to 20 language and cultural groups: 11 Athabaskan language groups plus Aleut, Alutiiq, Yupik, Siberian Yupik, Inupiat, Eyak, Tlingit, Tsimshian, and Haida (Rennick, 1996).

Although the Yupik, Siberian Yupik, and Inupiat are commonly referred to as "Eskimo," it is preferable to use the specific cultural names. The term *Eskimo* literally means "raw flesh eater" and may be perceived as pejorative by some people (Herring, 1999). The Inuit of Canada belong to the same cultural group—the terms *Inupiat* and *Inuit* both mean "the people" (Adams, 1995; Maracle, 1994). It is important to note that calling someone by the wrong specific group may be quite offensive (e.g., calling someone "Eskimo" who is Alutiiq, for example; Pullar, 1996). On the other hand, some Inupiat people refer to themselves as Eskimo (Swan Reimer, 1999). Thus, as a general rule, even when I know the specific term, I usually wait and listen for how clients describe themselves before using it.

However, even when clients use a term to describe themselves, it is not always OK for the therapist to use it. Toward the goal of asserting the right to name themselves, some minority groups have reclaimed terms that were once used in a derogatory way by members of the dominant culture (e.g., "queer" for gay and lesbian people, "crip" for people who have disabilities). This decision to take back the dominant culture's labels and define them for oneself is a powerful act (Watt, 1999), as Williams (1999a) explained in relation to her biracial identity:

> The idea that individuals have a right to define their own experience, to create their own personal meanings, to frame their own identity, to claim an "I" that is uniquely their own, shakes up many people's most dearly held beliefs about race. Courage to claim one's own experience despite resistance and judgment from others allows biracial people like me to begin to forge an authentic self. (p. 34)

When used by members of a particular group in reference to themselves, these terms become a form of "in-language." On rare occasions it may be acceptable for nonmembers to use these terms; however, as a general rule it is not.

When I do workshops incorporating the preceding information, this is usually the point at which someone in the audience says, in a tone of controlled exasperation, "Honestly, Pam, how do you expect us to remember all of this?" My answer is, I don't. Or at least, not right away. What I do hope is that rather than becoming overwhelmed with the memorization of terms and names, therapists will commit to the ongoing process of learning about cultures of which they are not a member.

I emphasize the process aspect of this learning because cultures and languages are changing all the time; as a consequence, what one needs to learn is continually changing. With regard to language in particular, it may be helpful to think of this learning process as involving a willingness to seek out information about the broader cultural meanings of terms; seek out information about the group—specific meanings of terms; listen for the terms each client uses; and, when appropriate, simply ask.

Conclusion

The range of influences and groups included in this book may seem overwhelming, but I believe that a broader focus is necessary if psychology is to move beyond unidimensional conceptualizations of culture and people. At first, recognition of the complexity of cultural influences is more difficult than either ignoring these influences or simplifying them into a singular dimension. But in the long run, recognizing this complexity can lead to a much deeper understanding of our clients and ourselves. Cultural diversity is less a problem than a challenge—a challenge that offers the potential for personal growth, creativity, and deeper human connections. The next chapter explores the practical aspects of this challenge in therapists' daily lives and work.

KEY IDEAS 1.	

Summary of Cultural Influences and Related Minority Groups Within the ADDRESSING Framework

Cultural Influences	Minority Groups
Age and generational influences	Children, adolescents, elders
Developmental and acquired Disabilities	People with developmental or acquired disabilities
Religion and spiritual orientation	Religious minority cultures
Ethnicity	Ethnic minority cultures
Socioeconomic status	People of lower status by class, education, occupation, income, rural or urban habitat, family name
Sexual orientation	Gay, lesbian, bisexual people
Indigenous heritage	Indigenous people
National origin	Refugees, immigrants, international students
Gender	Women, transgender people

Note: Adapted from Hays, P. A. (1996). Addressing the complexities of culture and gender in counseling. *Journal of Counseling and Development,* 74 March/April 1996, pp. 332–338, copyright American Counseling Association. Reprinted with permission. No further reproduction authorized without written permission of the American Counseling Association.

II | SELF-ASSESSMENT

Becoming a Culturally Responsive Therapist

2

Awareness is learning to keep yourself company. (Geneen Roth, quoted in Lamott, 1994, p. 31)

In looking for wisdom about how life can best be lived, Smith (1991) examined the world's major religions: Hinduism, Buddhism, Confucianism, Taoism, Islam, Judaism, Christianity, and Aboriginal Australian spirituality. He concluded that these traditions share an emphasis on three elements, or what he calls "virtues":

humility, charity, and veracity. Humility is not self-abasement. It is the capacity to regard oneself in the company of others as one, but not more than one. Charity shifts that shoe to the other foot; it is to regard one's neighbor as likewise one, as fully one as oneself. As for veracity, it extends beyond the minimum of truth-telling to sublime objectivity, the capacity to see things exactly as they are. To conform one's life to the way things are is to live authentically. (p. 387)

It seems to me that these characteristics are equally important in becoming an effective therapist. Humility helps me to avoid judging difference as inferior. Compassion, or an attitude of charity toward others, enables me to work with and appreciate people who challenge my beliefs and values. And critical thinking skills, which can guide one toward truths, help me to continually question my assumptions and look for explanations that go beyond what appears self-evident.

Before one can apply these qualities in therapeutic work, it is important to be familiar with a knowledge base concerning the relationship between individual and social biases, cultural values, and power structures. An understanding of these relationships is essential in cultivating a humble, compassionate, and critical approach to one's work. Let's begin with the example of Elaine, a Euroamerican therapist in her early 30s.

Elaine received a call from a local physician who wished to obtain counseling for his patient, Mrs. Sok, a 50-year-old Cambodian (Khmer) widow who had been crying, sleeping poorly, and losing weight since learning three weeks earlier that her apartment building was scheduled to be demolished. The physician gave Elaine the name and phone number of Mrs. Sok's interpreter, Han, who would bring Mrs. Sok with her to the mental health center.

Elaine called Han and made arrangements for an initial assessment to be attended by Mrs. Sok, Elaine, and Han. During their meeting, Mrs. Sok spoke in a soft voice and made little eye contact with Elaine. Mrs. Sok could not provide her age, the date, or the name of the building in which they were meeting. Han explained that Mrs. Sok had never learned to read or write in her own language and that she did not keep track of dates by the "Western" calendar. Elaine quickly realized it would be meaningless to ask the other mental status questions she would normally ask in an assessment of this sort (e.g., to spell a word backward, recall three objects, or draw geometric designs). Instead, she chose to focus on obtaining more information about Mrs. Sok's medical and social history.

With Han interpreting her questions, Elaine learned that Mrs. Sok had been widowed since her husband was killed in the war in Cambodia during the late 1970s and that four of her six children (at the time) also died or were killed. During the several-year period in which she lived in a refugee camp in Thailand, Mrs. Sok had another child by a man whose whereabouts she no longer knew. In the late 1980s, Mrs. Sok and her three surviving children (now ages 16, 22, and 23) emigrated to the United States, where they had been living in an apartment building next door to two other Cambodian families. The family managed to live on public assistance and the money her 23-year-old son earned from a part-time job in a restaurant.

As Elaine obtained this information, she began to notice that Mrs. Sok's responses in Khmer were much shorter than Han's subsequent interpretations in English. Elaine asked Han if she was adding information, and Han said yes, because she knew Mrs. Sok well and was trying to help by including information that Mrs. Sok was leaving out. When Elaine asked Han in a firm tone to interpret exactly what was said with no additions or deletions and explained that this would allow her to gain a more accurate assessment of Mrs. Sok, Han agreed but appeared uncomfortable.

Although Mrs. Sok showed little emotional response to questions about her history, she became tearful when Elaine asked about the impending loss of her apartment. She said that her friends were there and that she didn't know where else she would go. Elaine made an empathic comment in response but did not ask any additional questions about the housing situation. Instead, she focused on obtaining more information about Mrs. Sok's experiences during the war. As their time was ending, Elaine told Mrs. Sok that she believed she could be of help and wanted Mrs. Sok to return with Han the next week. She added that she would like Mrs. Sok to also see the psychiatrist, who might recommend some medicine to help her sleep. Mrs. Sok nodded her head in agreement. At this point, the session had already taken two hours and another client was waiting outside, so Elaine scheduled their second meeting, and they all said good-bye. The next week, Mrs. Sok and Han did not appear for their appointment, and when Elaine telephoned Han to find out why, Han told her that Mrs. Sok did not want to return.

This anecdote describes a situation not at all unusual in mental health practice today. A compassionate and well-meaning therapist tries to understand a new client's needs and how the therapist might be of help. At the same time, an individual seeking assistance attempts to understand the rules of therapy; assess the trustworthiness and competence of this relative stranger, the therapist; and determine whether the benefits of counseling will outweigh the time, effort, and embarrassment involved. For one or more reasons, the client often decides that therapy will not be helpful and so does not return.

From Mrs. Sok's perspective, Elaine seemed young to be in her position of authority and not especially sensitive to those around her; Elaine's pressing questions about Mrs. Sok's past and Han's apparent discomfort at something Elaine said made Mrs. Sok feel protective of Han and cautious about trusting Elaine. Mrs. Sok had had no prior experience with a counselor or psychotherapist, and when her physician and Han had told her that "counseling can help you," she assumed that such help would address her most pressing problem, namely, the destruction of her home.

Although Elaine was at least minimally aware that Mrs. Sok's and Han's Cambodian heritage influenced how they perceived and presented Mrs. Sok's needs, she did not think carefully about how these influences were relevant to the assessment. Had Elaine systematically considered the role of culture in Mrs. Sok's situation, she might have recognized her own lack of experience and knowledge regarding Cambodian culture, refugees, and older Cambodian women (50 years being "older" among people who survived the war). This realization could have led her to treat Han less as an assistant and more as a peer in the recognition that Han's knowledge of Cambodian people was as extensive as Elaine's knowledge of the mental health field. She might then have seen the need to consult with Han before and after the assessment, an action that would have helped her gain the trust and respect of Han and thus, indirectly, of Mrs. Sok (see Bradford & Munoz, 1993, and Leigh, Corbett, Gutman, & Morere, 1996, regarding the importance of pre- and postassessment meetings with interpreters).

Additionally, rapport could have been facilitated if Elaine had systematically considered the ways in which her own personal and professional experiences might be influencing her conceptualization of Mrs. Sok's situation. For example, Elaine's theoretical orientation and her personal beliefs about trauma led her to assume that Mrs. Sok's current symptoms were due to past trauma. As a result, she focused on eliciting information about Mrs. Sok's war-related experiences, despite the fact that both Mrs. Sok and Han were asking for help with something else. If Elaine had recognized the legitimacy of Mrs. Sok's conceptualization, she might then have focused on what Mrs. Sok considered central—that is, the threatened loss of her home—and Mrs. Sok might have felt more understood. (See Struwe, 1994, regarding clinical interviewing with refugees, and Criddle, 1992, for accounts of Khmer people's resettlement experiences.)

In turn, if Mrs. Sok had felt understood, she would have been more likely to return. With further assessment, it might have become apparent that past trauma was contributing to Mrs. Sok's distress, and in this case Elaine would understandably want to address the subject. However, because rapport and trust were not established and Mrs. Sok did not return, the opportunity for helping the client in this or any other way was lost.

Understanding Bias

One way to think about the mistakes Elaine made is in terms of bias, albeit well intentioned. Although Elaine could have conceptualized Mrs. Sok's case in a variety of ways, her experiences and training biased her toward a particular view that then inclined her to take certain actions, but not others. Although Elaine would have been open to considering these biases if someone had pointed them out, she did not see them on her own. Largely because she thought of bias in dichotomous terms (i.e., that one is either biased or not), the possibility that she might be biased did not even occur to her.

A more helpful way to think about bias is simply as a tendency—a tendency to think, act, or feel in a particular way. In some cases, these tendencies may guide us toward more accurate hypotheses and a quicker understanding of someone. In other situations, they may lead to embarrassingly wrong assumptions, as I experienced in the following situation.

I was visiting a small Unitarian group in a rural area. The circle was talkative and cheery, with the exception of one man. Dressed in a plaid shirt, jeans, and hiking boots, he appeared to be Euroamerican and had a long, unshaven beard. His facial expression was somber, and he didn't say a word, although he seemed to be listening intently. The word "Unibomber" popped into my head. During the coffee hour afterward, I avoided eye contact with him when I was speaking.

As I was driving home with a friend, I asked her about this man. She said, "Oh, he's a very interesting guy. He works full-time as a biologist, and he's a professional musician. He gets up at 4:00 every morning to practice his music before work. He's also a Quaker, so he doesn't say much in the service, but when he does, it's always interesting." Ouch

Clearly, my biases did not facilitate helpful hypotheses about this man. On the contrary, they sent me in the opposite direction—toward inaccurate assumptions that then led me to behave in a way that reinforced these assumptions. By avoiding eye contact with him, I was denied the opportunity to learn anything from him that might have contradicted my misunderstanding.

At the individual level, biases emerge in tandem with two other cognitive processes, those of categorization and generalization. The abilities to categorize information and then generalize this data to new situations help us in organizing the vast amounts of information we encounter on a daily basis (Hamilton & Trolier, 1986; Stephan, 1989). Usually these cognitive processes facilitate our learning and social interactions, but they can also contribute to the formation of inaccurate assumptions, as in my example above. When these assumptions become rigid, we may develop what Holiman and Lauver (1987) called "hardening of the categories," or a tendency toward stereotyping.

To avoid making inaccurate assumptions about their clients, therapists may decide that the best approach is to assume nothing about a client's culture and allow the client to share whatever she or he believes is important. Although such an approach is well motivated, it contains a problematic assumption, namely, that therapists are able to assume nothing about their clients if they choose. The idea that one can "turn off" preconceptions about groups of people is appealing. However, given the subtle and pervasive nature of our assumptions, such control is extremely difficult if not impossible. What is more likely to occur when one attempts to ignore the presence of assumptions is decreased awareness that one is making them (Pedersen, 1987).

A Euroamerican colleague described his own experience with the power of assumptions in his internship with a woman suffering from anxiety. At the time, the therapist knew that his client identified herself as a Christian; he too had been brought up in a Christian environment, although he was no longer practicing.

> I asked her what was exceptional about those times when anxiety was not a problem, [and] she said that her breathing was different. I jumped at this and launched into what I thought was a very erudite bit of psychoeducation on the subject of meditation. When I had finished, she politely informed me that her religion believed that meditation was the "devil's work." (Darling, 1996)

If, as in this case, rapport and trust have been established, then clients will often give the therapist the benefit of the doubt and overlook or forgive inaccurate assumptions. However, in most initial assessments, therapists do not have the benefit of having established a solid working relationship with the client. Rather, upon meeting an individual or family for the first time, they must establish rapport and trust in a relatively short period or risk losing the opportunity to help. Knowledge of a client's culture can facilitate this early work, because it enables the therapist to formulate hypotheses and ask questions that more closely address the client's real experience. The deeper and broader a therapist's knowledge of and experience with a client's culture, the more accurate and relevant these hypotheses and questions will be (S. Sue, 1998). In turn, well-informed hypotheses and questions often increase clients' trust and confidence in the therapist.

Social Bias and Power

The above case examples describe bias at the level of cognitive structures that predispose all human beings to the development of prejudice and stereotypes (Stephan, 1989). However, bias at the individual level cannot be fully understood without a knowledge of sociocultural influences (Gaines & Reed, 1995). Perhaps the most central concept to an understanding of the influence of sociocultural biases is that of power.

Because high-status groups hold more power, they can exert more control over their own situations and the situations of lower status groups. One of the ways in which powerful groups exert control is through stereotypes (Fiske, 1993). Stereotypes can be described in terms of two key functions. Descriptive stereotypes define how most people in a particular group behave, what they prefer, and where their competence lies. Descriptive stereotypes exert control because they create a starting point for people's expectations. That is, the stereotyped person must choose to either stay within the boundaries of these expectations or go outside of them; in either case, the stereotype places a burden on the person and his or her interactions with others. Adding to the effect of descriptive stereotypes, prescriptive stereotypes define "how certain groups *should* think, feel, and behave" (Fiske, 1993, p. 623).

Stereotypes, prejudice, and bias, when combined with power, form systems of privilege known as the "isms" (e.g., racism, sexism, classism, heterosexism, ageism, ableism, colonialism; Hays, 1996a). Unprivileged members of these systems are socialized to be acutely aware of the lines separating those who have privilege from those who do not. Unprivileged people need to pay more attention to differences and rules, because the outcomes of their lives are more dependent on those who hold power (Fiske, 1993).

In contrast, powerful groups are not socialized to see the differences and the lines, largely because they do not need to; oppressed groups have little impact on their daily lives. For example,

> There are many things that an African American child can do that will get him or her characterized as "acting Black" or "acting White," but there is very little that a European American child can do that will prompt such labeling. . . . Living in a White-dominated society, the average African American child is made aware implicitly and explicitly of these categorizations on a daily basis . . . [whereas] the average European American child rarely is made aware of anything having to do with these categories. (Gaines & Reed, 1995, p. 98)

In the United States, systems of privilege and oppression are intimately tied to capitalism. Sexism and racism support the view of women and people of color as "a surplus labor force" that "can be pushed in and out of employment in keeping with current needs of the economy (depression, expansion, wartime, or a period of union-busting)" (Blood, Tuttle, & Lakey, 1995, p. 156). Corporate capitalism also pressures men, who, if they are too demanding, can be easily replaced by women or people of color who cost less. Gender and racial stereotypes, aided by the media, educational institutions, and the legal system, reinforce the belief that this arrangement is fair and natural (Blood et al., 1995).

Members of dominant groups often find it painful to acknowledge the existence of systems of privilege, because the idea goes against fundamental Western beliefs in meritocracy (e.g., "if you work hard enough, you'll succeed") and democracy (e.g., "majority rule is fair") (Robinson, 1999). It is easier to believe that instances of prejudice and discrimination are primarily the fault of individual "bad apples." From his perspective as a Euroamerican man, Croteau (1999) explained,

> To me, racist attitudes and behaviors were solely about the moral or psychological failures or shortcomings of individual White people. Although I probably would not have explained it in a way that sounded this judgmental, it really came down to my seeing racism as what "bad" White people do to people of color. I desperately wanted to be a "good" White person. In retrospect, I realize that this exclusively individualistic and highly judgmental perspective on racism left my fragile ego on the line with every interpersonal interaction I had across racial lines. . . . Seeing racism solely through the lens of individualism was an unforgiving perspective that failed to take into account the reality of socially learned racism. (p. 30)

As Croteau suggested, systems of privilege harm those who hold privilege as well as those who do not (Locke & Kiselica, 1999). Systems of privilege can separate whole domains of information, knowledge, and skills from the members of dominant groups who might also benefit. For instance, traditional healing practices, many of which do not involve the side effects of Euroamerican medication and medical practices, were seen as inferior by the dominant medical establishment until 1978, when the World Health Organization and

UNICEF officially recognized traditional practitioners (Jilek, 1994). As a result, Euroamerican physicians have been slow to accept such practices, which continue to be relatively unavailable to patients in U.S. health care settings.

At the level of personal growth and development, privilege can also lead to the internalization of feelings of superiority and elitism, resulting in a sense of "alienation" and restriction of "one's capacities for love, trust, empathy, and openness" (Hertzberg, 1990, p. 279). Privilege (e.g., in the form of money or powerful social connections) may prevent a person from developing the coping abilities that less privileged individuals must develop in order to survive (McIntosh, 1998). At present, older Euroamerican men have the highest suicide rate in the United States (Richmond, 1999); this negative buffer effect of privilege may be one reason why.

Although it may never be possible to completely escape the influence of societal biases, it is possible to gain an awareness and knowledge base that can allow us to recognize the influence of these biases on ourselves and others. Such awareness and knowledge increase the likelihood that our decisions, beliefs, and behaviors will be conscious and well informed. The key lies in one's commitment to assessing—on an ongoing basis—one's own experiences, beliefs, values, knowledge, and information sources (Boyd Franklin, 1989; Brown, 1994; López et al., 1989; Pedersen, 1987; Williams, 1999a). Let's turn now to a consideration of the three elements mentioned earlier—humility, compassion, and critical thinking skills—that provide a foundation for this work.

Staying Humble While Thinking Critically

Over the course of my professional life, I have asked various people what they believe is the most important quality or characteristic for someone doing cross-cultural work. The most common response I've received is that the person needs to be humble. As Davis (1993) noted, "People with genuine humility are effective helpers, because they are realistic about what they have to offer, aware of their own limitations and accepting of the contribution of others" (p. 55).

It may seem that the idea of critical thinking is opposed to that of humility, because the term *critical* is often equated with negativity or confrontation. However, critical thinking skills are essential to humility because they involve the abilities to identify and challenge assumptions (one's own as well as those of others), examine contextual influences (on one's own thinking too), and imagine and explore alternatives (Brookfield, 1987).

For example, I consider myself a feminist, and while I recognize the limitations of this philosophy (particularly its ethnocentric applications), I still subscribe to many of its tenets. Among my values is the belief that women are better off if they can support themselves economically; this has something to do with personal empowerment and my desire for egalitarian relationships.

When I was in my mid-20s, I spent several months interviewing Arab women living in three different environments in North Africa: (a) the cosmopolitan capital city of Tunis, (b) a midsized village that was conservative and traditional in its values and mores, and (c) an impoverished Bedouin community that had gone from a nomadic to a settled agricultural life in the previous generation. As part of this research, I wanted to learn how Tunisian women's lives had changed since the country gained independence in 1956 and enacted laws aimed at improving the status of women. I expected to find some forms of economic independence to be associated with greater satisfaction and freedoms, at least for middle-class women. What I found was a bit more complicated (Hays, 1987; Hays & Zouari, 1995).

Nearly all of the middle-class urban women were employed outside the home. They cited mixed reasons for this, namely, that they liked working outside, but that they also needed to bring in extra money due to a higher cost of living in the city. Of course, the Bedouin women were poor and had always worked outside the home, in the fields alongside their husbands. This was extremely hard work—bending over for long periods in the hot sun, often with a baby tied to one's back. Not surprisingly, this kind of work did not lead the Bedouin women to feel greater satisfaction with their lives; rather, they expressed the most frustration.

It was the middle-class women in the village who surprised me by their disinterest in outside employment or a personal income. Granted, occupational opportunities were limited, but among those women who did have some personal income, whether by inheritance or sewing, the money was considered theirs. A common attitude was summarized by one woman: "I already do all the work at home [as one job]. Why would I want two?" She added that she liked having time in the afternoon to do embroidery and visit with her sisters, her mother, and her friends. She was astonished at how hard I chose to work; I think that she even thought I was a little nutty. My learning from her and the other women I spent time with led to me to think more critically about my beliefs about women's roles, men's roles, personal empowerment, and relationships. Seeing women who were satisfied with lifestyles that contradicted some of my most firmly held beliefs was humbling, to say the least.

In this way, humility and critical thinking often operate in a reciprocal relationship. Whereas humility opens one to new forms of learning and diverse sources of knowledge, critical thinking about one's knowledge base, sources of information, and ways of learning, along with constant testing of alternative hypotheses, can help one to stay open (López et al., 1989).

Sound clinical judgments require both humility and critical thinking. Because a willingness to question oneself is communicated in nonverbal ways, both have the added benefit of facilitating rapport. Consider the example of a Euroamerican male therapist working with a single woman of Mexican American heritage and her three children, ages 6, 8, and 12. Following her divorce, the client, who had a two-year college degree, received no child support and had to move to a lower-income apartment and find a job that would support them all. She came to counseling to obtain help in dealing with her 6-year-old son's bed-wetting. The therapist began working with her to help her son; however, he also had concerns about the 12-year-old daughter, whom he saw as a "parentified child" (i.e., in the role of the mother's confidante and partner in raising the two younger children).

Because the daughter had no academic or behavioral problems, the therapist decided to consult with a Latina therapist before sharing these concerns with the mother. Through the consultation, he began to realize how his own cultural heritage was influencing his views of what constitutes healthy child rearing. He began to see the possibility that in this family's case, the child's role might not be pathological. Although his concerns did not disappear completely, he did begin to see the family in a more accepting way, an attitude that manifested itself in behaviors that were respectful of the mother and all that she was doing for her children. (See Arroyo, 1997, and Garcia-Preto, 1996, for more on child-rearing in Mexican American families.)

There are a number of questions that therapists can ask themselves to prevent premature judgments. These include the following:

- How did I come to this understanding? How do I know that this is true?
- Are there alternative explanations or opinions that might be equally valid in this situation?
- How might my view of the client's situation be influenced by my own context, for example, my age or generational experiences, my ethnic background, my socioeconomic status (i.e., the ADDRESSING influences)?
- Might there be some information that lends validity to the view with which I disagree?
- Might there be a positive, culturally related purpose for the behavior, belief, or feeling that I judge to be dysfunctional or unhealthy?

These sorts of questions do not prevent therapists from making clinical judgments; however, they do slow down the process by encouraging a consideration of the client's context. In addition, they increase the likelihood that the therapist's hypotheses will be closer to the client's real experience.

Returning to my learning from the Tunisian women, although I still hold my feminist beliefs, I now realize that my values are directly related to my identity, my opportunities, and my context. Trying to think critically about my beliefs and why I believe what I believe helps me to be more open to people who hold values that I might see as contrary to mine. The more open I am, the more compassionate and understanding I am of others, which in turn helps me to be a better therapist.

OBSTACLES TO COMPASSION

The centrality of compassion in becoming a healthier and happier human being (and thus therapist) was explained by the Dalai Lama, the Buddhist spiritual leader of Tibet:

> If you maintain a feeling of compassion, loving kindness, then something automatically opens your inner door. Through that, you can communicate much more easily with other people. And that feeling of warmth creates a kind of openness. . . . Then there's less need to hide things, and as a result, feelings of fear, self-doubt, and insecurity are automatically dispelled. Also, it creates a feeling of trust from other people.
>
> . . . Anger, violence, and aggression may certainly rise, but I think it's on a secondary or more superficial level; in a sense, they arise when we're frustrated in our efforts to achieve love and affection. (His Holiness the Dalai Lama & Cutler, 1999, pp. 40, 54–55)

The concept of compassion is not unique to Buddhism, but because I've found Buddhist ideas on the subject so clearly outlined and easy to understand, I've chosen to explain compassion using these concepts. In my studies, I also came across the work of Patanjali, a 2nd-century BC scholar and author of part of the Yoga Sutras. He posited the following five obstacles to growth: fear, ignorance, aversion (i.e., from pain), desire, and egoism, defined as "the identification of the Self with the body and thoughts" leading to "fear, desire, and a sense of limitation" (Frager & Fadiman, 1998, p. 501). In relation to therapeutic work, I find it helpful to think of these as defensiveness, fear, ignorance, pain, and attachment—all of which can be seen as obstacles to compassion.

Defensiveness can be thought of as the cognitive and emotional rigidity that occurs when one feels threatened or attacked. As Williams (1999a) noted, it is a frequent reaction among counselors when talking about racial issues across racial groups (and I would add across the other ADDRESSING identities as well). In the therapeutic setting, feelings of defensiveness may lead therapists to focus on the justification of their own ideas, thus lessening their concern for the client's experience. This shift in one's primary concern is easily perceived by clients, who may then engage in self-protective behaviors such as emotionally distancing themselves from the therapist.

It is probably impossible to eliminate defensive feelings; it may also be undesirable because emotions often serve as cues that something is amiss. However, it is possible and frequently desirable to refrain from engaging in defensive behaviors, particularly if these behaviors interfere with one's acceptance of and concern for another person.

Defensiveness is just one of several normal human responses that can prevent therapists from developing and maintaining compassion. A related obstacle to compassion is *fear*. In a cross-cultural therapeutic relationship, a therapist's fear may or may not be related to the cultural differences involved. For example, a therapist may fear on an intellectual level that the culturally different client will realize how little the therapist knows about the client's culture. Fear may also be less conscious, as in the case of a Euroamerican therapist who experienced an initial fear of her client for no other reason than his apparent identity as an African American man (Boyd-Franklin, 1989, p. 98).

Fear may be related to *ignorance*, a third obstacle in the development of compassion. In a study of the developmental stages counselors experience in learning about culture, López and colleagues (1989) found the first stage to be characterized by a complete lack of awareness of cultural influences on clients' lives. Therapists in this stage did not entertain hypotheses about cultural influences, even when they were present. I think it is helpful to imagine this sort of ignorance as a blank spot or hole within one's self. As long as this hole is unfilled by direct personal experience with people of a particular group, it is vulnerable to being filled by dominant cultural assumptions and biases about that group.

Returning to the example of the woman therapist who feared her African American client, she may have had no frightening experiences with African American men; for that matter, she may have had no significant encounters of any kind with African American men. This lack of experience left her open to absorbing the fears about African American men so common in Euroamerican culture.

A fourth obstacle to compassion is *pain*. At present, there is a great deal of pain surrounding cultural issues. With the best of intentions, therapists may elicit this pain from their clients. For example, the therapist may ask questions about a person's cultural heritage with the only intention of learning more about what he values; however, the client may have been asked such questions by people who wanted to know exactly "what he is" before deciding how to treat him (Root, 1996; Williams, 1999a). When this happens, the client may shut down emotionally or distance himself.

Therapists may react similarly out of their own pain. For example, a nondisabled, Euroamerican male therapist may have been repeatedly hurt by others' assumptions that he is lacking in compassion for people of minority identities. As he attempts to understand the meaning of a particular client's disability from the client's perspective, he finds himself to be the target of the client's anger. If he then focuses on his own pain and anger, he will be more inclined to make automatic interpretations (e.g., that the client is overreacting) that do not facilitate a deeper understanding of the client's experience.

On the basis of their work with families of people who have disabilities, Hulnick and Hulnick (1989) suggested the following:

> We have observed many times that there is a sequence that always seems to be present at times of emotional upset. It goes like this. Whenever anger is present and we look beneath the anger, we always find hurt. Anger turns out to largely be a reaction occurring when we feel hurt. And when we look beneath the hurt, we always find caring. We are only hurt when something or someone we care about has been, in some way, desecrated or violated.

> This sequence gives us the key for effectively handling these types of situations. It is this. Give a client full permission to express his or her deepest pain. In fact, assist clients by actively encouraging them in expressing it. (p. 68)

A fifth obstacle to humility may be the therapist's attachment to a particular theoretical orientation or outcome. From a Buddhist perspective, attachment to one viewpoint, conceptualization, or idea often leads to unnecessary suffering (Rao, 1988). In the therapeutic setting, allowing one's theoretical orientation to take precedence over a client's concerns may result in an inaccurate assessment or an intervention that is inappropriate or ineffective.

For example, in working with a client who has anxiety about an impending move, a present-oriented, cognitive-behavioral therapist might overlook the importance of the family's multigenerational migration history. Alternatively, in response to a client's request for skills in dealing with coworkers' racist comments, a psychodynamically oriented therapist might make the mistake of overemphasizing the client's early upbringing in his feelings about the current situation.

In sum, therapists are advised to be on the lookout for these obstacles to compassion: defensive behaviors, fear, ignorance, pain, and attachment to one theoretical perspective. When a therapist recognizes any of these in herself or himself, there are specific steps she or he can take to prevent interference with the assessment process.

PREVENTING DEFENSIVE BEHAVIORS

My friend Bob was the principal of a high school in a Siberian Yupik village in Alaska. One day a Euroamerican male teacher (all of the teachers were Euroamerican) came in to see him. The teacher was furious because he said that he had corrected one of his students, and the boy had just laughed at him. The teacher considered the boy's behavior to be a sign of disrespect. Bob suggested that he bring the boy in, which the teacher did. As the teacher repeated his complaint in a loud angry voice, the boy began laughing again. Bob told the teacher to leave. When they were alone, Bob asked the boy what had happened, and the boy dissolved into tears.

The boy hadn't meant to laugh, but like all the students there, he spoke English as a second language and just didn't understand what the teacher had wanted him to do. His laughter was out of embarrassment at the teacher's angry focus on him. Unfortunately, the teacher was too stuck in his own defensiveness to stop the downward spiral of their inter-actions (i.e., the more the teacher shouted, the more the boy laughed). If Bob had accepted the teacher's (dominant cultural) view of the problem, the opportunity for seeing what was really happening would have been missed. But by staying open and looking for alter-native explanations, Bob opened the way for a deeper understanding of the boy.

A first step toward sustaining openness is to become more aware of one's experience in the moment, a process known as mindfulness in Buddhist psychology. The importance of mindfulness in resolving defensive feelings has been described as follows by the Vietnamese monk Thich Nhat Hanh (1992):

> The word *samyojana* refers to internal formations, fetters, or knots. When someone says something unkind to us, for example, if we do not understand why he said it and we become irritated, a knot will be tied in us. The lack of understanding is the basis for every internal knot. If we practice mindfulness, we can learn the skill of recognizing a knot the moment it is tied in us and finding ways to untie it. Internal formations need our full attention as soon as they form, while they are still loosely tied, so that the work of untying them will be easy. If we do not untie our knots when they form, they will grow tighter and stronger. (p. 48)

These "knots" may be experienced as physiological sensations that accompany one's feelings of defensiveness, fear, and pain. These sensations can then serve as cues that one is focusing more on oneself than on one's client. If possible, identifying the precipitants of these sensations and feelings may help the therapist predict his or her inclination to behave in a way that will work against his or her real intentions (e.g., to communicate respect, to obtain an accurate assessment).

For example, in a session with an older client, a young therapist may begin to experience tension in his forehead and upper back. He may use these sensations as cues to recognize that he feels some fear about working with a client who is much older than he is. In recog-nizing this fear, he may then be able to refrain from behaviors that he would normally unconsciously engage in when he feels afraid and inadequate. Rather than describing his qualifications in such a way that the client perceives him to be bragging (and consequently feels less connected to him), the therapist might openly discuss with the client how his younger age might limit his understanding of the client's situation. Because the latter behavior makes the therapist vulnerable and thus communicates his "humanness," it is more likely to facilitate a sense of connection between the two (Kiselica, 1998).

When confronted with feelings of discomfort in an assessment, it may be helpful to take a deep breath, exhale slowly, and then focus for a few seconds on your breath. This emphasis on breathing as a way of grounding oneself is found in Yogic and Buddhist meditation practice, as well as in their behavioral descendent, relaxation training. With this focus, it may then be more possible to ask yourself about the presumed need for two parties to hold the same view. That is, must a client conceptualize a situation in the same way that the therapist does? It may also be constructive to ask yourself if there are alternative opinions that may be as valid or useful as your own. Might there be some information or experiences that would allow you to appreciate these different perspectives? Finally, how might you go about getting the information or experiences that could lead to a broader vision and understanding of the client and her or his situation? Note that these questions parallel those offered earlier for thinking critically while staying humble.

To summarize, we can never eliminate defensive feelings. However, we can decrease defensive behaviors by following these steps:

- Be aware of the physical sensations that accompany feelings of defensiveness, fear, and pain.
- If possible, identify the precipitants of these sensations and feelings to help you predict defensive behaviors before they occur.
- Use these physical sensations as cues to what you are feeling.
- When you feel defensive sensations and feelings arise, take a deep breath, exhale slowly, and then focus for a few seconds on your breath.
- Refrain from defensive behaviors (e.g., talking too much, emphasizing your own accomplishments, emotional distancing).
- Question the need for clients' views to match your own. Are there equally valid alternative opinions?
- Recognize your need for additional information and experiences.
- If appropriate, discuss the limitations of your knowledge and experience with the client.

KEEPING A SENSE OF HUMOR

Humor provides an opportunity to step out of one's cognitive set, even if only for a few moments (Mahrer & Gervaise, 1994). This shift can allow one to see a new perspective or to appreciate other people even if they hold beliefs with which one disagrees (Lemma, 2000). I am continually reminded in my day-to-day experiences of the ways in which humor enables people to connect. For instance, I was asked to see Mr. Smith, a married man in his 70s, for questions about depression and cognitive difficulties. As I approached his hospital room, I could hear what sounded like an argument between him and his physician:

Physician: Now, George, you're gonna have to start listening to what I'm telling you. If you don't do this, you're going to have bigger problems. Are you listening to me?

Mr. Smith: Oh, why don't you just go find somebody else to pester?

Cringing a little inside, I knocked on the open door, then walked in and introduced myself. Mr. Smith was in a wheelchair and hooked up to an IV; he was hunched over (from osteoporosis, or depression, or just angrily facing the floor?). The physician gave me a warm smile and said, "Well, George, I guess you're the lucky one who gets to stay here and talk with Dr. Hays, so I'll just be heading out." Mr. Smith grumbled something; I couldn't see his face. Just then, the physician turned away to make a quick note in his chart. In that moment, Mr. Smith raised his head, looked right at me, winked, and put his head back down. I immediately relaxed and let go of the negative expectations and defensive feelings I'd been building since approaching the door.

ONGOING DILEMMAS

Therapists who can incorporate these suggestions into their cross-cultural practices will still encounter situations in which finding a good solution remains difficult. One such dilemma is that in which a client says something that would generally be considered racist or similarly offensive. If the comment is the main point and intentionally derogatory, it can often be addressed directly. For example, asking about a male client's homophobic feelings would be relevant if he uses a slur to describe his gay employer who he believes is treating him unfairly.

However, if the client's comment is incidental to her main point and not intentionally derogatory, then the decision to say something can be more difficult, because it involves pulling the client back to the offensive remark and prioritizing the therapist's feelings about it. For example, during the Gulf War, I saw a client who was telling me about her son who was a part of the military action, and as she was talking she made a negative comment about Arab people. Her comment was completely incidental to her main point, and I doubt that she had any idea that what she said was offensive. At the time, I was married to an Arab man, and we were both involved in protesting the war. I had many strong feelings in reaction to her comment, but I chose to say nothing, in part because it seemed to me that saying something would have been calling attention to my issues rather than to the client's. Also, this conversation took place during an assessment, and I had not yet established a relationship with the woman. At the same time, the value I place on the need to speak out against racist and other oppressive attitudes created pressure inside me to say something.

One guideline for therapist self-disclosure is whether it primarily benefits the therapist or the client (see chapter 5 on establishing a respectful relationship). Responding to a client's incidental remark seems to lean more toward benefiting the therapist. I could have addressed the woman's comment without disclosing my personal situation; however, simply calling attention to her comment would have made my political views fairly transparent. However, one could argue that it is to the client's advantage to know that she is offending others with her language; also, ultimately, racist attitudes hurt and limit the person who holds them (Hertzberg, 1990). It is important to note that the therapeutic relationship and the therapist's identity are also considerations. For example, if I were Arab and the client made the derogatory comment knowing this, I would want to find out why (e.g., was she feeling angry toward me, or did she think I might be biased against her?) see Chin, 1994; Perez Foster, 1996).

The complexity of dilemmas like these means that solutions will be highly situation specific. To increase the likelihood that you will make the best decision possible, the first step is to have thought about such issues beforehand as a part of your own ongoing cultural self-assessment (Greene, 1994). (This process and the relationship between therapists' values and their work is explored in chapter 3, followed by a more detailed discussion of cross-cultural transference and countertransference in chapter 4.) Once you are engaged in the self-assessment process, when difficult dilemmas occur, using the preceding guidelines regarding defensive behaviors can help you make a decision about how to respond in that particular moment. Afterward, whenever possible, I try to consult with a colleague who belongs to the cultural group being referenced; even if it is too late to do something, at least I can learn from the feedback.

Also, in the moment, when I personally feel offended, it helps me to pay attention to the speaker's intentions. If they mean well, I try to go with that. In turn, I hope that when I make mistakes, listeners will be generous in their judgments of me. Still, this "coming to critical consciousness" is, as the writer bell hooks (1998) noted,

> a difficult, "trying" process, one that demands that we give up set ways of thinking and being, that we shift our paradigms, that we open ourselves to the unknown, the unfamiliar. Undergoing this process, we learn what it means to struggle and in this effort we experience the dignity and integrity of being that comes with revolutionary change. (p. 584)

Conclusion

Humility, compassion, and critical thinking skills provide a foundation for learning more about diverse cultural influences on oneself and one's clients. However, they do not ensure culturally responsive practice. There is still the need for therapists to be aware of their own particular knowledge gaps and areas of bias. This topic is explored in the next chapter.

KEY IDEAS 2.

Becoming a Culturally Responsive Therapist

1. Bias is best thought of as a tendency to think, act, or feel in a particular way, sometimes guiding us toward more accurate hypotheses, but sometimes not.

2. When bias is reinforced by powerful groups and social structures, the results are systems of privilege and oppression (racism, sexism, classism, heterosexism, ableism, ageism, and colonialism).

3. Unprivileged members of these systems are socialized to be acutely aware of the lines separating those who have privilege from those who do not, because the outcomes of their lives are more dependent on those who hold power.

4. Privileged members are socialized to be less aware of the lines and differences related to privilege.

5. Humility, compassion, and critical thinking skills are qualities that facilitate therapists' work across lines of privilege and oppression.

6. Five obstacles to compassion are defensiveness, fear, ignorance, pain, and attachment to a particular theoretical orientation or outcome.

7. Although defensive feelings can never be eliminated and may even be helpful as cues, defensive behaviors often create emotional distance between the therapist and client.

8. Steps that can be taken to minimize defensive behaviors include maintaining mindful awareness of the physiological sensations that accompany one's defensive feelings, focusing on one's breath in the moment, and questioning the need for a client to see things in the same way as the therapist.

9. Cross-cultural work is fraught with challenging dilemmas; the best solution for one situation may not be the best for another.

10. Following a cross-cultural mistake or misunderstanding, it can be helpful to consult with a colleague who belongs to the cultural group being referenced.

Looking Into the Clinician's Mirror: Cultural Self-Assessment 3

Dime con quien andas y te diré quien eres [Tell me who your friends are, and I'll tell you who you are]—Spanish saying

One of my friends was in a spiritual growth group whose members became quite close. They provided each other with a warm, supportive environment to share their joy and pain. Everyone except my friend and her husband were Euroamerican, but this did not seem to be an issue until one meeting when my friend shared her pain about what she believed to be a racist comment from someone outside the group. Rather than validate her experience, the group asked questions aimed at explaining why the person would make such a comment. They seemed to be looking for a way to justify it and, in the process, implied that she was overreacting. As the tension built, one member objected to the time being spent on this issue, saying, "You know, this is a spiritual growth group, not an antiracism group." My friend replied, "But racism is a spiritual issue for me." Unfortunately, the group members were unanimous in their inability to see this situation from my friend's perspective; the result was that she and her husband decided to leave the group.

The dictionary defines *privilege* as a "right or immunity" that gives the individual a distinct advantage or favor; in contrast, the term *oppressed* is described as the state of being burdened spiritually or mentally, or suppressed or crushed by an abuse of power (Merriam-Webster, 1983). McIntosh (1998) compared White privilege to an invisible knapsack that White people can count on to make life easier. For example, Euroamericans can usually choose to be in the company of their own race when they want to be, they are not asked to speak for their race, they rarely have trouble finding housing because of their race, and so on.

However, as discussed earlier, privilege also tends to isolate people, to cut them off from information and experiences related to specific minority groups that could be helpful and enrich their lives. In my friend's case, the privilege experienced by the Euroamericans in the group led them to believe that racism was not the problem, and because they all agreed with each other, their position of "rightness" was affirmed. The only information they had to contradict their belief was that provided by my friend and her husband, whose views were easily dismissed because they were in the minority.

We all have our own unique identities and experiences, and consequently the areas in which we hold privilege vary. In general, though, these privileged areas are often those in which we hold the least awareness. The challenge then is to recognize our areas of privilege and commit ourselves to the extra work that is required to fill in our knowledge gaps (Akamatsu, 1998). Toward this goal, there are a number of practical steps therapists can take to increase their self-awareness and knowledge. These include, but are not limited to, the following:

- investigating our own cultural heritage
- paying attention to the influence of privilege on our understanding of cultural issues, and hence on our work with clients
- educating ourselves through diverse sources of information
- developing diverse relationships and understanding the influence of sociocultural contexts.

Work in each of these areas can be facilitated through the use of the ADDRESSING framework.

Investigating Your Own Cultural Heritage

One way to begin thinking about the influence that diverse cultural factors have had on you is by doing the following exercise (Hays, 1996a): First, take a lined piece of paper; on the left side, write the acronym ADDRESSING vertically, leaving space to the right of and below each letter. Next, record a brief description of the influences you consider salient for yourself in each category. If current influences are different from those that influenced you growing up, note the salient influences and identities in relation first to your upbringing, and then to your current contexts. Also, fill in every category, even those for which you hold a dominant cultural identity, because this too is meaningful information.

Table 3.1 illustrates this process, using as an example a therapist, Olivia. Under Age and generational influences, Olivia wrote, "52 years old; third-generation U.S. American; member of politically active generation of Chicanos and Chicanas in California; first generation affected by post-Civil Rights academic and employment opportunities in the 1970s." On the line for disabilities, she wrote, "Chronic knee problems since early adulthood, including multiple surgeries; sometimes use crutches to walk." She continued through the

TABLE 3.1.

The Therapist's Cultural Self-Assessment: Example of Olivia

Cultural Influences	Olivia's Self-Assessment
*Age and generational influences	52 years old; third-generation U.S. American; member of politically active generation of Chicanos and Chicanas in California; first generation affected by post-Civil Rights academic and employment opportunities in the 1970s.
Developmental or acquired Disabilities	Chronic knee problems since early adulthood, including multiple surgeries; sometimes use crutches to walk.
*Religion and spiritual orientation	Mother is a practicing Catholic, father nonpracticing Presbyterian; my current beliefs are a mixture of Catholic and secular; I don't attend mass.
Ethnicity	Mother and father both of mixed Mexican (Spanish and Indian) heritage, both U.S. born; my own identity is Chicana; I speak Spanish, but my primary language is English.
*Socioeconomic status	Parents urban, working, lower-middle-class members of an ethnic minority culture; however, my identity is as a university-educated Chicana; I identify with working-class people, although my occupation and income are middle class.
*Sexual orientation	Heterosexual
Indigenous heritage	My maternal grandmother was Indian and immigrated to the United States from Mexico with my grandfather when they were young adults; what I know about this part of my heritage came from her, but she died when I was 10.
*National origin	U.S., but deep understanding of the immigration experience from my grandparents.
Gender	Woman, Chicana, divorced, mother of two children.

Note. * = holds dominant cultural identity.

list, with some overlap between categories, providing a general sketch of both minority and dominant cultural influences and identities salient for her.

The degree to which this exercise is helpful depends on how far one takes the exploration of these influences and identities. For instance, in the first area, age and generational influences, simply recognizing your age is not particularly informative. However, exploring the generational influences—including historical and sociocultural contexts related to your age and particular developmental phases—offers a rich source of material regarding the meanings of these influences and identities (Brown, 1990).

The following general questions can help elicit the meanings of age and generational influences during the therapist's self-evaluation:

- When I was born, what were the social expectations for a person of my identity?
- When I was a teenager, what were the norms, values, and gender roles supported within my family, by my peers, in my culture, and in the dominant culture?
- How was my view of the world shaped by the social movements of my teenage years?
- When I was a young adult, what educational and occupational opportunities were available to me? And now?

The specific details of these questions will be shaped by each therapist's particular identity, experiences, and contexts. Returning to the example of the therapist above, her specific questions were

- When I was born (1948), what were the social expectations for a Chicana growing up in California?
- When I was a teenager (1960s), what were the norms, values, and gender roles supported within my family, by my peers, in Chicana culture, and in the dominant culture?
- How was my view of the world shaped by the social movements of my teenage years (e.g., protests by Chicano farm workers, the Civil Rights movement, the women's liberation movement, and the Vietnam War)?
- When I was a young adult (early 1970s), what were the educational and occupational opportunities available to me? More recently, in my early 40s (late 1980s and early 1990s), what did the economic recession and anti-immigration movement in California mean for me when I lost my job and was supporting two children? And how about now that I am a 52-year-old Chicana, with a disability, living in a time when affirmative action programs are being challenged and overturned?

The initial part of this work is individual, but the development of questions aimed at exploring the meaning of diverse influences can be facilitated by participation in a group aimed at increasing self-awareness (see Aponte, 1994, regarding the importance of groups in cross-cultural training). With large groups, I find it most helpful to divide participants into triads. Individuals in these smaller groups help one another explore the questions, then return to the large group to share their insights and obtain feedback. In classes, guest speakers of diverse minority identities bring additional perspectives. Films may be used for the same purpose; for examples, see Williams 1999b.

How Privilege and Culture Affect Your Work

In the ongoing process of cultural self-assessment, an understanding of the role of privilege in relation to one's own identity and opportunities is essential. The next exercise can help you recognize the ways in which privilege affects you. I focus on privilege here (rather than oppression) because I have found that therapists' areas of privilege are usually those in which they are less knowledgeable and aware. In contrast, people are usually very aware of the areas in which they feel oppressed, because they've spent a great deal of time thinking about their experiences of oppression and are more connected to people with similar experiences.

So, for this next step, return to your ADDRESSING outline. Look back over each category. Next to the areas in which you hold a dominant cultural identity, put a little star (*) (see Table 3.1). For example, if you are between 30 and 60 years of age, put a star next to *Age and generational influences. If you do not have a disability (i.e. if you are a member of the nondisabled majority), put a star next to *Developmental and acquired Disabilities. If you grew up in a secular or Christian home, put a star next to *Religion. Continue on down the list, starring *Ethnicity if you are of Euroamerican heritage, *Socioeconomic status if you were brought up in a middle- or upper-class family or are currently of middle- or upper-class status, *Sexual orientation if you are heterosexual, *Indigenous heritage if you are not of Indigenous heritage, *National origin if you live in the country in which you were born and grew up, and *Gender if you are male.

Now look at your ADDRESSING self-description with attention to the stars. Every individual has a different constellation. However, because a majority of therapists in North America hold membership in dominant ethnic, educational, and socioeconomic groups (Hammond & Yung, 1993), when I do this exercise in North American groups, people are often surprised by how many stars—that is, how much privilege—they have. This is true even for therapists who hold a particular minority identity (e.g., are members of an ethnic minority community), but who hold privilege in a variety of other areas (e.g., generational status, educational level, socioeconomic status, sexual orientation, or physical abilities).

But as you may notice, even this task of recognizing the areas in which you hold privilege involves complexities. For one, what constitutes a privileged group depends on the larger sociocultural context. For example, on the west coast of Canada, a middle-class, 65-year-old man of Chinese heritage may hold little status in the eyes of Anglo or French Canadians because of his age and ethnic heritage. However, within the Chinese Canadian community, the same man's age, gender, and socioeconomic standing may give him privilege. In fact, he may be seen as quite powerful in his particular environment.

Perceiving one's own privileges can be as difficult as seeing one's own assumptions. As Akamatsu (1998) noted,

> the underlying duality—the coexistence of one's own privileged and targeted positions—is not easy to apprehend emotionally. It requires a more complex view of identity, in which contradictory experiences of advantage and disadvantage form ragged layers. This demands a particular sort of "both-and" holding that relies on the ability to "contain opposites." (p. 138)

Values

As systems of privilege work to maintain the status quo, they also reinforce the values of powerful groups. Because the field of psychology is a privileged profession, its values are often enmeshed with those of the dominant culture (Moghaddam, 1990). In turn, many therapists, while recognizing that biases occur in the larger culture, believe that their particular approaches are relatively value free (Kantrowitz & Ballou, 1992). These therapists are vulnerable to making assumptions without being aware that they are doing so. On the other end of the continuum are therapists who believe that their political and social values are "the healing elements of their therapies"; problems arise when these individuals believe that their views concerning social roles and personal morality are the "therapeutically correct standards for healthy functioning" (Aponte, 1994, p. 170).

Not surprisingly, there is evidence that clinicians' personal beliefs and lifestyles are reflected in their values concerning therapy. In one study, religiously oriented therapists rated religious values as more important in mental health than did less religious therapists (Jensen & Bergin, 1988). Practitioners in their first marriage valued marriage more highly. Psychiatrists and older therapists "valued self maintenance and physical fitness more than did non-physicians and younger professionals." And psychodynamically oriented practitioners believed "self-awareness and growth values were more salient to mental health and psychotherapy than did behavior therapists" (Bergin, Payne, & Richards, 1996, p. 306).

But because the psychotherapy field is so dominated by Euroamerican practitioners, Euroamerican values are often simply not perceived. Take the example of individualism. In a random sample of 229 psychologists (96% non-Hispanic White), individualistic values were clearly endorsed over others (Fowers, Tredinnick, & Applegate, 1997, p. 214). This emphasis contrasts sharply with the greater weight given to interdependence, group cohesion, and harmonic relationships in other cultures (S. C. Kim, 1985; Matheson, 1986).

Individualistic values even influence the concepts used to measure success in therapy—for example, "*self*-awareness, *self*-fulfillment, and *self*-discovery" (Pedersen, 1987, p. 18—italics added). Although family systems theories offer a potential solution to this individual focus, they too suffer from Euroamerican biases. For example, the value placed on the individuation of family members may lead a therapist to diagnose an East Indian family as "enmeshed," despite the normality of their behavior within an Indian context (see Rastogi & Wampler, 1998).

Self-disclosure and emotional expressiveness are similarly valued by the field and often seen as central for progress in therapy. However, many clients are cautious about sharing information that could damage their families' reputation. Among Asian Americans, such reserve is best viewed as a culturally appropriate sign of maturity and self-control rather than as pathological resistance (S. C. Kim, 1985). With African American clients, "resistance" to therapeutic work may be a reflection of the "difficulties of balancing parenting, household tasks, and one or more jobs" (Moore Hines & Boyd-Franklin, 1996, p. 80).

Although behavioral change is often the goal of psychotherapy, clients of minority cultures and religions (and even some clients of dominant groups) may be more interested in obtaining emotional support or developing patience. Helping clients with the process of letting go of the need to control events

> is not a process of passivity, resignation, dependency on authoritarian direction, or obedience to some guru. It is rather a turning loose of the uncontrollable and the unnecessary, a positive spiritual realignment of one's life and a joining of one's resources with healing and life-enhancing processes of reality. (Kelly, 1995, p. 221)

In their exploration of values with clients, Bergin et al. (1996) gave attention to five specific areas of work that I've found to be equally relevant to therapists' cultural self-exploration. Two of these areas are value clarification, or the articulation of one's commitments, and value discovery, or the exploration of unconscious values that may be expressed through behaviors and words without awareness. To engage therapists with these processes, I ask members of the triads described above to first answer the question, "What do you value?" Common answers for therapists are hard work, education, family relationships, community, honesty, and a spiritual orientation to life.

You may share some of these values but also hold others that are related to your particular cultural identity, family, and experiences. I remember asking the question of one triad, which coincidentally consisted of three women of Scandinavian backgrounds. They laughingly said that they were all taught, "Work hard, save your money, and don't enjoy it!" Although humorous, they went on to talk about how this message affected their lives in the form of a certain seriousness and stoicism that were helpful to them in some situations but unhelpful in others.

A third area for exploration is that of value ordering, or prioritizing and recognizing one's priorities (Bergin et al., 1996). Often, what appears to be a value conflict between a therapist and client is related to differences in the degree to which something is valued. For example, in working with couples, a common question for therapists to pose is, "Which do you value more—the happiness of each individual or the maintenance of the relationship?" Clearly, most therapists value both and so do most clients; any differences are primarily related to the degree to which one is valued over the other. Recognizing the shared aspect of these values (i.e., the middle ground) can help therapists and clients of different belief systems to work together more effectively.

A fourth area, value realization, involves a consideration of the congruence (or incongruence) between one's stated values and what one actually does (Bergin et al., 1996). For example, a therapist may believe that not imposing her values on clients is the right thing to do; however, her particular theoretical orientation is laced with assumptions about what is important. Looking for more effective ways of implementing one's values, or "value enhancement" (Bergin et al., 1996), is the fifth area of attention, which for this therapist might involve reading cross-cultural critiques of her preferred theory and discussing them with colleagues of different cultural backgrounds.

To further explore therapists' values, a second question I ask triad members to discuss is, "How does a particular value affect your work with clients who may not share this value?" The challenge in this question is to begin to see value differences less judgmentally and more with an attitude of interest in understanding oneself and others. For instance, the value that many therapists place on hard work (in school and employment) may not be rewarded in the culture of a client who comes from an extremely harsh environment where there are few jobs, low pay, and no opportunities for advancement (Aponte, 1994; Boyd-Franklin, 1989). Moreover, the person who works hard in such a situation may even be seen as identifying with the dominant culture and be punished for trying to separate herself or himself from the group. Recognizing the reasons that clients hold the values they do can help therapists increase their compassion for and understanding of their clients.

More specific questions aimed at exploring how culturally related values affect one's work with clients include the following:

▪ How have these cultural influences shaped who I am, how I see myself, and how clients see me?
▪ How do these influences affect my comfort level in certain groups and my feelings about particular clients?
▪ What is the relationship between my visible identity and my self-identification, and how is this influenced by my cultural context?
▪ What kinds of assumptions are clients likely to make about me based on my visible identity, my sociocultural context, and what I choose to share about myself?
▪ How might my areas of privilege affect my work (e.g., my clinical judgments, theoretical preferences, view of clients, beliefs about health care)? (The concept of "countertransference" in relation to particular clients is discussed in chapter 4.)

The Case of Don

To give a better idea of how this process of self-exploration can work, consider the responses to these questions given by a particular therapist. Don would generally be seen as a middle-aged, middle-class, White man; however, his identity is much more complex when considered via the ADDRESSING framework. His example is a good one for illustrating the point that cultural influences affect all of us in complex ways, whatever our identities.

Table 3.2 summarizes the ADDRESSING influences in Don's life. The following interview summary provides the background for understanding the meaning of Don's self-description in Table 3.2.

▪ How have these cultural influences shaped who you are, how you see yourself, and how clients see you?

Well, clearly they've all influenced me in a great way. I think the most significant factor in my life would probably be having been . . . adopted; I'm hesitating, because the word that comes to mind is "abandoned," and I do think that that's a significant piece, because I think the abandonment stuff has been pretty big in my life.

I was adopted by my Irish Catholic family at the age of 10 months. My sister was also adopted, but she was 100% Irish. I've known my whole life that I was adopted, but I did not find out more about my background until high school. Then, much later, I did a legal search, not to get in contact with my biological parents, but because I wanted more of a cultural identity, more of a sense of who I was. And that's how I found out about the French Canadian and Seneca piece.

[As for the meaning of this for me,] it's a mixed blessing. Because I found it out as an adult, with a fair amount of education behind me and an interest already in diversity, the first thing that it did was that it slapped me in the face with my own prejudice. What I felt was a lot of pain because I realized how much I had bought

TABLE 3.2.	
The Therapist's Cultural Self-Assessment: Example of Don	
Cultural Influences	**Don's Self-Assessment**
*Age and generational influences	Mid-40s, post-World War II baby boomer; I identify with the sense of hopefulness of my generation and a shared history of political and social upheaval in early adult years (grew up near Berkeley).
*Developmental or acquired Disabilities	No current disability, but I once had cataracts on both eyes that hindered my work for 1 year; also, I was the primary caregiver for parents who both had heart attack and/or stroke in their 50s.
*Religion and spiritual orientation	Grew up in a fairly religious Irish Roman Catholic family; currently a "recovered" Catholic with a strong sense of spirituality, belief in reincarnation, Buddhist philosophy, and earth-based spiritualities.
*Ethnicity	1/2 Irish, 1/4 French Canadian, 1/4 Seneca Indian; adopted at birth and reared in Irish American family; as an adult, reconnected to Native heritage through legal search, academic study, professional work, and social relationships.
*Socioeconomic status	Adopted into a middle-class family that made it into upper middle class; currently upper middle class.
Sexual orientation	Gay, with some bisexual leanings; was married to a woman in my early 20s, had a child with her, then divorced; currently with a male partner and politically active in the gay community.
Indigenous heritage	See Ethnicity above.
*National origin	Born and reared in United States; English is first language.
*Gender	Male; active roles as son, brother, and partner.

Note. * = holds dominant cultural identity.

into stereotypes growing up. I lived in a family with a father who was pretty bigoted, my mother less so, but still influenced by her culture. I was raised in a pretty privileged, White, upper-middle-class environment on the East Coast, in the Midwest, in the South, and then in California. I went to junior high and high school in Oakland, and that was very diverse; the schools were about 60% students of color. That introduced me to a whole lot more. But I still lived in a White neighborhood.

In finding out more about my ethnic heritage, I had fairly avoidant behaviors, particularly around Native Americans. One, because growing up in the East and

Midwest, I didn't see them; even in California, the Native population was not very visible. Seattle is the first city I've lived in where there is a much larger Native population that is urban. I also had a painful awareness of how I had these internalized stereotypes of people who were lazy, who were drunk, who didn't parent very well. And then having to discover that there was a part of me that fit into that group was really hard, and it still is.

I've never felt a part of my family, so to some degree I feel more connected now that I have a sense of my ethnic heritage. But I still feel pretty isolated from a community. Through my adoptive family, I can connect to my Celtic heritage, but there's still this other half of me. I'm trying to find ways to connect with that in more meaningful ways. I battle with feeling like an outsider because, basically, I am. I have been putting out feelers to the Seneca tribe, which is one of the more decimated groups of the Iroquois Nation. They are primarily in upper New York State, Ontario, and Quebec. But they've lost their land and don't really have a place.

I've also made some strong connections in the Seattle community. I completed the Native American mental health specialist certification and did a lot of work with the Seattle Indian Health Board, which gave me more of a sense of how to work. I have also spent a lot of time in some rural areas of Mexico, particularly with Zapotec Indians. I did observations with their healers, studying with a translator, as part of my dissertation work.

I had these interests even before I knew the details of my heritage. But it was still pretty painful for me to see that, despite all of that, there was still part of me that avoided Indian people. I don't have this problem when I'm someplace else. But in my own home community, I really have to push myself to change that. It's still a struggle in that I generally want to feel connected, but I also feel like a fraud, because I was not raised with the identity. And clearly the other piece for me is that I look White.

▪ How do these influences affect your comfort level in certain groups and your feelings about particular clients?

There's a double-edged sword. On one hand, they allow me to feel fairly comfortable about being with people I don't know. I resort back to being the quiet observer at the beginning before I move in. The flip side of it is that I can get so introspective and so conscious about how I can best connect, that I get in the way of opportunities that are available. It's the fraud thing. I would hate for any person or group of people to think that I'm co-opting them or attempting for all the wrong reasons to be a part of them.

▪ What is the relationship between your visible identity and your self-identification?

Today, they are much more congruent. But I would say historically, I was really good at having a facade of being personable and present, when internally I experienced myself differently. I did a really good job of acting. But I didn't feel as confident inside.

▪ How has your self-identification been influenced by your cultural context?

A lot. I think there's a cultural thing with being an adult adoptee. It comes out in the part of me that realizes the male White privilege I have and how uncomfortable I can feel about that sometimes. Even though I realize it's somewhat uncontrollable. And adding to it is the recognition that I had all of that, and then finding out that I'm not really that at some level, or not all of me. I mean, in the purest sense, I'm not this

White middle-class straight male. And that's a whole thing that we haven't even touched on—the gay aspect.

▪ Was there a parallel between the time that you began to recognize that you were gay and the time that you started to learn about your ethnic identity?

The gay part happened much earlier. I mean, I knew, but I didn't have a word for it. But I knew that I was attracted to other boys at about age 6 to 8. Certainly, culturally, it was not just my family, but also the world around me. I didn't really get it—that there were gay people—until I was in college. And that says something about the interaction between the social and family system. I mean, I grew up in the Bay Area, and I had no clue until I moved here. And I spent lots of time in San Francisco, and so like, where was I? I have no idea. I dated women, and I had these full-blown attractions to men. And I was comfortable about it, but I knew you couldn't talk about it.

I think the hard thing now in my life is that although I feel so much more congruent, I am more aware when I act in opposition to this desire to be authentic. I don't have to or want to hide parts of myself. There are certainly places and situations where I come up against that—hiding myself—where it feels very clear that I should keep my mouth shut, for safety. However, I am no longer willing to consciously lie. Now, I might find creative ways around it that feel safe. Still, being more conscious means being aware of my discomfort.

But that's contemporary, and it's been true for the past 10 to 15 years. Previous to that, it was a real struggle, I mean, my homophobic stuff played itself out, in terms of finding ways to avoid having to deal with it. I didn't want to lie but I didn't want to get in trouble either, and I could pass as straight really well. To me, it was particularly evident not so much in my own life and how it had an impact on me, but in the sense that I wouldn't say anything when other people were making jokes or cracks. And now I feel ashamed that I didn't say something—which I'm no longer willing to do, about anybody. And that's true in terms of my ethnic relations stuff too. If I have anything in my life that haunts me now, that's it—that for a long chunk of time I didn't stand up and say "This is not okay."

▪ What kind of assumptions are clients likely to make about you based on your visible identity, your sociocultural context, and what you choose to share about yourself?

I think that my clients are attracted to me because they experience me as being genuine, which includes being willing to talk about my experience openly. And at the same time, I'm willing to say, I need to learn more about this. So when I'm working with someone who has such a different experience from me, I'm pretty open about the fact that I don't know what those experiences are, and I really want to understand. I think that's why I've had a fair amount of success with diverse clients.

▪ When clients first meet you, and know nothing about you, do you have an awareness of how they perceive you?

I suspect that they perceive me as this middle-aged—oh, I don't like to say that word—this youthful, middle-aged, White guy, and assume that I'm straight. I think that once we've chatted for a little while, they have a sense of me that's deeper. And it's not so much about whether my exterior has changed, but their sense of my being that's shifted.

■ How might your areas of privilege affect your work (e.g., your clinical judgments, theoretical preferences, view of clients, beliefs about health care)?

The biggest piece for me, and I try to keep really conscious of this, is the biases that come out of the givens of my life. It's something that I always have to pay attention to, in terms of the expectations I have of people. In other words, when someone is clearly different from me, it's much easier for me to step out of my biases because I think I'm more conscious of them. I actually struggle more with people who look like me, or are more like me, because then it's easier to make assumptions that I shouldn't make about their experience. On one level, I really do believe that we all have the capacity to do whatever we want to do. And, I think that there are tremendous obstacles based on history and all these "isms" we're talking about.

But underneath that, I still really believe the idea that we can all transcend ourselves in some way, even if it's just our attitude. So sometimes I have to be careful that I'm not leaving things out, like the obstacles; that has happened, and I have to catch myself that I don't make these assumptions.

The other thing to pay attention to is values, with people of particular backgrounds. The biggest place I get caught is between the value of the group versus the value of the individual, to stay conscious of not placing importance on the individual only. I've also been in situations where there's so much value placed on the group that the individual gets lost. It's not that it's right or wrong, it's just priorities.

■ How about in terms of your theoretical preferences?

I can't help but assume that because I was raised in this Western culture as a White male, that that's influenced me to some degree. I've certainly known that early on, for me, a cognitive-behavioral training program was attractive because it was rational. It was about changing thinking, and that made sense to me. Even though that's not how I operate very well, but I got caught in it and I was good at it.

I also think that my later attraction to existentialism was influenced by Western culture, which values the individual more than the group. And I think that I was attracted to Zen Buddhism for the same reason. Zen Buddhism is a very rational, individually oriented kind of thing, and I think it's also larger than that. It's about the individual within a group context. When I talk to people who were raised in Buddhist cultures, they have a very different slant on it than I do, yet this doesn't diminish the usefulness of this perspective for me.

I also have a firm belief that both of these theoretical leanings I have, have lots of room to be widened. I think that there are elements of each that address societies and groups and not just the individual. But that has to be conscious, something you do with it, which is most of the work I'm trying to do now. Clearly I'm still influenced by my experience, which I can't change.

And that's the other big thing I've come to realize: I can't leave behind my context, so how do I adapt it? I think it's a trend now to want to throw it out, because it's "bad," but I can't. We see this now in how many Westerners attempt to co-opt Eastern thought without truly understanding the context. In the process, they have once again done this Western dualistic split—Eastern is good, Western is not.

I can change what I think about things, but I can't change who I am. So I have a hard time with folks out there throwing everything off of their Euro/White, Christian culture and trying to be something they're not. I think we can learn from lots of other things, but we're always going to interpret it in a Western way. We can live in another country for years, and there's still going to be a way in which we perceive things. I think that's one of the reasons why both Zen Buddhism and existentialism offer me so much, because the one thing they do similarly and really well is that they hold the paradox. To me that's so essential. It's not about leaving one behind and moving to another, or either/or. It's about both/and.

Clearly, Don is a person who had thought deeply about cultural influences on himself before being asked these questions. But even when one is highly experienced in the area of diversity, there are always areas in which one can grow further. Exploring these questions by oneself and within a group setting are parts of a process that can contribute to therapists' ongoing cultural self-assessment (see Aponte, 1994; López et al., 1989).

Seeking New and Diverse Sources of Information

After carefully considering the questions and ideas outlined so far, you will come to recognize the key gaps in your experience and knowledge base regarding particular groups. The next step is to begin to search for information that will educate you about the groups with which you have little experience. This search can lead to books, magazines, newspapers, films, theater, workshops, and culture-specific community events. Of course, most of us already use these sources of information; what turns them into culture-specific learning opportunities is how we think about them and the questions we ask—that is, our critical thinking.

Critical thinking about one's sources of information involves questions that challenge the information itself and simultaneously expand one's perceptions, beliefs, and attitudes (Brookfield, 1987). For example, when you read newspaper articles about ethnic minority cultures, do you read between the lines for information about the authors' identities and political orientations? Does it occur to you that many articles about minority cultures are written by members of dominant groups, often without comment from members of the group being discussed? The following questions may help you in thinking critically about information sources:

- Who are the authors, producers, or editors of this information? What are their identities, political orientations, and alignments?
- Are people of minority identities and views represented?
- Is this information directly *from* people of minority groups or only *about* them?
- Where can I obtain information from more direct or alternative sources?

The views and experiences of people of minority cultures are routinely excluded from the mainstream media. Consider the number of popular films that focus on the love story of a person who has a disability, a hero who is Hindu, or the lives of ethnic minority elders. When minority groups are discussed, it is often from the perspective of members of the dominant culture. For example, despite the plethora of films about the Vietnam War, I have yet to see one written or directed by a Vietnamese person.

To counter this imbalance, look for publications and information emanating from minority communities themselves (e.g., elders' groups, organizations of people who have disabilities, religious and ethnic communities, sexual minorities, and women's groups). In cities and even in many smaller communities, minority groups publish their own newsletters or newspapers. Large newsstands and bookstores sell magazines and newspapers from various countries that provide news and perspectives on events often completely ignored by U.S. reporters. And films from Asia, Latin America, and India are available in many video stores.

Psychotherapists increasingly have an enormous resource in their efforts to become cross-culturally informed: the large and growing research base on people of diverse minority groups. However, there continue to be gaps, and one of the most obvious is the dearth of information regarding social class and people of lower socioeconomic status (Robinson & Howard-Hamilton, 2000). There are several reasons for this neglect. For one, people of lower socioeconomic status have commonly been labeled poor candidates for psychotherapy (Jones, 1974). The disinterest in investigating this stereotype and in developing approaches, if indicated, that are more effective is no doubt related to the lack of money in working with people who have limited or no income.

In addition, therapists are, by education, occupation, and usually income, middle- or upper middle-class and usually hold values consistent with their status (Acosta, Yamamoto, Evans, & Wilcox, 1982; Robinson & Howard-Hamilton, 2000). This observation applies to therapists and researchers of ethnic and other minority identities as well as those of dominant cultural identities. As Aponte (1994) noted, today's therapeutic models often carry strong social messages and philosophies "that reflect the world of the intellectual and the academic" and contrast sharply with the "traditional customs, lifestyles, and religious beliefs" (p. 246) that many clients of low socioeconomic status hold. These differences make it difficult for many therapists to understand and effectively help clients of low socioeconomic status (Acosta et al., 1982).

Within the multicultural literature, I believe that there is another reason for the lesser interest in social class. One of the primary purposes of multicultural counseling research and coursework has been to counter stereotypes about people of color (see Locke & Kiselica, 1999). Among these stereotypes is that of the poor, uneducated ethnic minority group member who holds values that are so antithetical to mainstream America that psychotherapy is assumed to be irrelevant. In attempting to overturn this stereotype, multicultural counseling research has focused more on middle-class people of color, particularly college students and middle-aged working people, who, not coincidentally, are more easily accessible to researchers.

Unfortunately, I do not believe psychology's relative disinterest in social class will change in the near future, which means that middle- and upper-middle-class therapists will need to work extra hard to find information that challenges their class-related biases. My suggestion for finding relevant written information (and one that I find personally helpful) is to read outside the field of psychology in the areas of political science, history, sociology, anthropology, social work, and some forms of literature (e.g., first-person novels by people who grew up in poverty or poor working-class environments).

To learn from, not simply about, people of diverse minority groups, knowledge of culture-specific organizations is also important. Examples of resources with which therapists will want to be familiar include religious institutions (mosques, synagogues, churches, temples, and meeting houses); support groups, educational institutions, and recreational centers for elders and people with disabilities and their families; culture-specific community organizations and language-specific social services; gay, lesbian, and bisexual counseling services and political action groups; university and community women's centers; and community support groups and activities for parents and children.

Relationships and the Influence of Sociocultural Contexts

As a field, psychology is oriented toward individualistic work. However, to increase one's cross-cultural competence, individually oriented work (e.g., introspection, self-questioning, reading, some forms of research) is necessary but not sufficient (Pedersen, Fukuyama, & Heath, 1989). Equally important are relationships with people of diverse identities and an understanding of how people in our social networks influence us. Interpersonal relationships contribute to our awareness of our limitations and biases. However, if the people around us hold similar identities and share the same privileges, then we may rarely question the "universal nature" of our beliefs, and become what Wrenn (1962) referred to as "culturally encapsulated counselors."

Because the therapist's role in itself confers authority and power (Holiman & Lauver, 1987), therapeutic practice—even with clients of diverse identities—will not necessarily increase one's self-awareness. Therapists need to look outside the therapy setting to individuals and groups who differ from themselves and who can facilitate the self-assessment process.

Here is another exercise. Take a minute to consider the people with whom you choose to spend most of your time. It can be helpful to make a list of these individuals (e.g., your partner, spouse, friends, co-workers, fellow students, and particular family members). Now look back at the ADDRESSING outline and the cultural influences you starred as areas of privilege. Think about the individuals in your intimate circle and ask yourself, How many in my circle differ from me in these areas of privilege? (Table 3.3). For example, if you are in your 30s, do you have any close friends who are in their 60s? If you do not have a disability, do you have any close relationships with people who do? If you grew up in a Christian or agnostic home, do you have any intimates who are Muslim, Buddhist, or Jewish? If you are heterosexual, is anyone in your closest circle gay, lesbian, or bisexual? If you are of Euroamerican heritage, do you have any confidantes of ethnic minority cultures?

Of course, everyone's situation will be different, but for many people, this exercise highlights the homogeneity of their social circles. This homogeneity is particularly common when one belongs to a dominant or majority group (e.g., consider professional circles in psychology; Hammond & Yung, 1993). Furthermore, research suggests that people tend to be attracted to those they perceive as similar to themselves, particularly with regard to mates (see Kail & Cavanaugh, 2000).

Although intercultural marriages and partnerships are increasing, "interracial" marriages between Euroamericans and African Americans, between Euroamericans and

TABLE 3.3.

Recognizing the Influence of Sociocultural Contexts

Cultural Influences: Are my confidantes different from me in:	Confidantes' Names				
	Jan	Habib	Max	José	Nadya
Age and generational influences?					
Developmental or acquired Disabilities?					
Religion and spiritual orientation?					
Ethnicity?					
Sexual orientation?					
Socioeconomic status?					
Indigenous heritage?					
National origin?					
Gender?					

American Indians, and between Asian Americans and African Americans constitute only about 2% of all marriages in the United States (Root, 1996) (a slight underestimate of relationships, because marriages do not include gay, lesbian, and nonmarital partnerships). However, people of minority groups have a much higher rate of intercultural marriage than Euroamericans: A 1993 Time magazine article stated that "65% of Japanese Americans and 70% of Native Americans married out of their ethnic communities" (Winndance Twine, 1996, p. 325).

One reason that minority groups have higher rates of intercultural marriages (and possibly other types of intimate relationships) is that because they are in the minority, they often have no choice but to develop relationships with people who are different from themselves. People of majority groups can usually find friends and partners of their own cultures because there are lots of them, and they are more likely to have the option to surround themselves with culturally similar people (e.g., a neighborhood) if they so choose (McIntosh, 1998).

Direct personal experience with people who differ from oneself culturally is an essential component for gaining cross-cultural sensitivity and understanding (Heppner & O'Brien, 1994; Mio, 1989). But it is not enough to simply be around people of diverse backgrounds. Interpersonal learning occurs through interaction. Traveling in various countries, eating in ethnic restaurants, and attending cultural events can set the stage for interaction, but deeper learning comes from relationships between people that are sustained over time.

In addition, it is important to remember that power differentials can affect what and how much is shared in a relationship. Relationships with people who are in a less powerful position than oneself (e.g., clients, students, support staff) may involve learning, but power differences generally mean that one person is in a more vulnerable position and thus often less inclined to speak freely. One can better learn from peer-level, intimate relationships in which both parties hold enough power to honestly and safely share their feelings and thoughts.

The development of such relationships is a natural outgrowth of the work described so far. However, if members of dominant cultural identities are not engaged in this type of work, attempts at relationships with people of minority identities can easily backfire. That is, choosing a friend because she or he holds a particular identity can be offensive because it suggests a greater interest in the person's culture than in the individual.

How Humor Can Help

Differences between people inevitably lead to disagreements, and humor can be a valuable tool in this regard. Humor can communicate an appreciation of someone but at the same time serve corrective or informative functions (Swinomish Tribal Community, 1991). In communities where daily life requires an ability to get along with others, the "face-saving" aspect of humor allows for the communication of sensitive information without offending the listener (Allen, 1998; Prerost, 1994). And humor can be an effective mechanism for decreasing tension and reducing conflict (Lemma, 2000).

For example, cross-cultural differences in behaviors regarding time lead to conflict for many people, particularly in work settings, and they have for me too. In my 16-year marriage to a Tunisian man, differences in our approaches to time were a rich source of disagreement. From my perspective, when we were in the United States, Jawed was late for almost everything. (When we were in Tunisia, it didn't matter.) From his perspective, I was obsessive about time; evidence of my problem included keeping my watch set five minutes ahead, my preference for being early to avoid being late, and my annoyance at waiting for him.

But one evening in Tunisia, after living several years in the United States, Jawed noticed how long it took to say goodbye and go out the door of his sister's house after dinner—approximately 2 hours. We started laughing about this, which reminded me of how long it took for my sister and me, living on the farm, to be ready when Dad asked, "Anybody wanna go to town?"—about 2 minutes, or we might miss an opportunity to get ice cream. After this experience, humor became connected to our differences regarding time, which helped to minimize the negative feelings. Over the years, Jawed became more aware of appointment times, and I came to see the positive side of his behavior: He was often late because he was focused on whomever was with him at that moment, whether colleague, friend, or student, which made that person feel important. Also, somewhere along the line, I started being late for meetings.

Conclusion

Culturally responsive practice begins with the therapist's commitment to a lifelong process of learning about diverse people across cultures and life spans. A first step in this process is to explore the influence of one's own cultural heritage on one's beliefs, views, and values. Related to this work is the need to recognize the ways in which privilege can limit one's experiences and knowledge base. Equally important is the willingness to seek out new sources of information that enable the therapist to learn from and with, and not simply about, people of minority cultures. Forming intimate relationships with people of diverse identities is an important part of this learning. The reward for these efforts is a deeper understanding of one's clients, an appreciation of the richness of diverse people's experiences, and an ability to provide more effective and culturally responsive mental health services.

KEY IDEAS 3.

Engaging in One's Own Cultural Self-Assessment

1. Recognizing the ADDRESSING influences on one's own life is a helpful first step in the exploration of one's cultural heritage.

2. Recognizing the areas in which one holds privilege is key in understanding the impact of these influences on one's work with clients.

3. Privilege is contextual: A privileged identity in one cultural context may not be privileged in another.

4. Because privilege tends to cut people off from information and experiences related to specific minority groups, the areas in which we hold privilege are usually those in which we hold the least awareness.

5. Psychology is a privileged profession that reinforces many dominant cultural values.

6. Therapists' personal beliefs and lifestyles are often reflected in their values concerning therapy.

7. Individually oriented work (e.g., introspection, self-questioning, reading, some forms of research) is necessary but not sufficient for increasing cross-cultural competence.

8. What turns mainstream sources of information into culture-specific learning opportunities is how we think about them and the questions we ask—that is, critical thinking.

9. Peer-level, intimate relationships with people of diverse identities are a rich source of cross-cultural learning.

10. Humor is a valuable tool in reducing the conflict that often comes with cross-cultural relationships and interactions.

III CONNECTING WITH YOUR CLIENT

Entering Another's World: Understanding Clients' Identities and Contexts

4

> I used to wonder why I have so often felt preoccupied with issues of boundaries and of identity. Why am I still startled when someone asks, yet again, What are you? Are you (fill in the blank racial/ethnic group, usually an incorrect one)? It can't be! Are you sure? Are you a woman first or a person of color/Asian American first? If this is a lesbian group, why do you keep talking about race? We are all women here! (K. M. Allman, 1996, p. 277)

During the past 20 years, psychologists have given a great deal of attention to describing the development of culturally related identities. Although this work initially focused on racially based identities of "Blacks" and "Whites" in the United States (see Helms, 1995, for an overview), more recently attention has been given to the development of identities related to ethnicity (Sue & Sue, 1999), gender (Downing & Roush, 1985; Kimmel & Messner, 1992; Wade, 1998), sexual orientation (Cass, 1979; McCarn & Fassinger, 1996; Troiden, 1979), disability (Olkin, 1999), and minority status in general (Atkinson, Morten, & Sue, 1993). One of the chief contributions of these new areas of knowledge has been a heightened awareness of individuals and groups that have been marginalized from and by mainstream psychology.

As briefly mentioned in chapter 1, much of the psychological research on identity continues to reflect dominant cultural conceptualizations, namely of identity as a unidimensional phenomenon (Reynolds & Pope, 1991). For example, research on sexual identity development among gay, lesbian, and bisexual people often assumes the following about the process of "coming out": (a) that it occurs in a linear progression of specific stages; (b) that it occurs only once in a person's lifetime (i.e., a person is either "out" or "still in the closet"); and (c) that the end result is usually positive (i.e., there is an increased self-acceptance and integration of one's sense of self) (Smith, 1997).

However, such approaches fail to consider contextual influences, such as membership in an ethnic minority community, that may make the coming out process a very different experience. More specifically, disclosure of one's sexual identity may involve the contradiction of cultural norms regarding personal and family privacy and the potential loss of support from one's cultural group. It may also add another form of oppression that, for an individual already affected by racism and possibly sexism, represents an unbearable burden (B. Greene, 1994). In such a context, the reluctance to disclose one's sexual identity may be an adaptive, self-protective response (Smith, 1997).

Much of the research regarding people of color, women, elders, and people with disabilities assumes a cultural homogeneity that simply does not exist (although feminist researchers recognized somewhat earlier the Eurocentric assumptions embedded in their theories). Only in the past few years have researchers begun to address the ways in which people of diverse minority and multicultural identities think about themselves and those around them (see Brown & Root, 1990; Comas-Díaz & Greene, 1994b; B. Greene, 1997; Gutiérrez & Dworkin, 1992; Hays, 1995, 1996a, 1996c; Robinson & Howard-Hamilton, 2000; Rungta, Margolis, & Westwood, 1993; Saravanabhavan & Marshall, 1994).

The Complexities of Identity

Using the concept of race and drawing from Anzaldua's (1987) ideas regarding "racial borders," Root (1996) offered a framework for understanding the experiences of people who hold biracial heritage:

> (1) an individual may solidly identify with both groups, simultaneously holding and merging multiple perspectives;
> (2) the individual may experience a shift in one identity, from foreground to background, depending on the sociocultural context, that is, in one setting, one identity may be experienced as primary, whereas in another setting, the other identity may be;
> (3) the individual may identify primarily as a biracial or multiracial person, thus using the "border between races" as a central reference point; or,
> (4) the biracial person may identify primarily with one group but, over an extended period of time, move in and out of identification with a number of other groups. (pp. xxi–xxii)

As Root noted, these various adaptations may also be useful in rethinking the dualities in conventional categorizations of gender and sexual orientation; I would add that they seem equally helpful in understanding people's identifications with diverse groups. Consider the example of Laura, a 45-year-old woman of bicultural heritage.

Laura's Euroamerican father met her mother, who was Japanese, in Japan. World War II had just ended, and the couple decided to settle in Hawaii, where mixed marriages were more accepted. Laura and her younger sister attended public schools, and the family lived in a neighborhood where bicultural children were so common as to be the norm. Looking back on her childhood, Laura remembered being referred to as "*hapa*," the Hawaiian word for part, meaning *part* Japanese. However, as she reached her teenage years, she was more inclined to see herself simply as "local," meaning born and reared in Hawaii. This identity gave her a feeling of comfort with friends of mixed ethnicities.

Laura experienced a noticeable shift in her identity when she left Hawaii to attend a university on the mainland. Her school was located in a rural area with few people of color. She was frequently asked where she was from and was not sure if the person meant "what state" or "what country." Although she perceived herself to be visibly bicultural, everyone seemed to assume that she was Asian. She began to think of herself more as Japanese American and became interested in connecting with the few Japanese American and Asian American students on campus.

After college, Laura moved to San Francisco, where she worked for a large bank. When she turned 30, she married a Chinese American man named Dan. Her daily interactions with Dan's large family, contrasted with her predominantly Anglo work environment, heightened Laura's sense of herself as an Asian American woman, although among her in-laws, she was also strongly aware of her Japanese roots.

In her late 30s, Laura experienced another major shift in her self-identification when, during the birth of her second child, she had a stroke caused by a brain aneurysm. Due to moderate cognitive and physical impairments and the paralysis of her right arm and leg, she had to go on disability leave from her work. Her mother came to stay with her and care for the children. Members of Dan's family came daily to bring meals and offer support.

Laura regained her cognitive abilities within a month. However, the right-sided paralysis persisted, and during this time Laura became depressed and anxious. She worried about whether she would ever regain the mobility she had had before. She worried about her ability to take care of her children over the long haul. And she worried about their finances, because although she was receiving disability insurance income, it did not match her previous salary. Her husband was clearly stressed from coping with the ordeal while maintaining his usual 55-hour-per-week job. It seemed that the disability dominated her entire existence, and only in negative ways.

Laura received both group and individual counseling through a rehabilitation program, which lasted 6 months. During this time she gained the use of her right arm, but her right leg remained weak. After 3 months in the program, her depression began to lift—not solely because her previous abilities were returning, but also because she began to see new ways of looking at her life. Through counseling, she realized that a big missing piece for her was a spiritual practice. She had been brought up in a Protestant church and, during college, was very interested in "the deeper questions," but she had let go of this part of herself when she entered the workforce. She could see now how she had been "caught up in the busy-ness" of working, rearing children, and maintaining a marriage and family relations and had had little time to think about the meaning of these activities for her.

After 1 year, Laura continued to use a cane to walk. She returned to work part time, and she and her husband and children moved into a smaller house to decrease their expenses. Laura became actively involved in a culturally diverse church that one of Dan's siblings attended. The new relationships she made with church members provided an additional sense of purpose and meaning in her life (see Royce-Davis, 2000). Despite the family's lowered income and her impairment, which she came to consider mild, Laura described herself as happy with her life.

With regard to her identity, Laura continued to experience shifts in her sense of self, depending on her situation. At her core, she still felt "local" (i.e., born and reared in Hawaii). More specifically, with Dan's family, she experienced her Japanese ethnicity as most salient because it contrasted with their Chinese culture. With friends who had disabilities, she was more aware of herself as an Asian American woman, but in her culturally diverse church group, she thought of herself more as a person with a disability.

As Laura's case illustrates, cultural identities are not necessarily mutually exclusive or linearly progressive in their development; the salience of one's identities often varies over time and across settings (McCarn & Fassinger, 1996). Moreover, changes in identity do not necessarily represent a switching of loyalties, but rather a response to the expectations and constraints of particular environments (Root, 1996).

The Significance of Identity in Assessment

Why is it important to be aware of the adaptive and varied identities clients experience? Perhaps the most obvious reason is that a knowledge of clients' salient identities gives the therapist clues about how clients see the world, what they value, how they may behave in certain situations, and how they are treated by others. The more a therapist knows about a particular client's cultures and the variations within, the closer her or his inferences and hypotheses will be to the client's reality, and, in turn, the better able the therapist will be to help that person (López et al., 1989). Consider another example.

An African American therapist was seeing a married, male client in his 30s who had recently immigrated to the United States with his family from Kenya. The assessment and two therapy sessions had gone well, and the therapist experienced a sense of mutual respect between them; because of their common African heritage, she also assumed that she held a deep understanding of his experiences in the United States. However, the therapist found herself becoming increasingly annoyed that the client called her a couple of times between each session to confirm some agreement or arrangement that the therapist had considered firm from their in-session discussion. These behaviors were not representative of any obsessive tendencies in the client; to the therapist, it felt as though the client did not consider her reliable and so was checking up on her.

During the third session, the therapist tactfully asked the client about his need to call. The client explained that in his country, he often had to remind people to do things they said they would do, especially people working in government or institutional settings. He added that things worked slowly and if you wanted something, you had to keep checking on it. The therapist, who had never been outside the United States, recognized the assumptions she held based on her own experiences with authorities in the United States: People in institutional settings usually do what they're supposed to do, even if it's slowly, and if they don't, there are usually alternatives. Her annoyance subsided as she and the client had a straightforward discussion of their different expectations regarding people's behaviors.

In an initial assessment, the simplest way to learn about a client's self-identification will often be to ask. However, at times, asking about a client's identity can be problematic. It is still considered impolite and even risky in many North American settings to discuss race, social class, sexual orientation, age, or certain disabilities. In an initial session, clients may assume that a therapist, regardless of her or his visible identity, holds the dominant culture's biases simply because the therapist is in a position of authority. Clients may fear that raising such topics will offend the therapist (B. Greene, 1994, p. 24).

In addition, the way in which an identity-related question is asked can subtly determine the client's response. Depending on the context, the question, "What is your ethnicity?" may be perceived as ridiculous or odd, because the client believes the answer to be obvious. Or, when the client's ethnic identity is not self-evident, such a question may be offensive because, in the dominant culture, questions about identity have historically been used to decide how people will be treated (Root, 1996). People of minority and mixed identities may be especially sensitive to such questions from a therapist who appears to belong to a dominant cultural group.

A less direct form of this question, such as, "Would you tell me about your cultural heritage or background?" is more likely to elicit helpful information without giving offense. Similarly, asking clients to describe their "religious upbringing" and then inquiring about their practice today allows for a richer response than simply asking, "What is your religion?" This suggested phrasing implies that heritage is not a unidimensional, static phenomenon by recognizing that one may have been brought up in a particular culture or group but currently identify with another. In addition, unlike more specific questions (e.g., "How is it for you as an African American in your school?") such phrasing does not expose the therapist to the risks of assuming an identity for the client that the client does not hold for himself or herself.

In working with people who have disabilities, Olkin (1999) recommended avoiding questions such as, "What's wrong with you?" or "What happened?" The first question assumes that only people without disabilities are normal, and the second suggests a search for something or someone to blame. Similarly offensive is the question, "How might you have been different without your disability?" which is like asking someone who they would be if they weren't a man, African American, Jewish, and so forth. More appropriate inquiries are, "What is the nature of your disability?" and, if the client has not brought up the subject of disability following a discussion of the presenting problem and current situation, "Are there ways in which your disability is part of this (presenting problem)?" (Olkin, 1999, p. 167). Exhibit 4.1 lists questions therapists can use to open discussion of cultural influences with clients.

Straightforward questions about a client's identity may also be inappropriate when clients perceive the concept of identity to be an abstraction unrelated to their presenting concerns. In fact, identity *is* an abstraction—one that may be useful to therapists but not necessarily to clients. Recall the case of Mrs. Sok (the Khmer woman in Chapter 2), who would no doubt have found a discussion of her identity to be even less relevant to her presenting complaint than the questions she was asked.

EXHIBIT 4.1.

Understanding Clients' Identities: Questions for Clients

1. How would you describe yourself?

2. Would you tell me about your cultural heritage or background? (Follow up with questions about ethnicity, racial identification, national origin, Indigenous heritage, and primary language, as relevant.)

3. What was your religious upbringing? Do you have a religious or spiritual practice now?

4. What was your family's economic situation growing up?

5. Do you have experience with disability, or have you been a caregiver for someone who does?

6. Are there ways in which your disability is a part of [your presenting problem]? (Olkin, 1999)

7. What did it mean to grow up as a girl (boy) in your culture and family? (L. S. Brown, 1990)

EXHIBIT 4.2.

Understanding Clients' Identities: Questions for Therapists

1. What are the ADDRESSING influences on this client (i.e., Age and generational influences, Developmental and acquired Disabilities, and so on)?

2. What are this client's salient identities related to each of these influences? What are the possible meanings of these identities in the dominant culture, in the client's culture, and from the personal perspective of the client?

3. How are my salient identities interacting with those of the client?
   a. How am I being perceived by this client, based on my visible identity?
   b. Am I knowledgeable about those groups with which the client identifies?
   c. How might my identity and related experiences, values, and beliefs limit my understanding of this client?

In general, when a client does not wish to explore the relationship of personal and cultural identities to his or her current situation, it is wise to respect this wish, especially before a trusting relationship has been built. However, this does not mean that the therapist should not consider identity issues and discuss these issues later in therapy, once a respectful relationship has been established. Assessment and therapy will invariably be facilitated by an understanding of clients' identities (Comas-Díaz & Greene, 1994a), as well as a consideration of the interaction between the therapist's own identity and that of the client (Pérez Foster, 1996) (Exhibit 4.2).

TURNING ASSUMPTIONS INTO QUESTIONS AND HYPOTHESES

At the beginning of any assessment, information about a client's identity and situation is usually provided by the referral source (e.g., "Mrs. Cheng is a 55-year-old, widowed, Asian

American woman who presents with . . .). Using this introductory information, the therapist then engages in "a continuous cycle of hypothesis formulation and hypothesis testing about the particular individual. Each item of information . . . suggests a hypothesis about the person, which will be either confirmed or refuted as other facts are gathered" (Anastasi, 1992, p. 611).

For example, a therapist who has experience with Asian American people would immediately recognize that this client's surname is Chinese. This realization would then allow him to begin to form hypotheses about the client's cultural context that are more likely to be useful (i.e., hypotheses that are relevant to a widowed Chinese American woman living in the area). At the same time, the therapist's experiences would keep him aware of the diversity of possible influences in this client's life, including, for example, the possibility that despite her name, the client is *not* Chinese American.

Of course, once the therapist and client meet, a great deal more information is usually available regarding a client's identity. The client's language fluency, national or regional accent, physical appearance, body posture, preferred physical distance during social interactions, mannerisms, clothes, grooming, and apparent age all serve as cues for the therapist's hypotheses about the client's possible identities. Here again, the usefulness of such information depends on the knowledge base and experience of the therapist.

Consider a less knowledgeable therapist's inferences regarding Mrs. Cheng's report that she was born in Vietnam and came to the United States with her husband and children at the age of 30. From the perspective of the second therapist, this piece of information would raise questions about the client's experiences of immigration and the Vietnam War and adjustment to life in a new country, and these would be reasonable areas of inquiry. However, because the therapist is unfamiliar with Asian names and people, her observation that Mrs. Cheng appears to be of Asian heritage, combined with Mrs. Cheng's statement that she was born in Vietnam, might lead the therapist to mistakenly assume that the client is ethnically Vietnamese, when in fact she is not. In this situation, the therapist's lack of knowledge of the existence of a Chinese minority culture within Vietnam (as well as any information about them) could lead to questions, hypotheses, or interventions that are irrelevant or inappropriate (e.g., consultation with a Vietnamese liaison who holds negative attitudes toward people of Chinese heritage). (See Rumbaut, 1985, for information on Chinese Vietnamese refugees.)

There is no substitute for culture-specific knowledge and experience in providing culturally responsive services. Moreover, what one needs to learn is also therapist specific, depending on the therapist's own cultural identifications, experiences, and contexts. For example, to work effectively with a gay African American client, a therapist who is gay and Euroamerican would in most cases need to expand his knowledge and experience in ways that are different from the ways in which a heterosexual African American therapist would need to expand his.

HOW THE ADDRESSING FRAMEWORK CAN HELP

For therapists engaged in the cross-cultural learning process, the most basic level of attention in an initial assessment involves simply considering what identities may be relevant for a given client. The ADDRESSING framework can be helpful with this systematic consideration, because it provides an easy-to-remember list of minority (and majority) identities that correspond to each of the ADDRESSING influences. The following example describes this systematic consideration of the ADDRESSING influences and related identities with one client.

Jean, a 35-year-old Haitian man, immigrated to Québec at the age of 15 with his uncle and the uncle's wife, who had no children of their own. Jean completed university in Montréal but had difficulty finding employment with his degree in political science. After many months he "settled" on a position as assistant manager of a large, nationally franchised hotel. He subsequently married a French Canadian woman who also worked in the hotel. They had a son, but after two years they divorced because, as Jean put it, "she looked down on my family."

Jean was referred to a counselor by his physician, who could find no medical reason for Jean's recurring migraines. Six months before the referral, Jean had taken a new position as manager of a mid-sized hotel, a significant move up. The position was so demanding that he had not had a weekend free in 3 months, and many times he stayed overnight at the hotel. His former wife was pressing to change their joint custody arrangement, because she knew Jean was frequently leaving their 8-year-old son with his aunt and uncle. Jean described his headaches as extremely painful and said that he had missed several days of work and was feeling anxiety and even some panic that he might lose the job.

In the initial assessment, the therapist, Marie, a 40-year-old French Canadian woman, spent the first few minutes talking socially with Jean. She told him that she had visited one of the French-speaking islands (St. Martin), which prompted Jean to talk about the similarities and differences between it and Haiti. Marie was aware of the prejudice toward Haitians in Québec (see Gopaul-McNicol, 1993) and the need for her, as a *Québecoise*, to demonstrate her respect for Jean fairly quickly. Because she knew he had a university degree, she asked him what he studied, thus acknowledging his educational status. His response allowed her to make a closer connection between their experiences, because her partner also had a degree in political science with a focus on immigration issues, and she shared this information with him.

Once a beginning rapport had been established, Marie explained the purpose of the assessment and asked Jean if he agreed to proceed. He did, so she went on to ask if he would describe himself to her, including "any information that you think I might need to know in order to understand you and your situation better." He replied,

> My father is a successful businessman in Port au Prince, and my mother was a
> teacher before she retired. I have one sister, who is also a teacher, and two brothers,
> who work with my father in his business. My brothers also attended university in
> Montréal, but they returned to live near our family. We have a large family, and I
> have many aunts, uncles, and cousins, and my grandparents are still living, too. I
> stayed here because my son is here.

Reviewing the ADDRESSING influences in her head, Marie noted those areas in which Jean provided information regarding his identity. The most consistent aspect of his summary was his emphasis on family. In addition, he provided information about his generational and socioeconomic status through the details about his parents' occupations, his sister being a teacher, and his brothers' university educations. From this brief description, as well as other observed cues (e.g., his physical appearance, dress, language abilities, and social skills), the therapist hypothesized that Jean's identity was closely tied to his family relationships, that he considered himself middle class, and that his national origin was a central part of his identity. These hypotheses were accurate primarily because they reflected the information Jean provided (Table 4.1).

Marie also noticed that Jean did not mention a religious identity, his sexual orientation, his gender, or the presence of any disability. She hypothesized that he had not mentioned gender, sexual orientation, or disability because he assumed that these were obvious. She also recognized that he might not conceptualize sexual orientation in the same way as the dominant culture (i.e., research suggests that for Haitians, sexual behavior between people of the same gender "is often not correlated with a self-definition as gay or bisexual"; Bibb & Casimir, 1996, p. 103). She asked if he had had a "partner" since his divorce, and he said that he had gone out with a few women but that he had not developed a serious relationship with anyone. Marie refrained from probing further in this initial assessment but still considered the possibility that Jean could be gay or bisexual. Later, as she learned more about his life and relationships, she ruled out this hypothesis.

TABLE 4.1.

ADDRESSING Client's Cultural Influences and Identities: The Case of Jean

Cultural Influences	Jean's influences, as noted by Marie
*Age and generational influences	35 years old; born in 1965 and grew up under the oppressive Duvalier governments (1957–1986).
*Developmental or acquired Disabilities	Not reported or apparent.
*Religion and spiritual orientation	Self-identifies as Catholic. I did not ask about, and he did not mention any voodoo belief or practices.
Ethnicity	Haitian; reports he "does not feel Canadian" although he has landed immigrant status (i.e., permanent residency).
*Socioeconomic status	Middle-class parents, has a university education, underemployed probably due to discrimination, speaks French fluently (a class-related ability).
*Sexual orientation	Probably Heterosexual.
*Indigenous heritage	None.
National origin	Haitian; speaks Haitian Creole and French fluently; immigrated to Québec in 1985.
*Gender	Male, single (divorced), father of one son also a brother and uncle.

Marie still needed to find out about religious influences in Jean's life, because this could be a source of support and positive coping behaviors. She asked, "What was your religious upbringing?" Jean said that he was Catholic but only attended mass when he was home (in Haiti), although he prayed "during hard times, like now." Marie was aware that many Haitians integrate voodoo rituals into Christianity and that such rituals might be helpful to him, providing some relief from the burden he was feeling. However, she also knew that voodoo is associated with lower social class, and Jean might interpret such questions as stereotyping or as an indirect way of checking his class status (Bibb & Casimir, 1996). So instead, she asked what he thought was contributing to his migraines, and what he had tried to change these factors or decrease the pain. He did not mention any voodoo beliefs or practices, so she refrained from asking more specifics at this point.

UNDERSTANDING THE MEANINGS OF IDENTITIES

Even when a therapist has a clear description of a client's self-identification, this information will not necessarily lead to a deeper understanding of the client. What is essential is a knowledge of the meaning of these identities (L. S. Brown, 1990). Depending on one's reference point, there may be more than one meaning for the same identity. That is, a particular identity may have one meaning in the dominant culture, another in a minority culture, and still another person-specific meaning for the individual.

Information about the person-specific meanings of identity usually comes from the client, either indirectly (through descriptive information and views shared by the client) or in response to direct questions (e.g., What does your identity as a Haitian man mean to you, in your present situation?). However, to understand these person-specific meanings, it is essential that therapists also understand their culture-specific meanings.

To understand the meaning of Jean's identity as a Haitian Canadian man, it was necessary to have at least a general knowledge of Haitian culture and history. Haiti became the world's first independent Black republic when slaves overthrew French colonizers in 1804. From 1915 to 1934, Haiti was occupied by the United States. From 1957 to 1986, Haitians endured the oppressive regimes of Papa Doc and his son Baby Doc Duvalier. The Tonton Macoutes, a secret military police, routinely tortured and politically persecuted dissenting professionals, politicians, and students. The first wave of immigration began during this period and consisted primarily of the well-educated upper and upper middle classes. A second wave, from the mid-1960s to 1971, consisted mainly of middle-class people such as Jean's aunt and uncle. The third wave of immigrants came during the 1980s; these individuals were mostly poor and nonliterate. It was this latter group that included the widely publicized cases of individuals with AIDS, contributing to the stereotypical association of Haitians with AIDS.

More recently, following the democratic election of Father Jean-Bertrand Aristide to the presidency in 1991, his reinstatement after a military coup, and the subsequent election of René Préval in 1996, the political situation is more stable. However, Haiti remains the poorest country in the Western Hemisphere. Class divisions among Haitians both inside and outside the country are strong. Fluency in French and lighter skin color, related to family histories of intermarriage with the French, and thus alignment with

French colonial values, are associated with higher social status. In Québec, Haitians who are fluent in French have the advantage of language. However, they are not accepted in the same way as French speakers of European origin; color-based job discrimination is not uncommon (summarized from Bibb & Casimir, 1996; Glasgow & Adaskin, 1990; Primedia, 2000).

Jean was a lighter-skinned, Haitian man, fluent in French and with a university degree, from a middle-class family. In his culture-of-origin, he held privilege and status. In contrast, in a Canadian context, the same cultural identities held a different meaning; being Haitian (or, from the dominant cultural perspective, Black) meant that he was seen primarily as an immigrant and a foreigner. The most salient aspects of his identity in Haiti, his gender and social class, were eclipsed by his ethnic identity, which visibly set him apart from the majority of Canadians.

Although it might at some point be appropriate for the therapist to ask Jean about his personal experience as a Haitian man living in Québec, it would not be appropriate for the therapist to expect Jean to educate her about the general cultural meanings of his identity. Nor would it be wise, because information about a whole culture from the client's sole perspective will often be quite limited. Obtaining this kind of information is part of a therapist's own personal learning, most of which should occur outside the therapy setting.

As an analogy, consider a therapist who has no direct experience with people who suffer from dissociative disorder; she would certainly not expect the first client she sees with this disorder to educate her about its common characteristics. Rather, she would obtain this information herself outside the therapeutic relationship and then use the assessment time to explore the client's personal experience of the disorder.

If, with regard to Jean, the therapist is unfamiliar with the general history and culture of Haiti, the impact of political events on Jean's generation, and the position of French-speaking "visible minority cultures" in Canada, she would be more likely to maintain her credibility by admitting these gaps, at the least to herself and, depending on the circumstances, possibly to her client as well. She could then commit herself to expanding her knowledge for the benefit of her client. This commitment would lead her to seek information and experiences outside the therapy setting and to educate herself about these general meanings. As her knowledge and experience increase, her understanding of Jean's identity would still be framed as hypotheses, but these hypotheses and the questions that emanate from them would be much closer to the realities of his life.

Understanding Client-Therapist Interactions: More Than Just Transference

Early psychoanalytic approaches emphasized the therapist's role as a blank slate or mirror upon which the client's feelings about parental figures could be projected. The client's emotional reactions to the therapist, known as transference, were seen as "projections by a client of expectations and distortions based on past experience" (Chin, 1994, p. 207). However, when one introduces the concept of culture into an analysis of therapist-client interactions, it is clear that the emotional reactions of clients to therapists, and vice versa, often reflect cultural differences and power imbalances in the real world.

As Pérez Foster (1996) noted, "the fact is that analysts are neither neutral screens nor simple clay for transferential transformation. They are, in fact, formidable characters who often have robust prejudices" (p. 15). A client's reaction to a therapist of another cultural identity may be less related to the client's feelings about her parents than to the client's daily experiences with people of the therapist's culture. Recognizing this reality, in recent years psychodynamic theorists have broadened definitions of transference and counter-transference in ways that open up a consideration of cultural influences (Chin, 1994). For example, from the perspective of self psychology, Hertzberg (1990) noted that the internal representations held by people of minority identities include "both the experience of self within a particular subculture, as well as the experience of the self as an outsider of a larger, dominant culture" (p. 276).

Consider the situation of a 60-year-old married woman of Guatemalan heritage who was referred to a much younger, Euroamerican woman therapist. Because the client's most intimate and long-lasting relationships have been with her husband and children, and because she is older than the therapist, she may be more likely to see the therapist as a daughter than as a parental figure. Similarly, the therapist's experience of the client may involve feelings associated with her own mother or grandmother. (See Newton & Jacobowitz, 1999, for more on transferential and countertransferential processes with older clients.)

But the reactions of this client and therapist to one another may be based on more complex identifications than age alone. For example, what if the therapist is from a well-educated, upper-middle-class family, and the client is from a poor, rural, Indigenous background? In this case, the client may remind the therapist more of the maid that she has hired to help with household responsibilities and child care, and the therapist may remind the client of the powerful Spanish-speaking landlords in Guatemala or of demanding employers in her new country. Conceptualizing the client's distrust as solely a projection of her feelings overlooks the client's history and day-to-day experiences of oppression by members of the therapist's culture (see Gleave & Manes, 1990, regarding Guatemalans in Canada).

Despite the negative emotions associated with the topic, it is important that therapists be able to bring up culture or race if it appears to be relevant to the therapeutic relationship. For example, a Euroamerican therapist's straightforward question to a Black family (e.g., "How do you feel about working with a White therapist?") makes available for discussion what is probably already on everyone's mind (Boyd-Franklin, 1989).

Of course, if the therapist does raise the topic, it is essential that she or he has "seriously thought through its relevance"; otherwise, the question may be perceived as patronizing (B. Greene, 1994). In addition,

> "White therapists need to be prepared for the possibility that this question may elicit feelings of anger, and some family members may even verbalize their reluctance to work with a White therapist. The more able a therapist is to remain nondefensive and nonapologetic while discussing this issue with the family, the greater the likelihood of a therapeutic connection." (Boyd-Franklin, 1989, p. 102)

Before raising these questions with clients, consultation and supervision with people of diverse identities can be helpful. As Williams (1999a) noted with regard to race, "the task in training White counselors is to desensitize them to talking about their feelings about race. For counselors and trainees of color, on the other hand, this usually is not the problem. Much of their experience . . . has been marked by frequent, lively discussions about racial issues with other people of color. However, what typically has been missing in these discussions is White people. The counselor education classroom or professional workshop, thus, becomes a forum for an unfamiliar enterprise that is rich with opportunity for growth for everyone: discussing race across racial groups." (pp. 34–35)

At the same time, therapists will not always want to bring up the topic with clients, at least initially. Many older people, of both dominant and minority cultures, grew up in a time when one was expected to hide or minimize differences related to race, social class, sexual orientation, and disabilities (Sang, 1992). In addition, many individuals are uncomfortable with direct discussion about another person's abilities or limitations, fearing that in the therapeutic setting such discussion might suggest that the therapist is not competent. Finally, as mentioned earlier in the case of Mrs. Sok, some clients will simply not see the relevance of the therapist's identity or their own, and making it an issue before a relationship is established may feel forced.

Just as clients' feelings about therapists may originate in their experiences with members of the therapist's culture, so also is the therapist influenced by his or her experiences with clients' cultures. Chin (1994) discussed common manifestations of countertransference in therapists of minority and dominant cultural identities. When the therapist is a person of color, countertransference may involve overidentifying with clients' experiences, and thus underdiagnosing or minimizing psychopathology when it is present. Therapists of color are also cautioned against "interventions that promote an agenda for personal change regarding cultural and gender roles that is not the client's" (Chin, p. 212). On the other hand, the strong identification of therapists of color with their clients frequently facilitates the therapeutic relationship.

In contrast, Chin (1994) noted that countertransference in Euroamerican therapists often involves issues related to power and difference. For example, out of a desire to form an alliance with clients of color, Euroamerican therapists may minimize cultural differences, and from a lack of knowledge, they may assume similarities that are not real. As a result, clients may feel misunderstood or alienated. A similar dynamic can occur with clients who are lesbian or have disabilities (see Boden, 1992, p. 173). On the other hand, countertransference may facilitate the therapeutic relationship if the therapist acknowledges the differences and her lack of knowledge regarding the client's culture, but also holds a strong willingness to be helpful and learn (Chin, pp. 212–213).

Returning to the case of Jean, the therapist's assessment could be facilitated by an understanding of the interaction between her own identity and that of Jean. She could first use the ADDRESSING acronym to identify those aspects of her identity that are different from Jean's and thus most salient in this particular setting; these would include religion, ethnicity, national origin, and gender.

Recognizing her own identity as a Canadian-born Québecoise, a feminist, and a woman, this therapist would want to think critically about how her inexperience with Haitian people increases her susceptibility to dominant cultural assumptions about Haitian men. She would want to consider the possibility that her own Euroamerican feminist philosophy, which she considers relatively unbiased, might contribute to any prejudice she holds (see Exhibit 4.2).

While the therapist might identify with Jean's experience as a member of a minority group because she holds minority status as a woman and as a French Canadian, she would want to be cautious about assuming similarities in this regard. When considered from a national perspective, her French Canadian ethnicity certainly constitutes a minority status. Francophones number approximately 5.4 million of the total Canadian population of 26 million, and as a group they have traditionally been in a subordinate position relative to the Anglophone majority (Elliott & Fleras, 1992, p. 202). However, within Quebec, French is the official language, and French Canadians constitute a powerful majority. Thus, relative to Jean, and in the context of Québec, the therapist is a member of the dominant culture.

Since the revision of discriminatory immigration laws in 1962, the proportion of European immigrants to Canada has decreased, and more people have arrived from Latin America, Asia, South Asia, the Middle East, the Caribbean, and Africa (Elliott & Fleras, 1992, pp. 231–236). Members of these later groups, referred to as "visible minorities" in Canada, commonly experience problems related to language, employment, finances, and the bureaucracies of the social services, health care, and immigration systems (Waxler-Morrison, 1990, p. 7). Although European immigrants experience these problems too, the barriers are often less formidable for their children, who physically resemble Anglo and French Canadians.

Along with this background, Marie's awareness of her perceived visible identity would help her to understand Jean's behavior in the therapeutic setting. If Jean initially appears defensive, Marie could consider the possibility that his self-protective behaviors may be in reaction to her visible identity as a *Québecoise*. Given the prejudice and discrimination he has experienced from members of her culture, it would not be surprising that he feels defensive with her. On the other hand, Jean's reaction may have more to do with the therapist's identity as a woman. What appears to be defensiveness may be discomfort about sharing his particular problems with a woman or with a woman who belongs to the dominant culture. Whatever the case, the more knowledgeable the therapist is regarding her own and Jean's identities, the more able she will be to understand his reactions and then behave in ways that facilitate their interactions. These facilitative behaviors are discussed in more detail in chapter 5.

Conclusion

Identity is a complex phenomenon that comprises both group-specific and person-specific meanings. Although the concept of identity is not always of interest to clients, it can be helpful to therapists who want a deeper understanding of their clients. Knowledge of a client's identity allows the therapist to more accurately infer what cultural influences have been important in that person's life. In turn, such information helps the therapist to form hypotheses and ask questions that are closer to the client's reality.

Although information about a client's personal experience of culture will usually come from the client, it is generally not fair to expect clients to educate the therapist about the broader cultural meanings of their identity. Obtaining the latter information is primarily the therapist's responsibility and will often involve work outside the therapeutic setting. The more committed a therapist is to this outside work, the more able she or he will be to use this background information to understand the client's personal experience and respond in ways that facilitate assessment and the therapeutic process.

KEY IDEAS 4.

Understanding Clients' Identities and Contexts

1. Identity is a multidimensional phenomenon that varies across cultures, contexts, and time.

2. A knowledge of clients' salient identities gives the therapist clues about how clients see the world, what they value, how they may behave in certain situations, and how they are treated by others.

3. In an initial assessment, the ADDRESSING framework can be helpful because it provides an easy-to-remember list of minority and majority identities that may be salient in a client's life.

4. Even if a client does not wish to explore the relationship of personal and cultural identities to his or her current situation, it is important that therapists consider identity issues, including the interaction between the therapist's own identities and those of the client.

5. A particular identity may have one meaning in the dominant culture, another in a minority culture, and still another person-specific meaning for the individual.

6. Information about the person-specific meanings of identity will usually come from the client; however, obtaining knowledge of culture-specific meanings of identity is a part of the therapist's own personal learning and ought to occur primarily outside the therapeutic relationship.

7. The reactions of clients and therapists to one another (transference and countertransference) often reflect cross-cultural relationships, conflicts, and power imbalances in the real world.

8. Awareness regarding one's own cultural identity is essential for understanding cross-cultural transference and countertransference in therapy.

9. The therapeutic relationship may be facilitated by an honest discussion of cultural differences between therapist and client, if the client is open to such a discussion.

10. Consultation, supervision, and ongoing self-assessment are important steps in building one's confidence and experience in addressing cross-cultural differences with clients.

Making Meaningful Connections: Establishing Respect and Rapport

5

To date, a great deal of research attention has been given to elucidating relationship-building behaviors in the therapeutic relationship. The focus of this work has been on the development of "microskills" that include attending, listening, influencing, focusing, and engaging in selective attention and confrontation. Most of this research originates from a Eurocentric frame of reference (Ivey, Ivey, & Simek-Morgan, 1993). For example, the skills taught to demonstrate attending and listening are those commonly valued in Euroamerican culture: "good" (i.e., direct and steady) eye contact; comfortable, forward-leaning posture (to indicate interest); and a neutral tone of voice, even when the client shares disturbing information. Dominant cultural norms are further reinforced by graduate schools that dictate expectations regarding "the importance of beginning and ending on time, whether first names or honorifics will be used, payment of fees, touch, therapist self-disclosure, and therapist availability between sessions" (L. S. Brown, 1994, p. 95).

The field's lack of attention to relationship-building behaviors and attitudes in other cultures is unfortunate because such knowledge could help therapists increase their effectiveness with clients of both minority and dominant cultural groups. Many of the dominant cultural behaviors used by therapists do not work for all people of Euroamerican cultures either. Let's look at some of these behaviors and attitudes, beginning with the case of Mr. Ortega.

Mr. Ortega, age 32 and of Costa Rican heritage, arrived for an appointment with the physician in his company's outpatient clinic. In fluent English with a Costa Rican accent, he explained that during the past 5 months he had had pains in his stomach, had not eaten well, and had lost about 20 pounds. The physician, a Euroamerican man in his 40s, did a thorough medical examination and concluded that Mr. Ortega's pain was due to esophageal reflux. He asked Mr. Ortega if he was experiencing some stress in his life. Mr. Ortega said yes, that he and his wife had not been getting along, that she had gone back to Costa Rica with their daughter to visit her family, and that he was afraid she might not come back. The physician responded that this sounded like a very stressful situation. He explained that Mr. Ortega's problem was heartburn, which can be aggravated by stress. While writing a prescription for medication, the physician asked Mr. Ortega if he would be willing to see the "nurse practitioner therapist" for a few minutes "to talk about stress and diet in relation to your stomach problems and get some suggestions regarding your health and what you can do to feel better." Mr. Ortega agreed, so the physician left for a few minutes to talk to the nurse practitioner, Sharon, returned to introduce her to Mr. Ortega, and left the two to talk.

Sharon, age 38 and of Italian American heritage, greeted Mr. Ortega with a firm handshake and some informal conversation about how difficult traffic had become in the two areas of town in which they each lived. Sharon's friendly manner and mention of traffic on the way to her children's day care led Mr. Ortega to talk about his own 2-year-old daughter. During the course of this conversation, he told Sharon that his first name was Manuel. Sharon observed to herself that Manuel was casually but neatly dressed and wearing dark-rimmed glasses. He showed a full range of affect and was friendly, although his facial expression and posture suggested anxiety.

Following this casual conversation, Sharon began the formal part of the assessment by describing her training as a nurse practitioner and psychotherapist who works with people who have stress-related problems. As she explained her particular, eclectic approach to therapy and gave a few examples of how she had helped people in the past, Manuel's facial expression became increasingly tense. He told Sharon that he had thought that this meeting "was just to talk to the nurse to get more information about my stomach problems; the doctor was the main one helping me." Sharon could see that he was feeling embarrassed about the suggestion that he might need counseling. She recognized her own feelings of embarrassment and irritation—embarrassment that he obviously didn't see how she could be of help, which felt like a jab at her competence, and irritation emanating from her belief—an assumption—that he wouldn't be reacting this way if she were a man.

Taking a deep breath to slow her own reactions, Sharon apologized for the misunderstanding about the meeting's purpose. She then validated Manuel's feelings by saying that she could see how he would be confused by the situation, that she and the physician had not been as clear as they could have been. This seemed to ease the tension slightly, so Sharon went on to explain that in their clinic, she and the physicians worked closely together, because so many health problems involve both the body and the mind. She talked about how "physical" problems like headaches, stomachaches, and body pains are often related to stress, for example, losing one's job, making a major move, or being in the middle of a family conflict. She also gave examples of problem-solving done in counseling that helped people feel less worried, which in turn decreased their physical symptoms. Manuel still appeared tense, but he was actively listening. Realizing the need to establish her own credibility, Sharon said she would like to ask the physician to join them for a few minutes.

Sharon went down the hall and returned with the physician, who also apologized to Manuel for the misunderstanding. The physician went on to repeat in his own words the clinic's intention to help people solve whatever problems might be affecting their health. He said that he and Sharon consulted regularly with each other to provide the best possible care for their patients and that if Manuel were willing to talk further with Sharon, he was sure she could give him some useful ideas on controlling his stomach pain and even eliminating the heartburn. Much of the tension subsided with this, and the physician left. Manuel indicated his willingness to stay for another half-hour to "consider" some of Sharon's suggestions. They talked informally again for a few minutes, and then resumed the assessment.

As this case illustrates, the establishment of some form of meaningful connection is an essential first step in the assessment process. With it, the therapist can proceed to gather information, but without it even the most basic questions may lead to the downward spiral of defensive behaviors. From the beginning, Sharon laid the foundation for a working relationship when she engaged in social conversation with Manuel. This initial accommodation to Manuel's culturally related expectation of *personalismo* (a friendly, personal approach—more on this below) and *respeto* (respect) increased the likelihood that he would stay engaged even if a conflict arose. When a conflict did occur, the therapist was able to set aside her own inclination to respond defensively and could think about what the client might need to feel more at ease. She hypothesized that Manuel might have more respect for the male physician (either because he was a physician or because he was male, or both), so she chose to involve the latter, despite the feelings that this brought up for her. (See Hernandez, 1996, for more on working with Costa Rican clients.)

The Importance of Respect

Euroamerican culture places great emphasis on egalitarianism in relationships. In individual interactions, differences in power related to social class, ethnicity, disability, and so on are supposedly ignored. Peer-oriented exchanges are preferred, and "talking down to" or interacting with someone in a patronizing way is considered just as undesirable as being patronized. It may be for this reason that (predominantly Euroamerican) psychotherapy researchers have focused primarily on rapport-building behaviors in their attempts to understand and find ways to facilitate the therapeutic relationship.

However, the concept of respect is just as important or more so than that of rapport in many cultures, including Latino, African American, Asian, Arab, and many Indigenous cultures (Boyd-Franklin, 1989; El-Islam, 1982; S. C. Kim, 1985; Matheson, 1986; E. S. Morales, 1992; Swinomish Tribal Community, 1991; Trimble & Fleming, 1989). This does not mean that respect is unimportant to Euroamericans, or that the concept of rapport is irrelevant to these cultures. But it does mean that what is considered a core element in a relationship may vary across cultures, as well as across individuals and families.

It can be helpful to think of respect in two ways: (a) as an internal orientation to the world (i.e., a set of attitudes or a worldview) and (b) as a set of overt behaviors. One of the best definitions I've found for the attitudinal form of respect is that of Matheson (1986). From an American Indian perspective, she describes the internal orientation of respect as

"a quality which one carries with him/her, as constantly as his/her heart or spine . . . not a re-active phenomenon, only stimulated in response to specifically measured behaviors or status . . . but a conscious and active awareness . . . between an individual and his/her universe." (p. 116)

What I like about this description is that the person starts by respecting others, rather than waiting for people to earn it.

Sometimes, the value placed on respect reflects traditional beliefs about the importance of honoring those in authority (Abudabbeh, 1996; S. C. Kim, 1985). For example, within Arab cultures, respect is determined by a number of interactive factors including age, type of work, family name and reputation, and socioeconomic status. Specifically, greater status and respect are accorded to older people, those with higher levels of education, and those seen as having personal integrity (e.g., families that have lived in the area for many generations, families with a good reputation because of their benevolent works or religious practice) (see Barakat, 1993).

In Mexican families, *respeto* is a central value in parent-child relationships and often connotes "more emotional dependence and dutifulness" than does the English "respect" (Falicov, 1996). *Respeto* may also be used to reinforce the authority of men over women and children Bernal & Shapiro, 1996), although increasingly, immigration and social changes have resulted in a wider variation of structures and processes in Latino marriages and family life (Bernal & Shapiro, 1996; Falicov, 1996; Martínez, 1999).

Among people of minority identities, a high value on respect may also be a response to repeated experiences of being disrespected by the dominant culture. For instance, African American adults may interpret the use of first names without permission as disrespectful, because such behavior is seen as related to the demeaning attitudes and behaviors of Euroamericans during and since slavery "who refused to use their names, renamed them, and referred to them with terms intended to convey low status (e.g., boy)" (Moore Hines & Boyd-Franklin, 1996, p. 79).

Assuming that one holds the attitudinal orientation of respect, how does one demonstrate it behaviorally? One of the most basic behaviors in the demonstration of respect is the form of address used in an initial encounter. However, what constitutes a respectful address varies as much within as across cultural groups. The dominant culture often assumes a first-name basis in an attempt to decrease the social distance between people (Pauwels, 1995). But many people of ethnic minority and Euroamerican heritage, particularly elders, consider such informality to be offensive (P. Morales, 1999). Due to the wide variation in customs regarding titles even within cultures, the general rules I go by are (a) to initially use a formal title with elders of any culture and (b) to ask clients at the initial meeting how they prefer to be addressed.

In his work with parents of children who have chronic illnesses or disabilities, Davis (1993) began with an attitude of honor toward parents for trusting him enough to share their lives with him for a brief period. Out of this attitude come the therapist behaviors of making parents the complete focus of attention during the time together, "allowing them to speak freely, listening to what they have to say and valuing it" (p. 54), even if he and the parents disagree. Davis noted that such respect involves using all of a therapist's knowledge and skills to help, but not "taking over for [clients] or denying their role in the process of change" (p. 54).

Inaccurate assumptions on the part of the therapist are a potential source of problems, because clients may interpret them as disrespectful. For example, an African American woman may judge a therapist to be disrespectful if she suspects that the therapist assumes she understands the woman's family based solely on a general knowledge of African American culture (Boyd-Franklin, 1989). The therapist's assumption that she understands without really knowing the client or her family suggests that the therapist is failing to recognize the enormous variations within African American culture—in other words, that she is stereotyping. In this situation, the therapist needs to distinguish between her general knowledge of African American culture and the person-specific and family-specific experiences of the client. Although she would not expect the client to educate her about the general cultural meanings of the client's identity, she would recognize her need to learn about the client's personal and familial experiences from the client.

The ADDRESSING framework can remind therapists of this within-group diversity. For example, with this African American client, it would be helpful to the therapist to consider the following kinds of questions:

- *Age and generational influences:* What are the age-related issues and generational influences on this client, keeping in mind her geographical origins? What have been the expectations, in both the African American and dominant cultures, of African American women during her lifetime?
- *Developmental and acquired Disabilities:* What is this woman's experience with disability? Might she have a disability that is not immediately apparent, or have experienced the impact of disability as a caregiver for a partner, parent, or child?
- *Religion and spiritual orientation:* What was her religious upbringing, and what are her current beliefs and practices? If she is Christian, what denomination? If she identifies as Jewish or Muslim or any other religion, what is her specific practice? Are her spiritual beliefs and religious community a source of support for her?
- *Ethnicity:* What is the meaning of her ethnic identity if, for example, she lives in a small town where African Americans make up only 1% of the population?
- *Socioeconomic status:* What is her current socioeconomic status as defined by her occupation, income, education, marital status, gender, ethnicity, community, and family name? Is this status different from that of her parents?
- *Sexual orientation:* What is the client's sexual orientation, and if she is lesbian or bisexual, what does this identity mean for her in her current context?
- *Indigenous heritage:* Does she have any Indigenous heritage (many African Americans do), and if so, is this a salient aspect of her ethnic identity?
- *National origin:* What is her national identity? Was she born in the United States? Were both of her parents American? What is her primary language?
- *Gender:* What gender-related information (e.g., regarding roles, expectations, and relationships) is significant given her cultural heritage and identity as a whole?

Therapist–Client Culture Match

To facilitate their relationships with clients, in addition to specific behaviors therapists also need to consider the effects of their own identities on the relationship. The vast majority of therapists are of dominant ethnic backgrounds (Hammond & Yung, 1993), which raises the question: Is the underutilization of mental health services by ethnic minority groups due to clients' preferences for ethnically similar counselors, of which there is a shortage?

A series of studies addressed this question with African American, Asian American, Euroamerican, Latino, and Native American college students (Atkinson, Furlong, & Poston, 1986; Atkinson, Poston, Furlong, & Mercado, 1989; Bennett & BigFoot-Sipes, 1991; Ponterotto, Alexander, & Hinkston, 1988). These researchers found that minority participants commonly ranked their preference for an ethnically similar counselor below one or more of the following: "(a) a counselor with similar attitudes and values, (b) a more educated counselor, (c) an older counselor, (d) a counselor with a similar personality, (e) a counselor with similar socioeconomic status, and (f) a same sex counselor" (Atkinson, Wampold, Lowe, Matthews, & Ahn, 1998, p. 103). For Native Americans, the type of problem also determined the ranking of participants' preferences; ethnic similarity was ranked as more important for counselors helping with academic problems than for those helping with personal problems (Bennett & Bigfoot-Sipes, 1991).

A follow-up study using more appropriate statistical methods found that Asian American students preferred a counselor with similar attitudes and values over an ethnically similar counselor (Atkinson et al., 1998). A separate study of Muslims, an ethnically mixed religious culture, found that only a slight majority (52.9%) preferred a Muslim counselor, whereas 75% said that if they had to go to a non-Muslim counselor, it was "somewhat" to "very important" that the counselor have "religious *values* similar to theirs" (Kelly, Aridi, & Bakhtiar, 1996, p. 211—italics added).

As Atkinson and colleagues (1998) pointed out, culture is defined largely "by the attitudes and values of the members of the cultural group" (p. 116). Earlier studies that used a simple choice methodology (e.g., Do you prefer an ethnically similar counselor to an ethnically dissimilar counselor?) often found that people chose the former. But clients may make such a choice because they assume that an ethnically similar counselor will have attitudes and values similar to their own (Coleman, Wampold, & Casali, 1995).

Some clients may specifically prefer a therapist who is dissimilar from themselves on particular dimensions. Among clients of minority identities, the preference for a therapist of the dominant culture may represent negative transference toward therapists seen as less competent or powerful because they are women or people of color (Chin, 1994; Tseng, 1999). In other situations, clients may prefer a therapist of any cultural group other than their own because their ethnic community is small and the confidentiality of the therapist is not fully understood or trusted (Tseng, 1999).

Studies have also investigated the relationship between treatment outcomes and ethnic match, addressing the question, "Do ethnically matched clients do better in therapy?" Controlling for a number of variables including social class, gender, age, and initial level of functioning, researchers found that "unacculturated" Asian Americans and Mexican

Americans did better when counselors were ethnically matched (S. Sue, Fujino, Hu, Takeuchi, & Zane, 1991). (Problems with the construct of acculturation are another issue, to be discussed in chapter 6.) However, treatment outcomes for African American and Euroamericans were not related to ethnic match (S. Sue et al., 1991). The reasons for these differences are unknown, but once again a hypothesis is that ethnicity is more of a demographic than a psychological variable and that psychological variables (e.g., identity, attitudes, beliefs, and personality) are of greater importance (S. Sue, 1998, p. 442).

Diverse Communication Styles

Common to many cultural and other minority groups is the expectation that informal social interaction will precede a formal procedure such as an assessment. This more casual type of interaction is known as *personalismo* in Latino cultures (recall the positive inter-action between Sharon and Manuel) (Ruiz & Padilla, 1979). It has also been described as the establishment of a sense of "mutuality" among older women (Greenberg & Motenko, 1994), a "person-to-person connection" among African Americans (Boyd-Franklin, 1989), and "respect and reciprocity" among American Indians (Matheson, 1986). Often, this expectation will take the form of what I call "who-you-know" exchanges. This form of interaction involves asking the other person if they know so and so, with the goals being to find common connections and gain a sense of the person's context. It is distinguished from the Euroamerican practice of "name dropping" in that it is generally not intended to impress or reinforce power.

I remember one such interaction between my friend and colleague Gwen, an African American woman, and a Native American man who were meeting for the first time. Both had lived in Seattle for many years and knew many Native people in the mental health field. The conversation went something like this:

"So, you're at Antioch. Do you know S?"
"No, but did he use to work at ----?"
"Yes."
"Oh. I had a friend who worked there for a couple years. Do you know her?"
"No, but I know her husband. He's at ----."

The exchange ended when they had found several people that they both knew; we then went on with the business parts of the meeting.

Hornby (1993, in Allen, 1998, p. 34) described this type of initial interaction among Lakota people as "common basing," which occurs with the shared understanding that "people and relationships are not viewed in isolation but instead as parts of an intercon-nected community" (Allen, 1998, p. 34). Upon meeting, people engage in casual conver-sation that may touch upon social events, activities, or people that the speakers have in common (Allen, 1998). Among people of Indigenous heritage, connections are often similarly made on the basis of one's geographical origin (e.g., see Cruikshank, 1990, regarding the importance of place among Athabaskan and Tlingit people). This form of connecting is also common among immigrants and among Euroamericans who grew up or live in rural areas.

With clients, however, who-you-know connections are tricky, because acknowledgment of the connection may imply that the therapist and the third party have a therapeutic relationship. In very small communities, this may be less of a problem because everyone knows everyone anyway, and a therapeutic relationship is not necessarily assumed. In other settings, when clients want to make such connections, it may be helpful to focus the discussion on events and places that one has in common, rather than people, and then if necessary to explain the limits of confidentiality as matter-of-factly as possible to avoid embarrassing the client. In any case, I mention such interactions because they are a very important form of communication for many people, and therapists will want to be aware of and prepared for this.

Directness is another behavior valued by the dominant culture. Research comparing more individualistic cultures with more collectivist cultures suggest that the latter more often use indirect forms of speech, particularly when conflict is possible, to avoid embarrassing others (see P. B. Smith & Bond, 1999, for a review). Reframing "indirectness" as "politeness" can help therapists to avoid judgmental assumptions about clients' responses; in addition, from the client's cultural perspective, such a view is often more accurate.

SELF-DISCLOSURE

Part of what distinguishes a more personalized approach from an engaging professional demeanor is the therapist's willingness to self-disclose. However, therapist self-disclosure has traditionally been viewed suspiciously, primarily related to early psychoanalytic assumptions about the processes of transference and countertransference. As Pérez Foster (1996) noted, "the trend in most analytic work has been to avoid exploration and weighted consideration of a patient's views of the therapist, outside of their transferential context" (p. 15).

I recall being chastised by a psychoanalytic supervisor once when I chatted about the weather with a very nervous 85-year-old woman client on our way from the lobby to my office. He told me that everything I said was material for therapy, so I should have waited until we were in the office to say anything to her. I understood his point from a psychoanalytic perspective; however, my client did not hold this worldview and seemed to need the reassurance of a more personal connection.

Comparing the roles of anthropologist and therapist, Fish (1996) noted that both are like a sunflower in a field of daisies: "It is easy when learning another culture to forget that you are an object of interest yourself" (p. 70). A therapist's sensitive self-disclosure gives the client an opportunity to assess the therapist's attitudes, awareness, and basic "humanness" (Allen, 1998, p. 34). In deciding what and how much to self-disclose, a useful question for therapists to ask themselves is, "How do I share personal information in a way that respects and empowers my clients?"

In some cases, asking this question may lead the therapist to share some personal information before beginning an assessment. In the earlier example, Sharon's comment about traffic on the way to her children's day care casually communicated the information that she had children—something she had in common with Manuel. Of course, she might not share such information with everyone, but Manuel was a regular patient of the clinic, a longtime employee of the referring company, and Sharon felt safe in sharing this piece of information with him. In turn, her willingness to share something about herself led to a more personalized interaction.

Opportunities for self-disclosure may also arise during the course of therapy. A common situation is one in which a client who is worried about the normality of certain behaviors or feelings asks the therapist, "Have you ever experienced this?" Often, such a question is simply an attempt by the client to normalize his or her behaviors in relation to a respected "standard" (i.e., the therapist). Flipping the question back onto the client (e.g., "Let's talk about why it is important to you to know this") may be perceived as insulting, patronizing, or making a mountain out of a molehill.

On the other hand, it may at times be therapeutic for the client to explore the meaning of the question, if the client can tolerate it. Lovinger (1996) advised taking this approach in work with religious clients, particularly Christian clients who ask, "Are you saved?" However, if the client is unable to explore the significance of the question, he advised not avoiding it and answering directly.

What a therapist chooses to share is highly person-specific and situation-specific. For example, while feminist therapy comes from a consumer orientation in which therapists are expected to share personal information that may inform their professional work, the extent of this sharing will vary depending on how the therapist defines her boundaries regarding privacy. Thus,

> One feminist therapist will be quite comfortable letting clients know that her capacity to work with incest survivors derives in some part from the fact that she is herself a survivor of incest; another will experience this level of sharing as a disrespect of self and will prefer to refer to other sources of knowledge. (L. S. Brown, 1994, p. 214)

Similarly, there will be specific clients with whom therapists may choose to share little or nothing personal about themselves (e.g., clients who are dangerous or potentially so).

Although sharing a personal experience that parallels the client's may be intended to communicate empathy, it may also be perceived as undercutting the uniqueness of, or pulling away from, the client's experience. Some clients prefer a more formal approach, and the therapist's self-disclosure may feel "intrusive" (Ivey, Ivey, & Simek-Morgan, 1993, p. 58).

L. S. Brown (1994) described three thematic characteristics of boundary violations for which therapists need to be on the lookout: (a) objectifying the client, (b) gratifying the therapist's impulses, and (c) excessively privileging the therapist's needs (pp. 215–217). To gauge this, I use the following as a guide: If it feels like what I'm sharing would help the client, then I usually share, but if the comment feels like it's more about helping me, then I don't. Also, when in doubt, consultation with a therapist of the client's culture can help to clarify what may work best. As Bergin, Payne, and Richards (1996) noted, disclosure of therapists' values and beliefs must be balanced by "respectful patience and non-interference" (p. 302), which allows for clients to make their own decisions and mistakes.

NONVERBAL COMMUNICATION

It is important to remember that therapists' self-disclosure may occur in nonverbal as well as verbal forms (Pauwels, 1995). The greater therapists' knowledge of and comfort level with different cultures, the more aware they will be of the nonverbal ways in which they are communicating and of the subtle types of information that people of different cultures look for.

An initial handshake can communicate a wealth of information. For example, in Euroamerican culture, a firm handshake is meant to convey a sense of self-assurance, or sincere happiness at seeing someone again, or (if very firm) an air of dominance. In contrast, among many American Indians, a handshake involves a more gentle touch, with the point being to *receive* information about the other person. Not realizing this, non-Indians may interpret an Indian handshake as weak or unfriendly, whereas the Indian person may interpret the non-Indian handshake as aggressive or disrespectful. Furthermore, an Indian client may assess a therapist's knowledge of and experience with Indian clients by their handshake. That is, "when a non-Indian shakes hands in the usual non-Indian manner with an Indian, the Indian person knows that this non-Indian is probably not very familiar with Indian culture" (Swinomish Tribal Community, 1991, p. 190).

Nonverbal communication may also take the form of bodily movements, preferences for physical space, and facial expressions (Berry, Poortinga, Segall, & Dasen, 1992). Physical gestures show considerable variability across ethnic cultures (P. B. Smith & Bond, 1999). In addition, people who have disabilities often use facial expressions and bodily movements to augment spoken or sign language (e.g., "guilt" is changed to "paranoia" in sign language by adding eye movements back and forth; Olkin, 1999, p. 194).

In Euroamerican culture, direct eye contact is commonly considered a measure of one's self-confidence or mental health. In therapeutic settings, indirect eye contact is often interpreted negatively as shyness, a lack of assertiveness, deception, or depression (D. W. Sue & D. Sue, 1999). However, in many cultures, indirect eye contact is not only normal, but considered the appropriate and even respectful behavior toward people in positions of authority (e.g., among Navajo students speaking to professors; Griffin-Pierce, 1997).

With regard to physical space, early research suggested that Arab, Latin American, and southern European cultures (i.e., those with Mediterranean roots) preferred less physical distance in personal interactions (Hall, 1966). However, subsequent research found significant intracultural differences on the basis of social class and situational determinants. For example, in one study, Japanese students sat farther apart when speaking in Japanese than did Venezuelans speaking Spanish. But when both spoke English, they sat at distances similar to those of students in the United States (Berry et al., 1992; Sussman & Rosenfeld, 1982).

With people who have disabilities, it is important to note the inappropriateness of touching someone's assistive device (e.g., a walker, wheelchair, or prosthetic) without permission. An assistive device functions as an extension of a person's body. As Olkin (1999) noted, "Wheelchairs are like one's legs, and I can only presume you don't rub a client's legs" (p. 194), so don't touch a person's wheelchair without being asked.

Adding to the cultural variations in preferences for physical space, individual and family differences make generalizations even more difficult. If you do not have experience with a client's particular cultural group, it is important to stay aware that there are differences, so that automatic misinterpretations are less likely to occur. It can be helpful for therapists to consider the arrangement of their office furniture, such as how close seats are placed and who sits where (D. W. Sue & D. Sue, 1999, p. 78), and to have chairs that are easily movable to allow for client- and family-specific adaptations.

Nonverbal communication may also occur in the form of silence. In Euroamerican culture, silence is often taken to be a sign of anger and may also indicate that the speaker is finished and the next person may speak. In contrast, in Chinese, Japanese, Alaska Native, and American Indian cultures, silence is often used to communicate respect (e.g., for elders); it may also be a signal that one is forming thoughts or waiting for a sign to speak (Allen, 1998; D. W. Sue & D. Sue, 1999; Sutton & Broken Nose, 1996). To avoid misinterpreting a client's silence, it may at times be helpful to ask the client about its meaning.

Related to silence is the phenomenon of "turn-taking" in conversation: "knowing when to talk and when to remain silent or pause, how long to talk for and how to indicate that one wants to talk" (Pauwels, 1995, p. 20). Overlapping speech in which the second person begins speaking before the first finishes, is common in many families and cultures. However, it is offensive to many people, who consider it "interrupting" (Pauwels, 1995). To avoid offending in this way, it may be helpful to allow the client to set the pace of the conversation (D. Brown, 1997; Trimble & Fleming, 1989).

Two other nonverbal behaviors are important to mention. One is note-taking by therapists in sessions. With American Indian and Alaska Native clients, taking notes may be perceived as disrespectful, because clients may assume that the therapist is not listening carefully (Herring, 1999, p. 37). Although it is often necessary to take notes during assessments, particularly in mental health centers, I try to keep my focus on the client as much as possible, even suspending the paperwork when clients are sharing particularly emotional information.

The other nonverbal behavior is that of giving gifts. In many cultures, giving gifts is an expression of appreciation. Turning down a small gift from a client may unnecessarily offend the client and is not recommended (P. Morales, 1999).

ENVIRONMENTAL CUES

Environmental cues are another form of nonverbal communication. For example, information about a therapist's cultural connections and relationship to the community may be communicated by the location and accessibility of her or his office. For example, when a therapist's office is accessible only by a flight of stairs, clearly, the therapist cannot see clients with certain types of disabilities there.

Within the therapist's office, the magazines in the waiting room, a calendar in a particular language, desk-top photographs, wall-hangings, and the books on the shelves all say something about the therapist's interests and concerns. When thinking about the range of clients who may be looking for the therapist's sensitivity to their own cultural contexts, it may be helpful to ask oneself, "How do aspects of my office communicate my awareness of and interest in people of different ages; people who have disabilities; religious or spiritually oriented people; people of various ethnicities; gay, lesbian, or bisexual people; and so on, using the ADDRESSING acronym?

Smell is another environmental cue that is rarely addressed in the cross-cultural counseling literature. I raise it here because misinterpretations of body smells can lead a therapist to draw inaccurate conclusions about a client. Specifically, body odor in the dominant culture is generally considered a sign of poor self-care, which is not the case in all cultures (P. B. Smith & Bond, 1999). An alternative perspective was provided by a pamphlet I found in the health clinic where I was working with Vietnamese, Lao, and Cambodian people, offering helpful hints to newly arrived refugees. One of these hints instructed readers that "Americans" are extremely sensitive to and do not like odors from themselves or others, and that they use soaps, deodorants, perfumes, and mouthwashes to hide their natural body smells; readers were advised to use such products to avoid offending their new neighbors.

TIME

One of the most common generalizations regarding time is that people of Indigenous, Latino, and Arab cultures are more past- or present-oriented, whereas Euroamericans are more future-oriented. The future orientation of the United States and Euroamericans was provided some support by the early work of Kluckhohn and Strodtbeck (1961) comparing value orientations in five cultures. However, subsequent research suggests a more complex situation. For example, the idea that Euroamericans are future-oriented is contradicted by "the massive violation of natural resources" to the neglect of future generations (Robinson & Howard-Hamilton, 2000, p. 30).

Within a particular culture, individuals of different ages may experience time differently. For example, how long a week feels to a young child, a middle-aged adult, and an older person may be quite different (Dator, 1979). People's experience of and the meanings they attach to time may also vary depending on the presence of a disability; the person's socioeconomic status, occupation, or religious culture; or what one is doing in the moment (Dator, 1979; Gonzalez & Zimbardo, 1985).

The profession of psychotherapy holds relatively rigid ideas about time, grounded in dominant cultural conceptions. Clients and therapists are expected to be on time for appointments and to meet during a set number of minutes (Holiman & Lauver, 1987). When clients do not follow the time rules for therapy, therapists may assume that they are not committed to change; clients, on the other hand, may feel that the therapist is disrespectfully rushing them (D. W. Sue & D. Sue, 1999).

There are many reasons why a client is not on time or fails to appear for an appointment. Low-income clients who do not have a car may use public transportation, which is not always on time; they may not have day care for children or older parents, or easy access to a telephone to cancel; and health and family crises understandably take priority over a one-hour appointment with the therapist (see Acosta, Yamamoto, Evans, & Wilcox, 1982; H. J. Aponte, 1994). Clients who have disabilities must also contend with the extra time it takes to do everything with a disability. Having a disability also creates tasks that require more time (e.g., ordering and buying a wheelchair or scooter, maintaining it, finding accessible services and entrances) (Olkin, 1999).

Given the variability of attitudes toward time, it is difficult to make accurate generalizations about how a client will perceive the time constraints embedded in psychotherapy. But keeping in mind the possibility of differences and clearly explaining to clients how flexible you can or cannot be will help to minimize misunderstandings.

HUMOR

Keeping in mind cultural differences (Goldstein, 2000), humor can be valuable in establishing rapport because it often decreases social tension and, in some cultures (e.g., among many American Indians), communicates an appreciation of the other person (Swinomish Tribal Community, 1991). Humor is an important element in many cultures, and often just what is needed to "break the ice" in an initial interaction (McGuire, 1999; Olson, 1994).

Humor can also be a useful diagnostic tool (Goldin & Bordan, 1999; McGuire, 1999). In my work with older adults, I often use a joke or humorous comment to gain a feeling for the person's general mood, which usually helps with building the relationship, too. Even if one of my jokes is not very funny (which of course never happens), a client's smile or smirk gives me some indication that their social skills are intact.

In therapy, humor serves a number of purposes. Humor can be used to create a cognitive shift in which the client experiences a brief relief from her or his symptoms and thus feels some hope that the stressful feelings can be changed (Mahrer & Gervaise, 1994). In the face of a situation that one cannot change, humor may help to create some distance from the problem, which then allows the person to view the situation more objectively, appraise it differently, and as a result, feel more in control; a sense of personal control is associated with better emotional well-being, better health, and better coping abilities (Lemma, 2000).

Of course, one needs to be careful not to use humor in a way that hurts or offends another person (Prerost, 1994). Dunkleblau (in McGuire, 1999) advised therapists to be aware of their own emotions and careful that they are not using humor sarcastically, or as a way to express anger or aggression. In addition, it is important not to use humor in a way that leads people to feel that they're not being taken seriously.

To distinguish harmful humor from therapeutic humor, Salameh (1983) noted that the latter:

(a) is concerned with the impact of humorous feedback on others;

(b) has an educational, corrective message;

(c) promotes the onset of a cognitive-emotional equilibrium;

(d) may question or amplify specific maladaptive *behaviors* but does not question the essential worth of all human beings;

(e) implies self- and other-awareness;

(f) has a gentle, healing, constructive quality;

(g) acts as an interpersonal lubricant and constitutes an asset;

(h) is based on acceptance;

(i) centers around clients' needs and welfare;

(j) strengthens, brightens, and alleviates; and

(k) aims to reveal and unblock alternatives. (p. 84).

Harmful humor is described as the opposite of these characteristics. To avoid misusing humor, Lemma (2000) suggested that therapists consider the meanings and underlying unconscious determinants of their humor as carefully as they think about any communication with clients. Lemma's book *Humour on the Couch* provides an exceptionally thorough discussion of humor-related issues in therapy (but be forewarned, it is not a funny book).

MINIMIZING PSYCHOLOGICAL JARGON

A potential barrier to establishing a comfortable working relationship with clients is that of language, particularly the use of psychological jargon (Holiman & Lauver, 1987). (The use of English as a second language in therapy is discussed in chapter 6.) Consider the use of the term "dysfunctional" to describe a particular pattern of family interactions. Although assumptions are often made about the meaning of this term, cultural norms that define functionality are rarely taken into account. But Westbrooks (1995) found that beliefs defined as "functional" in the family systems literature were not necessarily functional in the contexts of many low-income African American and Euroamerican families. For example, the dominant cultural definition of functional communication as that which is open and direct was challenged by some of these families' belief that "Communication involves a time to speak and a time to be silent" (Westbrooks, p. 141).

To understand the meaning behind a client's use of language, it may be necessary to ask the client to define a term (e.g., "Tell me what you mean by a 'functional' family or a 'dysfunctional' one"). This sort of inquiry is equally important for therapists to ask themselves. Therapists' use of theoretically-based terms or concepts (e.g., "providing a container" for clients, outlining "contingencies," or specifying "cognitive distortions") may be familiar and comfortable for therapists, but alienating to clients. Equally obscure from many clients' perspectives are phrases such as "getting in touch with your feelings," "sharing personal issues," and "learning to accept all parts of yourself."

Whether the use of theoretically-based language and idioms originates with the therapist or the client, it is important to consider the assumptions underlying such phrases (e.g., "What does 'being in touch with one's feelings' mean, and how do I know if I am or am not?") (Holiman & Lauver, 1987). It can be helpful for therapists to ask the questions, "What does that mean? How do I know?" For instance, once when I used the term "manipulative" to describe a client, my supervisor questioned what I meant by the word. I said something to the effect of "trying to get one's needs met, and not caring if you take something away from someone else in the process." However, my supervisor pointed out that we all have needs that we're trying to fulfill, but some people have less education, less effective social skills, or a brain impairment, or live in a particular environment that decreases their ability to meet their needs in subtle ways or in ways that do not infringe on other people. Clearly, the judgmental tone of this word did not facilitate my understanding of, or compassion for, the client.

Conclusion

With clients of diverse identities, making meaningful connections is complex, requiring familiarity with a wide range of relationship-building behaviors and attitudes. Of particular importance are the abilities to be respectful of and responsive to diverse communication styles, language preferences, and value systems. When clients feel respected and appreciated, they are more likely to share pertinent and accurate information, and to be open to the possibility of therapeutic intervention. Although a meaningful connection does not guarantee the accuracy of an assessment or the effectiveness of therapy, it is certainly an essential element.

KEY IDEAS 5.

Guidelines for Establishing Respect and Rapport

1. In working with clients, keep in mind the centrality of respect in many cultures.

2. Don't assume a title of address; ask the client what he or she prefers (e.g., Mr., Mrs., Ms., Dr., family or given name).

3. Even if you are knowledgeable about the client's culture, do not assume that you are therefore knowledgeable about the client's personal experience of her or his culture and identity. Use the ADDRESSING acronym to remind yourself of within-group variations.

4. Use self-disclosure in a way that allows clients to assess your ability to help them.

5. Stay aware of the different meanings of physical gestures, eye contact, silence, and other forms of nonverbal communication.

6. Be aware of differences in preferences for physical space, including your own; if possible, use easily movable furniture to allow for different preferences.

7. Do not touch the assistive device (e.g., a walker, wheelchair, prosthetic) of a person who has a disability without asking.

8. Consider what your office location, accessibility, and furnishings communicate about your awareness of people of different ages; people who have disabilities; religious or spiritually oriented people; people of various ethnicities; people who are gay, lesbian, or bisexual; and so on, using the ADDRESSING acronym.

9. Think about the meanings and intentions in your use of humor as carefully as you think about any other communication with clients.

10. Avoid psychological jargon.

11. Ask the client about the meaning of his or her use of a particular term.

12. Continually use critical thinking skills to think about your own assumptions in relation to clients' communication styles, including verbal and nonverbal communication.

IV | CULTURALLY RESPONSIVE ASSESSMENT AND DIAGNOSIS

Sorting Things Out: Culturally Response Assessment

6

I became 18 years old at the close of World War II. It was a time when men came back from the war to reclaim their "rightful" place in society, i.e., one of dominance. A new wave of homophobia swept the nation as men sought the jobs held by women during the war, expecting the women to return to their previous subservient roles. College deans expelled students for lesbian attachments; my college was no exception. . . . I isolated myself from fellow students and was terrified that discovery of my sexual orientation would end my hopes for a medical career. If even the word homosexual was used in my presence my mouth got dry and my heart pounded. I carefully wiped out any traces of a personal life in my conversations with co-workers, and refused all social invitations. I continued to be alone with my shame (Schoonmaker, 1993, p. 27).

In the preceding chapters, we considered several steps and processes that precede a culturally responsive assessment, including:

- an ongoing involvement in one's own cultural self-assessment and learning about other cultures
- recognition of the possible significance of diverse cultural identities and influences in a client's life
- consideration of the interaction between the therapist's and the client's identities
- the establishment of meaningful connections with clients

When these initial conditions are met, therapists can turn their attention to specific actions to increase their effectiveness and accuracy during the assessment process. This chapter discusses these actions, with attention to work with clients who do not speak English as a first language, as well as those who do. The chapter emphasizes a strengths-oriented approach in which therapists actively look for culturally related strengths and supports within and outside the individual. Because information-gathering is the initial task in most assessments, let's begin with suggestions for obtaining a client's history in a culturally responsive way.

Obtaining Clients' Histories

The first step in a culturally responsive assessment is that of gathering information, or taking the client's history. Standardized approaches to history-taking maintain a passive stance toward culturally related information. But consider the example of the older lesbian woman quoted above and how difficult it would be for a therapist to understand her as a person, without knowing the historical and sociocultural influences across her lifespan. A culturally responsive assessment would take an active approach toward learning about these influences and the multiple, overlapping systems relevant to her life, including extended family members, non-kin relationships, cultural and political contexts, and physical and natural environments (American Psychological Association, 1993).

USING MULTIPLE SOURCES

Taking cultural influences and systems into account involves obtaining information about the client's history from multiple sources whenever possible. Reliance on the client's report as one's sole source is risky, especially when the client is distressed and thus thinking narrowly about her or his situation. Multiple perspectives help the therapist to gain a fuller picture of the client's needs and strengths (Suzuki & Kugler, 1995).

Clinicians working with children and elders are especially attuned to the need for multiple perspectives in assessment. With children, Johnson-Powell (1997) noted that "a comprehensive assessment requires information from the school, the parents, significant family members, and the child," (p. 350), in addition to culturally related information. Similarly, the assessment of older adults is commonly expected to include information from "multiple sources (the elderly clients, their family, concerned others), in multiple ways (interviews, standardized testing, behavioral observation), about multiple areas (functional and social competencies, physical and emotional health, financial status, social and environmental supports and stresses)" (Lewinsohn, Teri, & Hautzinger, 1984, p. 194). Such an approach can enhance one's work with diverse clients of other age groups, too, as in the following example.

Gloria, a 40-year-old, divorced, bicultural woman (her deceased father, Irish American and Catholic; her mother, second-generation Cuban American and also Catholic), came to counseling for help in coping with chronic pain. Following a minor car accident 2 months earlier, Gloria reported experiencing a low-grade headache and pains in her upper back and neck muscles. She was on a 3-month disability leave from work and reported spending most of her time at home "lying around and feeling low because of the pain." She said that "every little thing" felt like "a major effort." Her two daughters, ages 13 and 15, helped make meals, and her mother, who lived down the street, came over every day to help with household chores. In addition, Gloria was not sleeping well.

The Euroamerican therapist, Sarah, had a sense that Gloria was being honest about her situation, but she noticed that Gloria smiled a couple of times when recounting funny things that her children had recently done. In this lighter moment, the therapist asked how the pain was, and Gloria immediately replied, "Oh, not as bad," but then within a minute said, "No, I think it's still there."

Recognizing the limitations of relying solely on Gloria's self-report, the therapist obtained a release of information to speak with her physician and a physical therapist that Gloria had seen twice in the week after the accident. The physician told Sarah that a thorough physical exam had ruled out any physiological problem. The physical therapist confirmed the physician's report but added that Gloria had been very tense and that her headaches and muscle pain seemed to be related to this tension. Sarah was somewhat puzzled by this, because Gloria did not report a high level of tension. She decided that it might be helpful to obtain more information from people closer to Gloria. She called Gloria and talked with her about the possibility of bringing her daughters and mother to the next meeting, as a way of helping Sarah to gain a broader view of Gloria's situation, and to help provide ideas for what might be helpful. Gloria agreed, and the four came in the next week.

During this second meeting, it quickly became apparent to Sarah that she had overlooked the significance of Gloria's divorce, which had been final, a year earlier. The daughters both talked about how much they missed their father, and Gloria's mother told the therapist that "marriage just doesn't mean the same thing to people anymore. They expect it to be happy all the time, and when it's not, they get divorced." Gloria's discomfort was visible as her mother spoke about the hardships in her own marriage and how she had just accepted the situation because she knew that it was the best thing for her children.

As she talked with Gloria and her family, Sarah became aware that she had made the assumption, based on Gloria's Euroamerican appearance, that Gloria's cultural reference points were similar to her own (i.e., Euroamerican, Protestant). She had not considered the influence of Gloria's Cuban and Catholic heritage in her current situation (specifically, norms regarding marriage, divorce, family relationships, work, and motherhood; see Bernal & Shapiro, 1996; Suárez, 1999; Vasquez, 1994). As she considered these influences, Sarah's view of Gloria began to shift from that of a depressed person who was "simply somaticizing," to one of a strong and self-sufficient woman whose emotional pain was contributing to her tension and headaches. Moreover, Sarah saw how Gloria's pain was being reinforced on a daily basis by her mother's comments, her children's complaints, and by Gloria's self-comparisons to a set of internalized standards.

In an individual session with Gloria the next week, Sarah described her impressions and Gloria said yes, this made sense, especially in that she had always seen herself as a hard-working "helper," as someone who follows through on her responsibilities. Recognition of the depression and grief as her primary problems allowed Gloria and the therapist to decide on a course of action that included antidepressant medications to improve her sleep and lift her mood and individual therapy. (Gloria did not want family therapy; she preferred to see Sarah alone.) The individual therapy was aimed at helping Gloria to grieve about her divorce-related losses, and to rethink cultural and religious norms, toward the goal of deciding which norms she wanted to hold on to and which ones she did not.

For example, although no longer a practicing Catholic, Gloria used the idea of God's grace to become more accepting of herself and her decisions, recognizing that although her life did not fit the preferred norm in her cultures, she was doing her best and that her best was quite good. (See Lovinger, 1996, on Catholic beliefs and their relevance to assessment and therapy.) In addition, she found the concept of forgiveness to be helpful in letting go of much of her anger toward her former husband. As her anger, sadness, and harsh judgments of herself decreased, Gloria's neck pain and headaches gradually subsided.

FAMILY MEMBERS AND SIGNIFICANT OTHERS

In Gloria's case, it is difficult to see how the therapist's understanding of her needs could have occurred without the family meeting. The therapist might have come to the same conclusions following extensive individual interviews, but the assessment would no doubt have taken much longer. Nor would the therapist have had the opportunity to connect with Gloria's family in a way that affirmed Gloria.

Whether or not one chooses to do individual therapy, family members and significant others can often provide new information and alternative perspectives. During my first meeting with a client, I may ask or suggest that he or she invite family members to an assessment. I explain that to gain a fuller picture of the person's situation, it can be helpful to have family members or significant others come in and give us their perspectives as well. I add that sometimes family members also have ideas that can help, and if they are an integral part of the client's problem situation, and the client agrees, they too may become a part of the therapy.

With some clients, including family members is inappropriate. For example, I would not normally ask a woman who is being abused by her husband to bring him in, particularly when her goal in therapy is to build her self-esteem and strength so that she can leave the marriage. (Although even this is a complicated issue with women of cultural minority groups; see Kanuha, 1994, for more detail.) There may also be other culturally related reasons why particular family members should be seen separately; for example, many people of Asian heritage (and some other cultures) would consider it inappropriate for parents to discuss their concerns with one another in front of the children (Hong, 1988).

With other clients, timing is a factor. Trust and respect may need to be established over a period of several sessions before a client feels comfortable enough to ask family members to attend a session. When the time is right, I ask clients if they want to invite the family member or if they'd like me to call the person. Clients usually choose the former option, which gives them more control, but if they choose the latter, I always obtain a release of information before calling.

During an assessment session to which family members have been invited, I usually begin by thanking the family members for coming, engage in conversation aimed at establishing rapport, and then ask the family members what the client told them about why we wanted them to join us. The family members' responses provide information for assessing the degree of communication between the client and family, as well as the family members' understanding of the client's needs. In addition, observing the client's reaction to the family members' explanations provides information about the client (e.g., Does the client sit quietly and listen, contradict, or argue with the family member about what the latter says?).

In many cases, clients will present as a family. This is often the case with children and parents and with older adults and their partners or adult children. When this is the case, I generally do not obtain a release of information; however, I explain the limits of confidentiality in relation to that particular situation and family. If I'm working primarily with one individual, and family members are present only for the purposes of the assessment, I may also obtain a release of information from the client so that I can speak with these family members with the client's permission. The formality of documentation makes explicit the client's agreement that I can talk with family members if they call me, although I tell the client before I plan to call a family member, even when the release has been signed.

For the purposes of an individual assessment, obtaining information from others requires special attention to respecting the client. This is especially true when family members have complaints about the client. For example, an older male client who is having memory lapses may trust his wife and be more comfortable having her present during an initial assessment with the therapist. However, if he feels defensive about her concerns, an initial meeting alone with the therapist may be less threatening (Hays, 1996c).

As a general rule, when more than one person comes to an initial assessment, I meet with whomever is there initially for at least a few minutes. However, depending on the makeup of the family, I often spend the remainder of the time meeting separately with each individual. The choice of whom to meet with (or speak to) first is an important one and should be determined via consideration of the cultural identities and ages of those involved (e.g., see Rastogi & Wampler, 1998). S. C. Kim (1985) advised following the family's current hierarchical arrangements, an idea I usually follow initially as a demonstration of respect.

HEALTH CARE PROVIDERS AND OTHER PROFESSIONALS

An equally important source of information is other health care providers (e.g., physician, nurse, physical therapist, occupational therapist, audiologist, speech therapist) and, in some cases, individuals in the client's community (e.g., a religious leader or teacher). With older clients, consultation with medical providers may be especially important, because many older people have a long-term relationship with their physician and expect the mental health therapist to talk with him or her about their care. Consulting the client's physician or other health care provider communicates respect for the client's physical complaints and provides the therapist with an opportunity to learn more about the client's specific needs (Sanders, Brockway, Ellis, Cotton, & Bredin, 1999). And because older clients are more likely to have physical problems and to be taking medication, a thorough medical examination is important to rule out or clarify the effects of physical illnesses, impairments, and medications on the client's mental health and cognitive functioning, (see Gatz, 1994). As with family members, releases of information are necessary before obtaining and sharing information with other care providers.

BEHAVIORAL OBSERVATIONS

Behavioral observations may be direct or indirect. Indirect observations, for the purposes of assessment, occur primarily in the form of self-reported psychological and neuropsychological test data. Because few standardized tests adequately address culture-specific variations, their use is complicated, particularly with people of ethnic minority cultures, people who are older, and those who have disabilities or little formal education. (Testing is the subject of chapter 7, which provides a more detailed discussion and specific suggestions.)

Direct observations of the client and significant others are made during interviews and testing procedures. Therapists note clients' behaviors in relation to the therapist (e.g., level of cooperation or defensiveness) and in relation to significant others, as well as behaviors during the completion of tests (e.g., frustration level, ability to learn by trial and error) (Suzuki & Kugler, 1995).

The usefulness of direct observations can be enhanced if made in the client's natural environment (e.g., school, home, nursing home). Home visits may be especially useful in the assessment of functional abilities, because the therapist is able to compare what clients do in their own environments with what clients and others report (Lewinsohn et al., 1984). In addition, home visits demonstrate caring and thus enhance the therapeutic relationship, increase the therapist's integration into the client's natural support system, and facilitate the involvement of other family members who cannot or will not come to an office (e.g., small children, people with disabilities, elders) (Swinomish Tribal Community, 1991, p. 227).

In sum, although it may not be possible or appropriate to obtain information from all of these sources for every client, setting this practice as a standard reinforces the view of clients' problems as multifaceted and complex. More "up front" work is involved (e.g., obtaining releases of information, making telephone calls, visiting clients in their homes), but in the long run the advantages usually outweigh the extra time. For one, the reliability of an assessment is increased when more than one source is consulted. Second, rapport with the client may be facilitated by the therapist's willingness to connect with significant individuals in the client's environment. And third, because the involvement of others can be used to reinforce therapeutic interventions later, the likelihood of success in therapy is often increased.

CLIENTS' AGE AND DEVELOPMENT IN RELATION TO HISTORICAL EVENTS

In mental health assessments, information about the client's personal history is commonly organized into developmental and social history, including education, family upbringing, significant relationships, and work experience, and medical and psychiatric history, including substance use and psychiatric or psychological treatment. Questions aimed at eliciting information in these categories tend to assume that a client's development is relatively unaffected by sociocultural historical events, or affected in the same way as members of the dominant group. However, it is difficult to understand an individual's personal history without an understanding of his or her larger cultural context and history.

To better understand a client's personal history, I have found it helpful to think about the client's age and development in relation to historical events with which I am familiar. To begin, this involves knowing a client's age and then calculating (in my head) the years or era during which the client experienced significant life transitions. Thinking about a client's development in relation to historical periods opens up numerous questions about the influence of cultural attitudes, views, and events on the client.

Take the case of a college-educated, married, 65-year-old Euroamerican man during an assessment conducted in 2000. Calculating the client's date of birth immediately yields information that the therapist can use to formulate questions, some of which might be appropriate to ask, but others not. (These questions are similar to those suggested for therapists in their own cultural self-assessments.) For example, this man was a young child during World War II, which raises questions about his family's relationship to the war. Did his father go off to fight and, if so, did he return? Was he disabled? What was the socioeconomic situation of the family before, during, and after the war? What were his parents' specific Euroamerican ethnic and religious roots—German? Russian? Christian? Jewish? And how did this affect his experience of the war and his experiences growing up?

Continuing these calculations based on the client's birth date, the therapist would recognize that the client was 10 years old at the end of the war and that he grew up during the 1940s and 1950s. The client turned 18 a few months before the Korean War armistice was signed in 1953; was he drafted or did he enlist and, if so, was he involved in military action? How did the general economic prosperity, strict gender roles, and assimilationist attitudes of the late 1940s and 1950s affect him? He moved from young to middle adulthood in the 1960s and 1970s. Keeping in mind the ADDRESSING influences on his identity, how was he affected by the Civil Rights, women's, and peace movements of this period? How did these events affect his family? For example, how did the women's movement affect his marriage? More recently, how has it been for him to move from middle age into the identity of an older White man during the current time period, when health care and social security systems are undergoing major changes, and women and ethnic minority groups are becoming more politically vocal and visible?

This example is a relatively simple one, because the cultural influences most pertinent to this client are primarily those of the dominant culture and thus likely to be known by most therapists. But consider the same historical periods in relation to a 65-year-old, college-educated, married man who is Japanese American. Calculating this second client's birth date while remaining conscious of his ethnic identity would facilitate the therapist's formulation of questions and hypotheses relevant to this client. Even a basic familiarity with the dominant cultural attitudes toward Japanese Americans during World War II, the probable internment of the client's family, and the socioeconomic losses of Japanese Americans after the war would lead the therapist to make very different hypotheses about the impact of World War II on the client.

This client also turned 18 a few months before the Korean War armistice was signed. Did he serve in the military and, if so, what was his experience as a visibly Asian American man? How did the assimilationist attitudes of the late 1940s and 1950s affect him? He was 29 when the Civil Rights Act became law in 1964; did this event have an impact on his employment opportunities? As an Asian American, what was his experience of the

Vietnam War? Recognizing the illegality of "interracial marriage" in many states until 1967 (Root, 1996), did he marry a Japanese American woman, and what did the women's movement in the dominant culture mean for his marriage?

The answers to these questions depend to a great extent on this client's immigration history, including where he, his parents, and his grandparents were born and grew up. Was the client issei (the first generation of Japanese American immigrants) or nisei (the second generation, first born in the United States)? Or might he be kibei, a subset of the nisei born in the United States but sent back to Japan for their education, who then returned to the United States (Matsui, 1996; Takaki, 1993)?

If he grew up in Hawaii, did his parents work in the sugar cane fields, as did many Japanese people living in Hawaii in the 1930s? Or were they immigrants to the mainland United States, which would have been during a time when anti-Japanese sentiment was building in the form of the San Francisco School Board Segregation Order of 1906, the California Alien Land Law prohibiting Japanese immigrants from buying land, and the Immigration Act of 1924, which essentially halted Japanese immigration to the United States (Matsui, 1996)? Finally, the therapist would want to think about and possibly ask the client how it has been for him to move into the identity of an older man within his own family, keeping in mind the variety of attitudes toward aging in Japanese, Japanese American, and Euroamerican cultures.

While the therapist might not know all the specific events mentioned above, all it takes is a few minutes after the session to look up a particular era in a history book to get a feeling for cultural events of the times. Takaki's (1993) and Zinn's (1995) books on the history of ethnic minority groups in the United States are excellent resources. For Canadians, I recommend *Unequal Relations: An Introduction to Race and Ethnic Dynamics in Canada* by Elliott and Fleras (1992). With regard to people who grew up in other countries, the *World Almanac* (Primedia, 2000) is a convenient resource with information on the languages, religions, economic conditions, ethnic identifications, and political events of every country in the world, updated every year. A handy resource for practical descriptions of different religions is *The World's Religions* by H. Smith (1991).

One way to organize historical influences is by constructing a timeline that also notes sociocultural events and time periods; Figure 6.1 provides an example. As with any timeline, a long line has intersecting marks that denote significant dates. When using this

FIGURE 6.1.

Example of Timeline for Older Japanese American Man

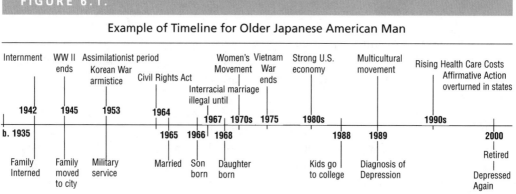

tool in sociocultural assessment, the therapist notes brief descriptions of events in the client's personal history underneath the line and relevant sociocultural events above the line. Some clients may like drawing the timeline with the therapist, and the longer legal-size paper or flip charts are convenient for this work. However, I want to emphasize again that most of the questions concerning the client's cultural history (i.e., the top side of the timeline) should not be asked directly; it is the therapist's responsibility to obtain this information outside assessment sessions.

MEDICAL AND PSYCHOLOGICAL INFORMATION

When gathering information about a client's medical, psychiatric, and psychological history, it is important that therapists also think about historical changes in conceptualizations of illness, health, and disability (Westermeyer & Janca, 1997). Within the dominant culture, certain behaviors that were viewed as normal or treated with a bemused tolerance in earlier decades (e.g., alcohol abuse and intoxication) are now seen as indicative of a serious problem. In contrast, some behaviors considered pathological in past years (e.g., sexual behavior between people of the same gender) are now viewed as normal.

Over the past decade, I have seen certain diagnostic trends among counseling interns that seem to correspond to popular interests in psychology. In the late 1980s and early 1990s, my students were inclined to overuse the diagnosis of what was then called "multiple personality disorder" (MPD, now known as dissociative identity disorder). In the mid-1990s, I noticed that MPD seemed to be declining in frequency, while borderline personality disorder was on the rise (primarily, that is, among women). In the late 1990s, I noticed a sudden increase in the diagnosis of attention deficit disorder in children and adults.

To some extent, these shifts may be attributable to increased awareness. However, this is obviously not the case when the same symptoms, characteristics, and histories are diagnosed differently during different eras. It is important to stay aware of the subtle ways in which the media and popular ideas interact with clients' presentations and the field's conceptualizations of psychopathology.

Therapists will also want to be aware of the diverse ways in which clients conceptualize illness, health, and disability, both within and across cultures. Understanding these conceptualizations (or what Kleinman, 1980, called "explanatory models") is important, because what a therapist sees as problematic may not be so from the client's perspective. Clients may engage in certain health care practices that to therapists appear useless or even dangerous; however, it is important that therapists recognize the possible function of these practices so as to avoid overpathologizing.

For example, although I've never seen anything written in the psychological literature about scarification (blood-letting) as a treatment for headaches, during a study I conducted on women's mental health in Tunisia, several Bedouin women told me how they use it (Hays, 1987). With a razor blade, they make small nicks in the forehead, right at the hairline where the cuts are difficult to see. The women then put caper leaves over the cuts, cover them with a headscarf, and take a nap. Although I've never tried this myself (and I'm not recommending it), the women told me that it helped, especially with headaches caused by working out in the hot sun.

Similarly, Muecke (1983b) described dermabrasive procedures commonly used by Khmer and Vietnamese people for a wide range of problems including headache, muscle pain, nausea, and cough. Subcutaneous hematomas (i.e., bruises) are made

> by firmly pinching the epidermis and the dermis between two fingers while pulling on the skin, by rubbing an oiled skin with the edge of a coin, spoon or piece of bamboo, or by placing a cup from which the oxygen has been burnt out over the affected area for 15 to 30 minutes; as the air in the cup cools, it contracts and draws the skin and "air" up and out, leaving an ecchymotic area on the skin. (p. 838)

Such practices reflect Asian theories about health as a state of balance and the role of hot and cold in maintaining this balance. Whether or not you believe they work, such self-care practices may help the person to feel nurtured and more in control (i.e., able to do something about the illness). And none of these practices do any permanent damage (Muecke, 1983a). Moreover, one needs to allow for the possibility that such practices really do work, even if Western medicine does not understand how.

Different conceptualizations of health, illness, and disability can occur even when cultural differences are not readily apparent. For example, as a person with a disability, Weeber (1999) talked about the different meanings that deciding to use a scooter had for her, her family, and the larger culture:

> We are taught that to walk, no matter how distorted or exhausting, is far more virtuous than using a chair—because it is closer to "normal." Never mind that my galumphing polio-gait twists my muscle into iron-like sinew that only the hardiest of masseuses can "unknot." Never mind that my shoulders and hands, never meant for walking, have their future usefulness limited by 40 years of misuse on crutches.
>
> . . . My using a scooter is an act that scares my family. They are afraid that somehow giving up walking will make me give up—period! It makes them think that I am losing ground, becoming dependent on the scooter, when they and society need me to act as if I am strong and virile.
>
> . . . I have begun to use a scooter for mobility. What an act of liberation—and resistance—this has been! I felt like a bird let out of a cage, the first time I used one! I could go and go and not be exhausted! I was able to fully participate in the conference I was attending, rather than just be dully present. (p. 22)

Even when therapists and clients agree on how they see a situation or problem, their solution preferences may vary depending on what they consider the origin of the problem to be. For example, in a situation where anxiety is clearly the problem, therapist and client may see its cause to be any of the following: (a) sinful thoughts or actions; (b) external stressors such as poverty, losing a job, or an oppressive work environment; (c) bad spirits or supernatural forces; (d) a deficit in the client's personality or character; (e) working too hard; (f) poor coping skills; (g) a lack of social support; or (h) a difficult upbringing. Obviously, whichever cause is perceived to be primary will strongly influence the course of action taken. To increase the likelihood that therapist and client are working together toward common goals, it is essential that therapists ask about clients' understandings and about their health care practices. This is not to say that therapists and clients must always agree on the cause; however, if they don't, it's better to know this from the beginning to avoid misunderstandings later.

FORMAL ASSESSMENT OF ACCULTURATION: PROCEED WITH CAUTION

A common recommendation among multicultural assessment researchers is to administer a measure of acculturation, identity, or language ability (or a combination) with clients of ethnic minority status. While this recommendation is well intentioned, I think it presents more problems than it offers to solve. First of all, how does one decide which "ethnic-minority" individuals will be asked to complete such a test? Many people would be offended at the suggestion that their culture needs assessing, particularly given that race and ethnicity are such loaded subjects these days. To avoid offending clients, therapists would need to be able to assess accurately *before* administering such a test whether or not the client is unacculturated enough for it to be useful; but if the therapist can do this, then why would she or he need a test?

A second, related issue involves time—both the therapist's and the client's. There may be settings in which it is possible to add one more test to the work a client is already doing. Although even this raises the question, For whose convenience are the tests being administered? In addition, in many settings, asking clients to fill out a test of their cultural identity would be seen as irrelevant to their presenting problem. Therapists obviously should assess the cultural influences on each client; however, I believe that it is more respectful to assess the meaning of the clients' identity via the more direct method of talking with them about it.

A third problem concerns the concept of acculturation and the instruments used to measure it. The most common way of looking at acculturation is as a linear process through which immigrants drop their own values, customs, and languages and take on those of the dominant culture (Azar, 1999). But such a model ignores the complexity of the acculturation process (Berry, 1997; Phinney, 1996). Essentially, no allowance is made "for the possibility that a person might retain elements of his or her culture of origin while simultaneously learning another culture" (Zane, interviewed in Azar, 1999, p. 14; also see Betancourt & López, 1993).

Given the enormous differences within groups, combined with the fact that minority and dominant cultures are continually mixing and changing, it is difficult to determine what constitutes a particular acculturation level for a culture. Furthermore, the amount of time it takes to design, standardize, and test any research instrument means that measures of acculturation may be out of date by the time they are published (Cuéllar, 1998). In sum, while the idea of assessing a client's level of acculturation is aimed at making therapy more helpful, the use of a test to do this seems less practical than simply training therapists to be more knowledgeable and experienced with the cultures of their clients.

CHOICE OF LANGUAGE: WORKING WITH INTERPRETERS

For a while, I had a tutor for Spanish. She was an Argentinean woman who was fluent in English but wanted help with some of the pickier points of English, so we exchanged services. (I got the better deal.) During one of our lessons, she was quite distressed about a series of events that had occurred. As she was describing her day (in English), she said something about feeling like she was just "going forth and back." I interrupted to tell her that in English, the phrase is "going back and forth." She was annoyed by this, and said, "Well, in Spanish, it's *'para adelante y para atrás,'* meaning 'going forward and then back,' because you cannot go back until you've gone forth." I could see her point; the English was confusing. Furthermore, the illogic of it only added to her annoyance and distress.

In the therapeutic setting, expecting a client to use his or her second language may lead to miscommunication (Del Castillo, 1970; Westermeyer, 1987). Furthermore, clients' emotional distress may limit their ability to describe a stressful or traumatic situation in a second language (Bradford & Munoz, 1993; Westermeyer & Janca, 1997). A greater reliance on pencil-and-paper tests in English will not resolve the language problem either; although clients can take their time reading, their results will still reflect language difficulties confounded with the abilities being measured (Geisinger, 1992; Kaufert & Shapiro, 1996; Wilgosh & Gibson, 1994).

When a therapist does not speak the client's primary language, the ideal solution will usually be a referral to a therapist who speaks the client's primary language. However, when such a person is unavailable, the therapist and client may need to work with an interpreter. Clients on public assistance often have case managers who act as their interpreters, also called "cultural liaisons". (Note that *interpretation* refers to spoken language and *translation* to the written form.)

There is currently no national body in the United States that certifies spoken-language interpreters, although a few states do, including Washington state (Bookda Gheisar, Executive Director, Cross Cultural Health Care Program, PacMed Clinics, Seattle, personal communication, February 1999; also see Department of Social and Health Services, State of Washington, 1999). In large hospitals, interpreters may be available through a central registry. Information about certified interpreters for the Deaf can be obtained through the Registry of Interpreters for the Deaf or the National Directory of TTY numbers, available through Telecommunications for the Deaf, Inc. (see Leigh, Corbett, Gutman, & Morere, 1996). In Australia, professional interpreters are accredited by the National Accreditation Authority for Translators and Interpreters and abide by a strict code of ethics regarding interpreter-mediated confidentiality (Pauwels, 1995, p. 141).

To ensure that interpreters are well qualified, it is important that they be certified or, in places where a certification system is not in place, evaluated by a qualified person. If you do not speak the client's language, and the interpreter turns out to be inappropriate or unprofessional in ways that are not visually evident, the client has no way of letting you know this. Ideally, interpreters will also have some training in mental health issues. And of course it is important that interpreters speak the particular dialect of any given language (Paniagua, 1998).

There are two main forms of interpretation: (a) concurrent or simultaneous, in which the interpreter speaks concurrently with the client, interpreting the client's words as the client speaks, and (b) sequential, in which the interpreter waits for the client or therapist to stop speaking before interpreting her or his words. Concurrent interpretation is probably ideal, as it is the favored method in the United Nations and has been shown to be effective in therapeutic practice (Bradford & Munoz, 1993).

But in the mental health world of limited resources, individuals with this high level of skill, plus mental health expertise, are not in great supply. I've conducted approximately

170 clinical interviews with eight different interpreters who spoke Khmer, Lao, Vietnamese, Tunisian Arabic, and Korean; all of these involved sequential interpretation, and while I do not have the experience with concurrent interpretation to make a fair comparison, I can say that I grew to like sequential interpretation because of the extra time it gave me (while the interpreter was speaking) to observe clients and their interactions with the interpreter.

A number of suggestions may be helpful in working with an interpreter. The first concerns the task of choosing an individual. To avoid problems with confidentiality, it is important that the interpreter not have a social relationship with the client. The use of family members as interpreters is almost never appropriate, because such an arrangement places an unfair load on the person acting as interpreter (M. K. Ho, 1987). It also risks offending older family members, who are placed in a lower position when children or grandchildren interpret for them (Itai & McRae, 1994). And family interpretation may even be dangerous, for example, in cases of domestic violence where the abuser assumes the role of interpreter for the victimized partner, child, or elder.

The second suggestion is to schedule a preassessment meeting with the interpreter to establish rapport and discuss expectations and goals (Bradford & Munoz, 1993). Ideally, this preassessment meeting will be face-to-face and held a day or two before the session with the client; sometimes, however, only a telephone conversation may be possible. Scheduling this initial meeting with the interpreter at a separate time eliminates the need for the therapist and interpreter to meet at the beginning of the assessment session, which would require the client to wait and could lead the client to feel as though she or he is being colluded against.

During the preassessment meeting, it is helpful to learn about the interpreter's background. If raised with polite interest, questions about the interpreter can help to increase rapport and demonstrate respect for the interpreter's expertise. At the same time, such information increases the therapist's understanding of any cultural, social class, or political differences that could inhibit the interpreter's work with a particular client (Sundberg & Sue, 1989). This is where the therapist's personal learning and information seeking outside the therapeutic setting is also important. For example, when I consulted with the leaders of a particular Vietnamese community in which I was going to work, I was advised that there were two main political groups and that if I hired an interpreter who was even loosely connected to one, I should also hire another who was not, because people aligned with the one group would not work with an interpreter who was aligned with the other.

Frequently, the gender of the interpreter is also important. With some groups, the choice of a male interpreter may add authority to the therapeutic endeavor, particularly if the therapist is a woman; e.g., see Landau, 1982). However, as a general rule, do not expect a woman client to share intimate relationship or physical health details with the therapist or interpreter if either one is male. (See Waxler-Morrison, Anderson, & Richardson, 1990, regarding gender preferences for health care providers in Cambodian, Lao, Vietnamese, Iranian, Central American, and other cultures.)

Whether concurrent or sequential interpretation is used, ask the interpreter to interpret everything the client says verbatim (Anderson, Waxler-Morrison, Richardson, Herbert, &

Murphy, 1990), but also to tell you if they think you or the client have misunderstood something due to language or conceptual inequivalencies. This is also a good time to be sure that the interpreter understands the commitment to confidentiality (Bradford & Munoz, 1993). Obviously, any information the interpreter can provide concerning the client's context will be helpful, particularly, for the purposes of mental status evaluation, information the client would be expected to know. (Chapter 7 provides more detail on testing.)

For the assessment session with the client and interpreter, scheduling extra time is necessary due to the extra speaking time involved (Paniagua, 1998). In addition, extra time allows for a get-acquainted conversation between the interpreter and client at the beginning of the session; the presence of an interpreter who shares the client's culture often decreases the client's anxiety in an initial interview (Kaufert & Shapiro, 1996). It can also help if the therapist re-states in front of the client the commitment to and limits of confidentiality for both the therapist and interpreter.

When the formal assessment or therapy session begins, try to avoid discussions between you and the interpreter. If the interpreter needs to explain a concept or idea that you have not understood, let the client know that this is what you are doing to avoid his or her wondering about why you are talking so much about the last reply given. Also, use short sentences and avoid complex language and terms (Paniagua, 1998; Struwe, 1994). For example, simple one-part questions are easier to interpret and answer than are two-part questions (e.g., "How often have you experienced this dizziness, and when did it start?") (Pauwels, 1995). With sequential interpretation, it is important to pause after each main idea is expressed to allow the interpreter time to interpret.

Finally, although it may be well intentioned, therapists are advised not to attempt to work in the client's language unless they have near-native fluency (Westermeyer, 1987). The poor use of a client's language puts the client in an awkward position; she or he may not want to insult the therapist by suggesting the need for an interpreter. The complexity involved in speaking a language was underscored by Pollard (1996) with regard to American Sign Language (ASL). Noting that ASL is a conceptually based language (i.e., not English or aurally based) with its own vocabulary, grammar, and patterns of discourse, Pollard observed,

> Like German, ASL verbs are often at the end of statements. Like Spanish, ASL adjectives follow the nouns they modify. Like Hebrew, ASL does not employ certain forms of the verb "to be." Like Japanese, feedback signals from the listener are expected in ASL. Like French, there is reflection in ASL sentences and discourse.
>
> . . . Too many individuals (and program administrators) wrongly assume that a few courses in "sign" enable one to converse with, or worse, interpret for, a primary user of ASL. (p. 391)

As a former student of mine noted, based on her experience as a Japanese–English interpreter, interpretation is a demanding job (P. Nagasaka, personal communication, January 1999). It is thus unfair to expect bilingual individuals who are not paid for their interpreting services to do interpretation on an "as needed" basis for agencies and hospitals. In this case, an informal approach to interpretation is another way in which people of minority cultures are expected to do extra work while the dominant culture fails to educate itself (see Exhibit 6.1).

EXHIBIT 6.1.

Guidelines for Working with Interpreters

1. Schedule extra time for the assessment.

2. If the interpreter is not the client's case manager (i.e., they do not have a prior professional relationship),

   a. be sure that the interpreter speaks the client's dialect (i.e., not just their language);

   b. be sure that the interpreter is certified whenever possible; and

   c. allow the interpreter and client time to talk together before the session begins to establish rapport and increase trust.

3. Do not use family members or social acquaintances as interpreters.

4. Arrange a preassessment meeting with the interpreter to

   a. discuss expectations and confidentiality;

   b. ask the interpreter to interpret verbatim and tell you when you may be misunderstanding the client due to conceptual or language difficulties; and

   c. obtain information about the client's particular context if the interpreter knows the client.

5. Reassure the client about confidentiality and its limits when both you and the interpreter are present.

6. Avoid discussions between you and the interpreter during the session. If such a discussion is necessary, let the client know that you are discussing a conceptual or linguistic difference.

7. Be concise. Avoid using complex terms (e.g., two-part questions) and language that is more difficult to interpret.

8. With sequential interpretation, pause after each main idea to give the interpreter time to interpret.

9. Be aware of cultural, class, and political differences between the interpreter and client that might affect the interpreter's work and rapport with the client.

10. Do not attempt to use a language in which you are not completely fluent.

Looking for Strengths

My sister Kim has taught fourth grade for 11 years on the Texas side of the Rio Grande River in an area known as the Valley. (This is the region that Anzaldua, 1987, wrote about in *Borderlands/La Frontera*.) The Valley is a politically conservative area with widespread poverty. Most of the children in Kim's classes speak English as a second language. Some are the children of migrant workers, and during harvest season, they move north with their families to states like Washington and Oregon to pick fruit on farms. Approximately 1.6

million people do this backbreaking work, and because many (about 40%) are in the United States illegally, they have little power to protest poor working and living conditions (Mapes, 1998).

After the harvest, the children return to their home schools in the Valley. Now that drugs and gangs are there, it's an even rougher place to grow up. On top of it, there is prejudice against the "migrant kids," who are often assumed to be poorer students because they move a lot. But Kim says that the exact opposite is true. They are the hardest workers and the most motivated. Their families instill a strong work ethic, respect for education, and most important, a sense of hope. They usually speak English more fluently because they have spent time in northern schools. And, Kim says, some even go on to college and return to the area to teach.

Because the dominant culture so often assumes the worst about people of minority identities, it is essential that therapists actively look for the strengths in their clients. Knowledge of a client's strengths and supports serves at least three purposes. First, it adds to the therapist's understanding of the client. Second, it allows the therapist and client to plan interventions that build on those aspects of the client's life that are already working. And third, with regard to culturally related strengths, it allows differences to be framed in positive terms (Stevenson & Renard, 1993).

It may be helpful to think of culturally related strengths and supports in terms of three categories. The first category, personal strengths, includes characteristics, beliefs, and abilities that reside within the individual—for example, pride in one's culture, belief in God or a Higher Power, a sense of humor, and artistic and language abilities. Spiritual beliefs may be central, providing the individual with meaning and purpose in life and a sense of connection to something bigger or greater than himself or herself (Royce-Davis, 2000). Personal strengths may also include coping abilities related directly to a person's minority status. As McIntosh (1998) noted,

> Those who do not depend on conferred dominance have traits and qualities that may never develop in those who do. . . . In some groups, those dominated have actually become strong through *not* having all of these unearned advantages, and this gives them a great deal to teach the others. (p. 83)

The second category consists of interpersonal supports. Included in this category are family, friends, group-specific networks, and activities that involve one's cultural group (e.g., traditional celebrations, political or social action groups, recreational activities). Family may include kinship networks that are broader than traditional definitions of family traced by bloodlines (Moore Hines & Boyd-Franklin, 1996). Because satisfaction with social support has been found to be a significant predictor of depression and general psychopathology (Fiore, Coppel, Becker, & Cox, 1986), knowledge of a client's social supports is essential for an understanding of her or his mental health. At the same time, therapists must be careful not to assume that people of color or other minority identities have good support networks. For example, in one study McAdoo (1978) found that African Americans of lower socioeconomic status had less activity within kin networks than did African Americans of higher socioeconomic status.

The third category includes sources of support and strength in the client's physical and natural environments. Some of these sources can be created—for example, an altar in one's home to honor ancestors, a space for prayer and meditation, or a garden where foods and medicinal plants are grown. Beyond cultural and taste preferences, culture-specific foods may also act as a protective factor in one's health (Marsella, Kaplan, & Suárez, in press).

Other sources of support may be anchored in the client's sense of place in the natural environment (e.g., see Cruikshank, 1990, and McClanahan, 1986, for richly described first-person accounts of the importance of place among Alaska Native elders.). For example, clients of rural origin or Indigenous heritage may find involvement with or nearness to animals, plants, mountains, and bodies of water to be important sources of spiritual strength (Sutton & Broken Nose, 1996).

Griffin-Pierce (1997) emphasized the importance of place to Navajo people in her description of the emotional trauma many Navajo individuals experience upon leaving their homeland for college or medical care. She noted that such trauma "goes beyond mere homesickness because it is based on an often unconscious sense of having violated the moral code of the universe" by leaving the land, which is considered "a vital source of spiritual strength" (p. 1). Similarly, the importance of understanding health and illness "in relation to dislocation from the land and the subsequent loss of cultural continuity this engendered" has been noted with regard to Aboriginal Australians (Acklin et al., 1999, p.9).

The importance of outdoor activities, including traditional (hunting, berry picking) and nontraditional (snow machining) activities among some Alaska Natives, was also documented by Minton and Soule (1990), who found these activities to be the most common response to the question, "What makes you happy?" When these activities are not available due to environmental changes (e.g., pollution, industrialization, or a person's institutionalization), therapists and clients may need to think creatively about alternative ways to get these needs met (e.g., visiting a park, setting up a bird feeder, finding a new place to go fishing, watching the stars at night).

As solution-focused therapists like to point out, even if solutions do not appear to be directly related to the problem, simply increasing the strengths and supports in a person's life will usually have a positive effect on their view of the problem, which in turn helps them to feel better (deShazer, 1985). Moreover, recent research in the area of positive psychology suggests that a sense of meaning, control, and optimism can be protective of one's physical as well as mental health (Taylor, Kemeny, Reed, Bower, & Gruenewald, 2000).

The simplest way to obtain information on culturally related supports and strengths will be to ask clients to describe their strengths and the supports in their lives. For clients who have difficulty spontaneously listing their strengths and supports, a review of the general categories listed in Table 6.1 can be helpful. Although clients may not frame their strengths as cultural, it is important that therapists stay aware of a possible cultural connection, to avoid overlooking or misinterpreting behaviors and attitudes that may be positive even if they do not fit dominant norms (Stevenson & Renard, 1993). To help with this process, therapists may review the possible strengths and supports related to each of the ADDRESSING influences in the client's life.

TABLE 6.1.	
Culturally Related Strengths and Supports	
Type of Strength	**Example**
Personal strengths	Pride in one's culture
	Religious faith or spirituality
	Artistic abilities
	Bilingual and multilingual skills
	Group-specific social skills
	Sense of humor
	Culturally-related knowledge and practical skills (e.g., fishing, hunting, farming, medicinal plants)
	Culture-specific beliefs that help one cope (e.g., with racism, prejudice, discrimination)
	Respectful attitude toward the natural environment
	Commitment to helping one's own group (i.e., through social action)
	Wisdom from experience
Interpersonal supports	Extended families, including non-blood-related kin
	Cultural or group-specific networks
	Religious communities
	Traditional celebrations and rituals
	Recreational, playful activities
	Story-telling activities that make meaning and pass on history of the group
	Involvement in political or social action group
Environmental conditions	An altar in one's home or room to honor deceased family members and ancestors
	A space for prayer and meditation
	Foods related to cultural preferences (cooking and eating)
	Animals to care for
	A gardening area
	Access to outdoors for subsistence or recreational fishing, hunting, farming, observing stars and constellations in the night sky

Assessing Unusual Perceptions and Experiences

Even if one takes a more behavioral approach, one of the most difficult tasks in cross-cultural evaluations involves the assessment of unusual beliefs and behaviors that may be seen as normal and even healthy in certain contexts (e.g., beliefs in the supernatural, communication with spirits, trance experiences). Westermeyer (1987) offered several criteria for distinguishing the latter, noting that they are "usually characterized by (a) community and family support; (b) time limitations from a few hours to a few days; (c) socially appropriate, productive, and coping behavior before and after the experience; (d) a resultant gain in self-esteem and social prestige; (e) the absence of psychopathological signs and symptoms and (f) culturally congruent visions or auditory experiences."(p. 473). Psychopathological conditions are distinguished by the opposites of these criteria.

Although clients' presentations will not always fit this list (in part, because some of the criteria apply to beliefs, some to behaviors, and others to experiences), the criteria can be useful as a general guide. Take the example of a Christian client who told his therapist that God speaks to him on a daily basis. This man was a member of a fundamentalist church that conceptualized the Bible as the literal word of God. His experience of direct communication with God was supported by his family and church community and was "contained" that is, the communication was of an expected duration and did not interfere with other activities. In addition, the content of the communication was constructive and perceived as helpful. Although the client was suffering from anxiety and depression, his spiritual experiences seemed to be a source of support and strength, not a maladaptive response. Attention to the cultural aspects of this client's presentation prevented the therapist from misinterpreting the client's experience as pathological.

In assessing the normality of behaviors and beliefs in children, it is important to consider the influence of developmental processes. For example, children may lack the verbal skills to express feelings of worthlessness and guilt, or the intellectual ability to understand or describe death or suicidal ideation (Yamamoto, Silva, Ferrari, & Nukariya, 1997). In addition, the ages at which social and verbal skills develop may vary depending on the cultural context.

Of course, just as the therapist risks overdiagnosing or pathologizing clients whose cultures are unfamiliar, the therapist may also underdiagnose or overlook pathology because she or he frames a belief, behavior, or experience as cultural and thus automatically accepts it (Paniagua, 1998). This mistake almost occurred on a geropsychiatry hospital unit when an older Filipina woman was admitted for treatment of "probable depression." Although the woman was noted to be "talking to the spirits of dead people," the intake nurse decided that these were not pathological hallucinations because she knew that "in some Asian cultures, people talk to their deceased relatives."

However, in this case, a little knowledge was misleading. A closer look at the accompanying behaviors and experiences of the client revealed that she was distressed by these "conversations," that she was coping poorly both before and after them, and that the voices inhibited her ability to care for herself and engage with her family and caregivers. In addition, the voices were telling her to do destructive things that were not congruent with her culture and Catholic faith.

A more thorough evaluation found the client to have a moderate dementia and hearing impairment that were contributing to her auditory hallucinations and depressed mood. Antidepressant medication was subsequently used to lift her mood, and antipsychotic medication eliminated the voices. The client refused to wear a hearing aid, but her impairments resulted in her admission to a nursing home where she had more auditory stimulation (i.e., more people around her who would speak loudly).

Kemp and Mallinckrodt (1996) discussed these sorts of problems in clinical judgment as (a) errors of omission (i.e., failing to ask about a crucial aspect of the client's life) and (b) errors of commission (focusing on an issue that is not especially important, although the therapist believes it is). With regard to people who have disabilities, one example of an error of omission is the failure of therapists to ask about clients' sexuality; therapists often mistakenly assume that people with disabilities are incapable of or not interested in sexual intimacy. In contrast, an error of commission would be focusing too heavily on the disability when it is not the client's presenting problem (Kemp & Mallinckrodt, p. 378). In either case, the more a therapist knows about a client's cultural history and context, the less likely she or he is to make such mistakes.

Conclusion

Effective assessment of clients of minority cultures and groups requires an understanding of clients' personal and cultural histories and contexts. Assuming that the therapist is actively engaged in an ongoing learning process about diverse cultures, this chapter has focused on specific steps he or she can take during the assessment. These involve the use of multiple sources of information, including information from health care providers and significant others, and direct and indirect observations. In addition, to facilitate an understanding of the client's personal history, the therapist needs to obtain information about relevant cultural histories and stay aware of changing conceptualizations of illness and health in different cultures. Toward this end, it can be helpful to calculate the eras during which a client experienced significant developmental phases and then think about the sociocultural influences during these time periods. Equally important is the use of a client's preferred language and a deliberate search for culturally related strengths at the individual, interpersonal, and environmental levels. All of this work sets the stage for the culturally responsive use of standardized questions and tests—the next chapter's topic.

KEY IDEAS 6.

Suggestions for Obtaining Accurate and Important Information in an Assessment

1. Seek out and use multiple sources of information.

2. Obtain information on clients' cultural histories outside the therapy setting.

3. Calculate the year or era when the client was a child, adolescent, young adult, and so on, and consider the dominant cultural perspective of these time periods.

4. Ask yourself (or find out later), What was happening in the client's culture during this year or time period?

5. Stay aware of changing conceptualizations of illness, health, and disability over time.

6. Ask about the client's conceptualization of her or his problem or situation and health care (including self-care) practices.

7. Be aware of the limitations of and problems with standardized measures of acculturation.

8. Facilitate the client's use of his or her preferred language, if necessary, via involvement with a well-qualified interpreter or referral.

9. Look for culturally related strengths at the individual, interpersonal, and environmental levels.

10. Consider the influence of culture on standardized assessment questions and tests (e.g., of mental status, intelligence, personality, behavior).

Putting Culture to the Test: Considerations With Standardized Testing

7

> Given the importance of tests and the emphasis on fairness in our culture, it is really remarkable how little research there is on the appropriateness and effectiveness of psychological assessment instruments when used cross-culturally.
>
> —Cuéllar (1998, p. 81)

My initial exposure to cultural issues in testing occurred during my doctoral studies at the University of Hawaii in the mid-1980s. My focus there was on cultural issues in clinical psychology. Through academic lectures and reading, I became aware of the continued lack of consensus on the definition of intelligence. I learned that definitions vary across cultures because different cultures value different skills and knowledge (Samuda, 1998). Moreover, within cultures, the most appreciated skills and knowledge often change over time (i.e., across historical periods and over the life span of each individual) (Anastasi, 1992).

Although it is possible, with deep knowledge of a culture, to delineate such skills and knowledge, nearly all of the tests currently being used for these purposes originate in Euroamerican culture and, as such, are culture specific (Dana, 1997; Greenfield, 1997; Wilgosh & Gibson, 1994). In addition, they are commonly standardized using "populations that explicitly exclude people with disabilities" (Olkin, 1999, p. 211). Although increasing attention is being given to the need for representative sampling in the development of norms, in most cases samples are either too small or matched on too few variables that could affect responses (as in the case of the MMPI and MMPI-2; see Dana, 1997). The translation of tests originally developed in English is equally problematic; even if linguistic equivalence can be ensured, conceptual and other forms of cultural equivalence do not necessarily follow (Reddy, Knowles, & Reddy, 1995).

With this knowledge in hand, I was granted a one-year practicum that primarily involved testing children in Hawaii public schools. The majority of these children were of Asian, Pacific Islander, or mixed cultures. After my first couple of months, I recall asking my supervisor, a thoughtful Japanese American woman with children of her own, about the ethics of using such Eurocentric tests with kids who were not Euroamerican. The gist of her reply was that this is not an ideal world, and if these kids were to get anywhere in life, they had to succeed in the present school system. She went on to say that the tests we were conducting helped to demonstrate their specific learning needs so that they could get the help they needed. I probably remember her words more than others because they fit with my own view that one needs to work toward a more just world but also, until the social changes occur, not overlook ways of getting people's needs met within the system.

This chapter begins with an overview of the four main responses to Eurocentric bias that have been presented in the testing literature. In reality, none of these responses completely solves the problem, although I believe that the fourth solution—a more fluid, dynamic approach aimed at understanding the reasons for clients' test performance— comes the closest. Building upon this fourth approach, the suggestions that follow move beyond critiques to describe ways to use standardized tests in a culturally responsive way. The chapter is organized by types of testing, including mental status and intelligence tests and neuropsychological assessment; a case example is described of an older Korean man brought in for an assessment by his adult daughter, who is concerned about his memory difficulties. Personality tests, whose use is particularly problematic with clients with minority identities, are discussed last.

Decreasing Eurocentrism and Other Biases in Standardized Tests

It seems to me that the present challenge with regard to the use of tests is to decide which tests are so biased that they should not be used at all, and then, of those tests that may be less biased, to determine how they can be used in ways that primarily benefit clients, rather than clinicians or the field. At this point, the testing literature proposes four solutions to the problem of Eurocentrism in standardized tests.

The first solution involves obtaining norms for a wide range of cultural groups, which can then be used to restandardize current instruments. This approach is probably the most common in the assessment field; one example is the extensive restandardization of the MMPI into the MMPI-2 (Graham, 1990). However, restandardization via the collection of culture-specific norms cannot change the fact that the original test items or questions were based on what Euroamerican researchers considered important at the time (Okazaki, 1998).

Even if such norms could be collected and used to adapt and change specific items, the immense amount of work involved in obtaining representative samples makes it unlikely that psychology will see this goal accomplished in the near future. Asian and Pacific Islander Americans "can trace their roots to 28 countries of origin or ethnic groups or to 25 identified Pacific Island cultures" (Okazaki, 1998, p. 56), while Indigenous people in North America alone belong to over 500 tribal groups and speak over 150 languages

(Choney, Berryhill-Paapke, & Robbins, 1995). And these are only two of the larger ethnic minority groups in North America.

The second solution to biases in testing against minority groups is to create new tests that emanate from the value systems specific to minority cultures (Lindsey, 1998). For example, an instrument aimed at assessing intellectual abilities in Samoan children would begin with a definition of intelligence from a Samoan cultural perspective and from there develop items that reflect those abilities. A similar approach could be taken in assessing affective constructs such as depression (Geisinger, 1992). Clearly, this is the preferable solution, and a few researchers have attempted to develop such measures. Examples include the Hispanic Stress Inventory (Cervantes, Padilla, & Salgado de Snyder, 1990), the Vietnamese Depression Scale (Kinzie et al., 1982), and some of the instruments described in the Handbook of Tests and Measurements for Black Populations (R. L. Jones, 1996). However, for the vast majority of cultures, such instruments do not exist or are not sufficiently developed to be of any practical clinical use. In addition, as with the first solution, the amount of work involved in developing such tests precludes substantive changes in the near future.

The third approach involves the use of an Index of Correction for Culture (ICC) (Cuéllar, 2000), which is derived by correlating a measure of acculturation with the criterion variable. An individual's score on the test is then adjusted by this correction factor. The greater the cultural difference between the person taking the test and the standardization sample, the greater the ICC. The direction of the correction is determined "by the direction of the correlation between acculturation and the criterion variable" for that ethnic group (Cuéllar, 2000, p. 124).

However, as Cuéllar (2000) noted, standardized procedures for this approach have not been established. And even if they are, such adjustments would tend to support the status quo by reinforcing the use of tests developed from a dominant cultural perspective (Dana, 2000b). Another problem with this method is the conceptualization of acculturation as a linear process, the limitations of which were discussed in chapter 6.

The fourth approach to biases in testing involves adopting a more fluid approach to assessing intelligence, personality, and behavior. Cuéllar (1998) described this "dynamic approach" as one in which specific strategies are adopted in addition to standardized procedures for the purpose of eliciting "additional qualitative data about the examinee" (p. 76). In many cases, this will involve replacing tests with more culturally acceptable approaches such as interviews and direct observation. (Note that a recent trend related to managed care is a reduction in the use of tests by psychologists; see Eisman et al., 2000; Piotrowski, Belter, & Keller, 1998). My own rule is that if information can be obtained directly, either by asking or observing the client, her or his family, or other health care providers, then I prefer the more direct approach.

Of course, in certain settings, it is currently impossible to eliminate standardized tests. For example, in schools, test results are required to obtain the resources necessary to facilitate a child's learning (Kamphaus, Petoskey, & Rowe, 2000). But there are ways to conceptualize and augment testing so that the results are meaningful. Consider the use of the IQ score in intelligence testing. Because the IQ represents a composite of one's scores on a variety of tasks, the total score is not especially useful in planning for the educational needs of a child. Moreover, the misguided equation of IQ with intelligence has led to the disproportionate classification of African American and Latino children as mentally retarded or learning disabled (Suzuki & Valencia, 1997). As Anastasi (1992) noted, "test scores tell us *how well* individuals perform at the time of testing, not why they perform as they do" (p. 612).

To gain an understanding of the reasons for a client's performance, a shift is needed from this focus on classification and rating (e.g., an IQ score) to one that emphasizes "description and prescription" (Samuda, 1998, p. 173). This latter approach involves dropping the concept of IQ and instead using the specific subtest results to provide details about what the individual can do, cannot do, and might be able to do with help. Such information is then used to plan strategies that facilitate learning in the current educational system (Samuda, 1998) or in rehabilitation programs with people who have disabilities.

The need for clinicians to take "reasonable steps" to ensure cross-cultural competence in test administration and interpretation was emphasized in the American Psychological Association's (1992) latest revision of the *Ethical Principles of Psychologists*. However, the revised code offers "no clarity on how to use cultural factors for test interpretations" or acknowledgment of the fact that the requested adjustments violate standard psychometric procedures (Dana, 1994, p. 352). This is probably because there are few empirically validated studies on the specifics of making such adjustments. The suggestions that follow are strategies I have learned through my clinical training and work conducting intellectual and neuropsychological assessments with children in schools and with adults and elders in rehabilitation, psychiatric, and geriatric inpatient and outpatient settings, along with some ideas from the testing literature.

Mental Status Testing and Intellectual Assessment

With regard to mental status evaluations, many of the questions included in standardized questionnaires are not reliable indicators of a client's functioning (Paniagua, 1998). For example, in a study of Native and non-Native elders in Manitoba, 45% of the Native elders had no formal schooling at all (Kaufert & Shapiro, 1996). In communities that did not routinely designate individual house addresses, participants had difficulty stating their street addresses. Similarly, dates were considered less important as time markers than events such as the beginning of hunting and fishing season. Native elders in this study also had difficulty naming the current and former prime ministers of Canada (questions on the adapted Mental Status Questionnaire developed by Kahn, Goldfarb, Pollack, & Peck, 1960). Even well-educated immigrant clients may have difficulty recalling such information as former heads of state in their adopted country.

In the same study, when Aboriginal (i.e., Native) elders were asked what year they gained voting rights and the community obtained electricity, relatively few could answer the first question, but a higher proportion answered the second correctly (Kaufert & Shapiro, 1996). The authors attributed these findings to the cultural and ecological significance of electrification; the hydroelectric dam that produced electricity also resulted in the flooding of hunting, trapping, and fishing territories, which in turn contributed to decreased self-sufficiency and a sense of alienation in community members.

One of the most commonly used questionnaires for assessing mental status is the Folstein mini mental status exam, or MMSE (Folstein, Anthony, Parhad, Duffy, & Gruenberg, 1985). But the MMSE has limitations in assessing individuals who have not had formal schooling in North America. For example, this test requires takers to draw geometrical designs as a screen for visuospatial perceptual difficulties, a difficult task for a nonliterate person who rarely uses a pencil. Even basic questions concerning orientation may be misleading for clients who do not use watches or the Christian calendar or follow a structured daily routine (Jewell, 1989).

For Spanish-speaking people in particular, the MMSE has been found to yield higher error rates on questions as simple as "Can you tell me the season?" and "What state are we in?" (Escobar et al., 1986). Many Spanish-speaking people come from tropical and subtropical areas, which have two seasons, rainy and dry, rather than the four seasons of temperate climates. The term "state" means both country and divisions within a country (Ardila, Rosselli, & Puentes, 1994).

TACIT KNOWLEDGE AND PRACTICAL INTELLIGENCE

What is needed is a way to test mental status that taps intellectual functions that clients use in their daily lives. A relatively new development in cognitive research is helpful in this regard, namely the distinction now being made between academic intelligence (used to solve academic questions, and typically measured by quantitatively oriented instruments) and practical intelligence (used to solve day-to-day problems and performance in real-life situations) (Sternberg, Wagner, Williams, & Horvath, 1995). Whereas academic intelligence is facilitated by academic knowledge, practical intelligence increases with one's tacit knowledge, or common sense.

Tacit knowledge is action oriented (i.e., it involves knowing how to do things); it is practical (in contrast to academic knowledge, which is often irrelevant to people's daily lives); and it is usually acquired without the help of others, which means that it is often unspoken and poorly articulated (unlike academic knowledge, which is reinforced by the academic environment and the dominant culture) (Sternberg et al., 1995). Research has shown that it is possible to develop measures of tacit knowledge relevant to job and school performance (Sternberg, Wagner, & Okagaki, 1993).

In assessing everyday-life functioning among Aboriginal Australians, Davidson (1995) further suggested that what is needed is an ideographic approach, in which the skills and knowledge used to assess the client's functioning are those considered important for that particular client and measured in relation to her or his baseline; thus, what is assessed may vary with each client.

> Those who quibble with the notion that cognitive assessment can be ideographic may consider the possibility of a psychologist asking the question "Which of these two individuals is more schizophrenic?" When it comes to clinical diagnosis we are more concerned about whether, and the extent to which, both individuals are functional in everyday-life contexts rather than whether one individual has *more* psychopathology than the other. Why then are we not prepared to adopt an

ideographic approach to cognitive assessment? The question in cognitive assessment should be, To what extent is the individual functioning cognitively in particular contexts? and not, Which of these two individuals is more cognitively capable? (Davidson, 1995, p. 32).

Obviously, such an approach sidesteps the issues involved with children in public schools. As my former supervisor said, at present it is important that children succeed in the dominant educational system so that they can have access to future opportunities, and thus it is still necessary to assess children's performance in relation to the dominant curricula. However, this is generally not the case with adults and elders. Moreover, even with children, an additional emphasis on practical intelligence can be helpful in calling attention to a child's strengths, avoiding pathologization of difficulties, and assessing the child's functioning more broadly than the tests measure.

Unfortunately, to date, there are no practical measures of tacit knowledge specific to clinical practice. This should not be surprising, given that such measures would by definition be culture specific or even person-specific. But clinicians can take steps to incorporate some aspects of ideographic testing into their assessments.

PREASSESSMENT MEETING WITH INTERPRETER OR CULTURAL LIAISON

As outlined in chapter 6, when the therapist encounters a client who was not educated in a Euroamerican school system, a useful first step is to arrange a preassessment meeting with the client's interpreter or cultural liaison. The purpose of this meeting is to gain an idea of the kinds of information the client would normally be expected to know in his or her environment (i.e., his or her tacit knowledge). With this information, the therapist can then work with the interpreter to develop a list of relevant and culturally responsive questions in advance. In working with an interpreter and a client who is Deaf or has a hearing impairment, Leigh, Corbett, Gutman, and Morere (1996) suggested holding such a meeting both before and after the counseling session to discuss expectations and actual results—a good idea in bilingual therapy with anyone.

Examples of information a therapist might seek from the interpreter or cultural liaison were described in the previously cited study of Manitoba elders (Kaufert & Shapiro, 1996). For example, in place of the standardized mental status questions about date, Cree elders were asked to identify the current season and the season in which breakup (i.e., of ice) begins. In addition, in an adapted question for assessing recall of reference persons, participants were asked to identify the local band chief, although even with this question there was variability, as elders living on reserves with highly visible leaders were more able to name them than were elders living outside reserves or in Métis settlements.

For another example, let's return to the case of the Cambodian (Khmer) woman, Mrs. Sok, described in chapter 2. Before attempting to assess Mrs. Sok's mental status, the therapist would have needed to talk with the interpreter alone to learn more about the cultural context in which Mrs. Sok grew up and lived. This meeting would have educated the therapist about the skills and knowledge valued in Khmer society over the course of Mrs. Sok's life and what she could reasonably be expected to know given her age and generation, experience with disability, religious beliefs, and so on. The therapist could still use the standard mental status categories (i.e., orientation, attention, speech, language, short-term memory, long-term memory, visuospatial abilities) to develop relevant questions. But the content of these questions would reflect Mrs. Sok's sociocultural upbringing and environment, rather than the tester's.

In addition, the questions would need to be ones for which the therapist could obtain confirmation of correct answers from the interpreter or another reliable source. Asking Mrs. Sok to recall her own or her children's birth dates as a screen for long-term memory difficulties would not be particularly helpful, because she probably wouldn't know this information and certainly not by the European calendar. On the other hand, asking about specifics such as the names of her father's sisters might be a reliable measure of her memory but would not be information that the interpreter would know; hence, there would be no way to confirm the accuracy of her answers.

Questions that would avoid both of these problems and give some indication of Mrs. Sok's memory might elicit the name of the place in Cambodia where she is from, the name of the internment camp where she lived prior to resettlement, the foods she uses to prepare a particular Khmer meal and how she would prepare it, and a description of her daily activities. Ideally, such an evaluation would be conducted in a home visit, which would allow the psychologist to observe Mrs. Sok's activities and ask questions about items in her home.

With clients who do not reference Euroamerican norms regarding time, Manson and Kleinman (1998) suggested the use of life history charts in which clients' symptoms are tied to significant events rather than dates. Events are chosen by the client and can be important for either personal reasons (e.g., "the crying started the year my husband died") or larger sociocultural reasons ("I remember first feeling that way just before the last harvest"). Visual symbols and pictures could be used to make the chart more comprehensible to nonliterate clients. The timeline described in chapter 6 could be modified to incorporate these ideas.

With regard to the assessment of clients who are culturally Deaf or who have a hearing impairment, Leigh and colleagues (1996) noted a number of important points. The use of written language to communicate (e.g., in an emergency room where no interpreters are immediately available) may seem like a reasonable solution but can lead to serious errors in clinical judgment. Because "ASL grammatical structures differ from English, written communication by Deaf signers who are weak in English may appear aphasic or psychotic to the unsophisticated practitioner" (Leigh et al., 1996, p. 367). Similarly, English-based tests of intellectual functioning may not accurately reflect the client's cognitive abilities and may rather be confounded with the client's English linguistic abilities. To decrease this confounding, Leigh et al. recommended the use of the WAIS-R Performance Scales (Wechsler, 1981) and the Raven's Progressive Matrices (Raven, 1960) for intellectual assessment. However, it is important to note that even these scales (including the updated WAIS-III-Wechsler, 1997) are not free of cultural biases (Samuda, 1998). To avoid misunderstandings and inaccurate diagnoses, Olkin (1999) stated that "Deaf clients are best served by Deaf therapists within the Deaf community" (p. 4).

Obviously, such a flexible and dynamic approach is more time consuming. But with clients such as Mrs. Sok, not taking this approach may result in an assessment that is essentially meaningless. On the positive side, the collaboration with an interpreter or liaison demonstrates respect for and a valuing of the interpreter's cultural expertise, increasing the likelihood that rapport will be established with both the interpreter and the client.

WHY A THOROUGH HISTORY IS ESSENTIAL IN TESTING

Chapter 6, on assessment, described ways to obtain a client's cultural history in order to better understand her or his personal history. Knowledge of the client's cultural history is also important in the accurate interpretation of test results. The most obvious example involves a client's educational background: How many years of school were completed, during what historical period, where geographically, and how well the person performed are all pieces of information necessary for estimating a client's premorbid level of cognitive functioning (Lezak, 1995).

For example, take the case of an older man who attended a strict Quranic school in Mali (East Africa) and who has experienced a stroke in his new country. No psychologist could possibly figure out whether the man was experiencing impairments from his original level of functioning without understanding his culture-specific educational history (i.e., what was taught in the Quranic school, how well he performed, what kind of work he was prepared to do, and whether he did it effectively). Such a client might be considered very well educated in his home community. But without this information, a psychologist could underestimate the client's premorbid level and thus the level of impairment from the stroke.

Neuropsychological Assessment

When mental status screening suggests the possibility of a cognitive problem, a neuropsychological assessment may be necessary. Neuropsychological assessment involves the evaluation of specific cognitive functions, including attention, concentration, short- and long-term memory, language, reasoning, visuospatial perceptual and constructive abilities, psychomotor functioning, and "higher level" functions such as abstraction, awareness, insight, judgment, planning, and goal-setting (Lezak, 1995).

For clinical purposes, neuropsychological assessment serves two main purposes. The first is to help in formulating a diagnosis, or more specifically, to clarify whether or not a cognitive impairment exists and to distinguish between impairment due to psychological problems such as depression and deficits related to dementia (Kubiszyn et al., 2000). The second purpose is to plan treatment after the diagnosis has been made, which requires detailed information concerning the client's cognitive abilities, strengths, and weaknesses, as well as her or his progress over time (Walsh, 1987). The latter information is important in planning rehabilitation strategies and in resolving placement issues (i.e., how independently the person can live).

The hypothesis-testing approach to neuropsychological assessment is similar to the single-subject design of experiments in research and provides a model for the use of standardized tests in general (Lezak, 1995; M. B. Shapiro, 1970; Walsh, 1987). The psychologist begins with an initial set of hypotheses based on the referral question, the client's history, and initial observations. The psychologist then chooses the specific tests that will best assess the client's capabilities. As testing progresses, the psychologist refines these general hypotheses into more specific ones. Gradually, the "successive elimination of alternative diagnostic possibilities" leads to a relatively conclusive diagnosis (Lezak, 1995, p. 112).

Until recently, research on neuropsychological assessment paid little attention to cultural influences, at least in part because neuropsychologists believed that such influences had little to do with the physiological processes of the brain they were measuring (Ardila et al., 1994; Cuéllar, 1998). But as Anastasi (1992) noted, tests measure only samples of behavior at a given time and cannot say why the person responded as he or she did. To find out, one needs to look at other variables such as the individual's culture, values, and beliefs (Campbell et al., 1996). Assuming that the psychologist has obtained cultural and personal histories for the client, a strategy known as "testing the limits" can be helpful in interpreting the results of neuropsychological tests as well as measures of mental status and intellectual functioning.

Testing the limits of standardized tests involves exploring, beyond standard administrative procedures, the possible reasons for a client's poor performance. Because it is performed after the standardized test procedure for an item, testing the limits does not affect standardized scores (Lezak, 1995). In addition, testing the limits offers the opportunity to move beyond the constraints of the test and, because the tester may ask clients why they think they missed an item, can also facilitate discussion and rapport with clients (Morris, 2000).

Take a specific example: the Picture Completion subtest of the Wechsler Adult Intelligence Scale (WAIS-III). This subtest asks the client to "name what important part is missing in this picture" for a series of different scenes within time limits. If a client is unable to provide correct answers to the items on this subtest and the psychologist simply accepts the client's incorrect answers as an assessment of his ability, she may be missing a great deal of potentially valuable information. If, however, she recognizes that a score does not indicate how or why the person has difficulty with this task, the psychologist could gain more information in the following ways.

First, following the standard administration, the psychologist may return to each item and ask the client to look at the picture again and describe in detail what he sees. The underlying hypothesis at this point is that the client is capable of seeing the missing piece, but simply missed it when asked.

Another question to be investigated concerns the influence of time pressure. For this, the psychologist can ask the client to try to answer each item again, but this time without time limits. Time limits may contribute to the underestimation of a person's true abilities, particularly in the case of those who require additional time because of age, disability, language differences, cultural factors, chronic illness, or simply nervousness (Lezak, 1995). When this is the case, testing without time limits is essential to give a fuller picture of the client's capabilities.

Granted, there generally are no normative data with which to compare time-free responses on certain items. However, the point is to find out whether or not the individual can perform the task at all. If the person can, it will then be necessary to figure out whether the real-life skills represented by this task are intact and whether their time-free performance is important. For example, in the case of an elder who can do Picture Completion only without time limits, does his performance represent a deficit that could be dangerous in an independent living situation? Or, given that he experiences little time pressure in his home environment, is the issue of time relatively unimportant in assessing his abilities?

In a third strategy, after the client has failed to answer the question correctly, the psychologist may inform him of the correct answer and ask if he can now see the missing piece. A look of surprised recognition is often apparent if the person then sees it; in addition, for some items, the psychologist may ask the client to point to the missing piece. Note that if the person needs to be retested within the next year, the use of this strategy is ruled out.

Fourth, the psychologist may ask the client directly if he has an idea why he had difficulty with a particular item on the subtest. The answer may be as simple as fatigue, disinterest, preoccupation with a problem, or physical pain that distracts the client periodically. Similarly, a misunderstanding of the directions or impaired vision or hearing can account for poor performance. As an intern in a Veterans Administration nursing home, I used the Geriatric Depression Scale in assessing some of the older male clients. The first question, "Are you basically satisfied with your life?" frequently elicited the response, "Oh, yeah, she's been a pretty good old gal." It only took two or three such responses before I learned to ask before testing whether a person used or needed a hearing aid or glasses.

Finally, less obvious reasons related to a client's history may be important in her or his test performance. For example, a person may have been educated in a non-Euroamerican educational system or, in the case of some older adults, may have little or no formal education (P. Morales, 1999). With regard to individuals who speak English as a second language, Cuéllar (1998) suggested that after administering the failed item in English, the psychologist may ask the client the same item in the client's native language. (Of course, this assumes that the psychologist can.) This questioning will indicate whether or not the problem is related to language comprehension. Similarly, on a broader scale, when assessing a bilingual child's ability to succeed in an English-language educational system, it can be helpful to assess the child in both languages; this approach provides the required data but also offers a fuller understanding of the child's real needs and strengths (Geisinger, 1992, p. 33).

The Case of Mr. Kim

The following example illustrates the preceding suggestions in the case of an older Korean man who was brought to a psychologist by his daughter. The psychologist was trained in standardized procedures; however, she recognized this assessment as one requiring a more dynamic approach. Because she was able to make adaptations in the moment, she was able to successfully assess the family's needs. The key questions she used in assessing this client's mental status in the moment are included (see also Exhibit 7.1).

EXHIBIT 7.1.

Questions for Assessing Mental Status and Intellectual Functioning

1. Does the client provide a detailed personal history, or does she or he become confused about the sequence of events being recounted?

2. Might the client's style of recounting his or her personal history differ from what I would expect, but still be normal in his or her cultural context (e.g., in terms of the content, or a style that is linear, circular, or some other form)?

3. Does the client know information that most people of her or his culture and age would know, and do I know enough about the client's particular cohort to assess this?

4. Does the client show communication problems such as word-finding difficulties or paraphasias (i.e., made-up or misused words), taking into account his or her fluency level in English?

5. Does the client show appropriate concern and knowledge about her or his health problems, consistent with her or his educational background?

6. How does the client interact with me (aggressive, hostile, disinterested, confused)? Might there be cross-cultural dynamics related to any of the ADDRESSING influences that account for this behavior?

7. Might there be cultural explanations related to any of the ADDRESSING influences for behaviors or beliefs that appear to me to be unusual or abnormal?

Mr. Kim, a 70-year-old, high-school-educated, second-generation Korean American man, was referred by his physician to a 37-year-old Latina psychologist for an assessment of "memory loss." Mr. Kim came to the mental health center accompanied by his 32-year-old daughter, who introduced herself as Insook. Upon meeting Mr. Kim, the psychologist was reminded of her own father, with whom she had a strained relationship. The psychologist felt uncomfortable asking Mr. Kim directly about his difficulties. She unintentionally directed several questions to Insook, whose eye contact with the psychologist was direct, whereas Mr. Kim mostly looked at the floor.

After obtaining answers to only a few questions about Mr. Kim's history, primarily from his daughter, the psychologist sensed that something was wrong. She asked Mr. Kim directly if he was experiencing memory problems. In a low voice with a slight accent, he said that he noticed "some" but that his daughter was "too bothered." This was the point at which the psychologist would normally ask the client questions to test his mental status. Taking into account Mr. Kim's educational level, language fluency, and second-generation status, the psychologist decided that the Folstein mini mental status exam would be an adequate screening measure.

However, because she sensed that the mental status questions would alienate Mr. Kim further, the psychologist said that she would like to take a 10-minute break followed by a brief interview alone with Mr. Kim and then, if it was all right with him, alone with his daughter. She offered Mr. Kim and Insook something to drink, excused herself for a few minutes, and returned with three cups of tea. During the break, the psychologist engaged Mr. Kim and Insook in a more socially oriented conversation. After the tension had subsided a little, the psychologist showed Insook to the waiting area and spoke with Mr. Kim alone for 30 minutes.

Despite her desire to ask the mental status questions, the psychologist refrained and instead engaged Mr. Kim in conversation about his family's medical history. With his help, she drew a genogram of his family on the board, which also gave them both something to look at (see McGoldrick & Gerson, 1985, regarding genograms). Mr. Kim told her what he knew about the health and social histories of extended family members, including his maternal grandparents who died in Korea. The psychologist also asked about his family's religion, which he described as Buddhist with Confucian teachings.

As Mr. Kim spoke, the psychologist realized that she had inadvertently assumed that he was more impaired than he was. Rather than ask him directly about his mental status, she watched for signs of cognitive dysfunction while they completed the genogram. She asked herself the following questions:

1. Does Mr. Kim provide a detailed personal history, or does he become confused about the sequence of events being recounted? He provided good details for past events but couldn't recall some dates that the psychologist considered important—for example, the year he was married. However, the psychologist thought that this might not be unusual for an older Korean man who had been married for over 30 years and widowed for 10.

2. Might his style of recounting his history differ from what I would expect, but still be normal in his cultural context (e.g., in terms of the content, or a style that is linear, circular, or some other form)? His style of recounting events was relatively chronological. None of his responses expressed feelings; rather, they were more focused on places, events, and experiences; the psychologist hypothesized that this was normal for an older Korean American man.

3. Does he know information that most Korean American men his age would know, and do I know enough about his particular cohort to assess this? The psychologist did not.

4. Does he show communication problems such as word-finding difficulties or paraphasias (i.e., made-up or misused words), taking into account his fluency level in English? He spoke English fluently with a slight accent and occasional grammatical errors that appeared related to his educational level.

5. Is his understanding of his health problems consistent with his educational background? It was.

6. How does he interact with me, and might there be a cross-cultural dynamic that accounts for his reaction? The psychologist realized that his reserved manner might be related to any combination of his Buddhist, Confucian, or Korean heritage; his older age; and his gender, in response to her identity as a younger Latina woman.

7. Might there be cultural explanations for behaviors or beliefs that appear to me to be unusual or abnormal, that is, explanations related to his age or generation, possible disability, religion or spiritual orientation, or any of the other ADDRESSING influences? She correctly interpreted his lesser eye contact as due to embarrassment about the situation; however, she overlooked her own part in their uncomfortable interactions. Otherwise, there were no beliefs or behaviors that she considered unusual.

Following the interview with Mr. Kim, the psychologist walked with him to the waiting area, offered him another cup of tea, and then met with Insook. Alone with the psychologist, Insook spoke more freely about the problems she had observed in her father (increased irritability, weight loss, and poor memory—evident in several incidents of lost keys and leaving the stove on). She also told the psychologist that she hadn't wanted to list all of these problems in front of her father, although he did seem to be aware of them at home.

In a brief closing period with Mr. Kim and Insook, the psychologist thanked them for their patience and cooperation and said that she would like to consult with a colleague who had more experience with situations such as theirs. This time, she directed her comments primarily to Mr. Kim. She added that she would like to meet with them for another shorter session the next week to complete the assessment. She asked Mr. Kim first, and then Insook, if they would be willing to return. Both agreed and seemed less tense as they said good-bye.

The success of this assessment was in jeopardy from the beginning, when the psychologist posed her initial questions to the daughter. As a Latina, she was aware that in her own and Korean cultures, younger people and children, including adult children, are expected to be respectful toward elders (B. L. C. Kim, 1996; B. S. K. Kim, 1996). Her intuition was good about not asking Mr. Kim directly about his difficulties, but her over-identification with the daughter led her to make the mistake of directing her questions to Insook in front of Mr. Kim. Clearly, this was embarrassing to both father and daughter, as Insook's later comments and Mr. Kim's behavior suggested (see B. L. C. Kim, 1996, regarding therapists' demonstration of respect with Korean families).

In addition, the psychologist initially misinterpreted the father's emotional restraint, lesser eye contact, and apparent acceptance of his difficulties as signs of dementia. She later learned that Mr. Kim's demeanor is not uncommon among people of Korean and Buddhist cultures, for whom emotional restraint is often seen as a sign of maturity and problems as a fact of life (Kim, Kim, & Rue, 1997; Murgatroyd, 1996).

But the psychologist was able to recover from her initial mistakes by taking a flexible, dynamic, hypothesis-testing approach to the situation. Her decision to meet separately with Mr. Kim and Insook, in that order, was a good one. When she did so, she immediately recognized her incorrect assumption that Mr. Kim was too impaired to speak for himself. She quickly let go of the internal demand to find out certain pieces of information in the way in which she had been trained, through direct test-type questions. Instead, she evaluated Mr. Kim through a more collaborative task—completion of the genogram and observation of his responses to less direct questions.

Via these observations and her own internal questioning, she developed her next working hypothesis—that Mr. Kim's cognitive deficits were due to depression. (Major depression, particularly in elders, can cause cognitive deficits that are reversible if the depression is successfully treated; see Cummings & Benson, 1992.) But because she realized her need for more culturally related information, she refrained from stating this hypothesis as the diagnosis. It would be a tentative one until she could consult with a Korean American clinician and possibly obtain more information via a neuropsychological evaluation.

Personality Tests

Personality is commonly thought to consist of personality traits, described as "enduring patterns of perceiving, relating to, and thinking about the environment and oneself that are exhibited in a wide range of social and personal contexts" (American Psychiatric Association, 1994, p. 630). Most standardized tests developed to assess these traits derive from Euroamerican cultural perspectives. Although personality tests (e.g., the MMPI-2, Rorschach, TAT) may be helpful with some clients to raise questions and ideas for the client's consideration, in general their use with clients of minority identities for diagnostic purposes is not advised.

THE MMPI AND MMPI-2

One of the most widely used personality tests is the Minnesota Multiphasic Personality Inventory, or MMPI, and its more recent version, the MMPI-2. For decades, the MMPI used norms based on an original standardization sample of 724 friends and relatives of patients at the University of Minnesota Hospitals. The entire sample was White, with the typical participant being married and about 35 years old, having 8 years of formal education, and residing in a small town or rural area (Graham, 1990). The MMPI-2 restandardization sample included Asian, Latino, Native and African Americans, but "their modest representation in this sample is insufficient to guarantee freedom from ethnic biases, particularly among persons without competence in English" (Nichols, Padilla, & Gomez-Macqueo, 2000, p. 262).

When the MMPI-2 is used with clients of minority cultures, the risk is that clients' personalities will be inaccurately pathologized, because what constitutes a "normal" personality in their cultures may not be so in Euroamerican culture (and vice versa). The tendency of the MMPI-2 to overpathologize has been documented with regard to people of many minority cultures, including those of Asian heritage (Okazaki & Sue, 1995). In addition, American Indian people have been found to score higher than Euroamericans on most of the MMPI-2 scales (Butcher, Dahlstrom, Graham, Tellegen, & Kaemmer, 1989, and Forey, 1996, in Allen, 1998, p. 19). Cultural differences have also been noted to influence most of the MMPI scales for Mexican Americans (Cuéllar, 1998). In a study by Timbrook and Graham (1994), the MMPI-2 underpredicted "the ratings of symptoms and problems of African Americans on the basis of five of the clinical scales", although when participants "were matched for age, education, and income, differences between the two groups decreased" (cited in Suzuki & Kugler, 1995, p. 503). (See Handel & Ben-Porath, 2000, for an overview of studies of the MMPI-2 with African Americans.) And with clients who are culturally Deaf or have a hearing impairment, the written English skills required by the MMPI have been noted to pose problems; "even when language is changed with care to ensure comprehension, a deaf client may respond in an atypical manner because of previous experiences rather than as a result of current psychological functioning" (Leigh et al., 1996, p. 368).

In general, cross-cultural research on the MMPI-2 also suffers from the inaccurate assumption that ethnic culture is synonymous with race. Surname and skin color, inaccurately assumed to represent race, are still commonly used to identify participants' ethnicities, despite the fact that these characteristics say nothing about a person's beliefs, values, attitudes, or behaviors (Greene, Gwin, & Staal, 1997).

Another problem involves the greater tendency of some groups (e.g., people who are of lower socioeconomic status, older, or of Mexican heritage) to give more socially acquiescent or acceptable responses to MMPI questions (Ross & Mirowski, 1984). The MMPI-2 now contains two scales to catch inconsistencies: the True Response Inconsistency (TRIN) scale (which identifies individuals who give true responses to items indiscriminately or false responses to items indiscriminately) and the Variable Response Inconsistency (VRIN) scale (which identifies responses typically due to not reading the items or responding in a random way) (Graham, 1990). But to date there are no studies of the effects of culture (e.g., ethnicity, socioeconomic status, or acculturation) on these scales (Cuéllar, 1998).

With regard to people who have disabilities, there is research suggesting that specific medical and physical conditions (e.g., stroke, multiple sclerosis, neurologic dysfunction, and physical disabilities) may predispose individuals to answer MMPI and MMPI-2 items in a way that results in biased scores. However, these studies contain a number of problematic assumptions (Greene et al., 1997). At this point, further research is needed on the use of the MMPI and MMPI-2 with people who have disabilities and specific medical conditions.

Clients' possible reactions to taking such a test may also preclude its use. For example, although many geropsychiatry hospital units routinely use the MMPI-2, asking people in their 70s, 80s, and 90s who may have health problems to answer over 500 questions may be overwhelming, particularly for depressed elders (Scogin, 1994). For the same reason, it is generally not advisable to ask clients who do not speak English comfortably to complete these tests. The use of translated versions is a possibility; however, "the MMPI/MMPI-2, which has been translated into a large number of different languages including many Spanish versions using unrecognized systematic procedures, has major unresolved translation problems" (Dana, 2000a, p. 10). (For further information on linguistic, conceptual, functional, and metric equivalence in cross-cultural applications of the MMPI-2, see Nichols et al., 2000.)

Finally, computer-generated reports should not be used with clients of minority identities (Suzuki & Kugler, 1995). For that matter, their inability to account for diverse sociocultural influences in general limits their use with anyone.

PERFORMANCE-BASED PERSONALITY (PROJECTIVE) TESTS

I use the term "performance-based personality" in place of the term "projective" because, unlike the MMPI, these tests require the individual to "perform a defined activity with an examiner (i.e., generate a story or identify images)," and there is evidence that such tests do not depend on or require projections, but rather reflect a person's "perceptions, classifications, and cognitive-emotional templates or internal representations" (Kubiszyn et al., 2000, p. 120). Hence, as Kubiszyn et al. noted, the descriptor *performance-based* is more accurate than that of *projective*.

Most of the widely used performance-based personality tests start from a Euroamerican cultural base and, as such, are also susceptible to cultural biases (Cuéllar, 1998; Costantino, Flanagan, & Malgady, 1995). For example, the Thematic Apperception Test (TAT) makes use of pictures that the client is asked to describe; the client's responses are considered indicative of his or her beliefs and views (i.e., which are "projected" onto the people in the picture). But the original TAT pictures were of characters and situations relevant primarily to Euroamerican culture. Over the years, the TAT pictures have been redrawn to depict people and situations of diverse cultures (see Costantino & Malgady, 2000, for an overview). However, the use of the TAT has declined significantly both in doctoral training programs and in general assessment practice (except with adolescents), and "optimism concerning TAT reliability and validity research has waned" (Dana, 1999, p. 178).

The Tell-Me-a-Story or TEMAS test (Costantino, Malgady, & Rogler, 1988; Costantino, Malgady, & Vasquez, 1981) "was developed to revive the TAT technique for culturally and linguistically diverse children and adolescents" (Costantino & Malgady, 2000, p. 484). Research using the TEMAS suggests that the cultural identity of characters does make a difference in clients' responses (Suzuki & Kugler, 1995). The TEMAS is currently the only "adequately validated multicultural thematic test employing cards to depict Hispanic or Black, Asian, and White adolescents" (Dana, 1998, p. 6). Picture story tests have been developed for Inupiat and Indian people; however, no scoring systems currently exist (Allen, 1998.)

The Rorschach Comprehensive System (RCS) avoids the problem of respondents' perceptions of characters' identities through the use of inkblots. However, although inkblots may be less culturally laden, the interpretation of clients' associations to these stimuli is especially susceptible to misunderstanding by clinicians whose cultures differ from their clients'. For example, the dark areas of the color cards have traditionally been associated with death and mourning, but in India "white, not black, is the color associated with mourning and death" (Jewell, 1989, p. 306).

As Ephraim (2000) observed, "Rorschach examiners tend to agree that common principles of Rorschach interpretation could be applied to protocols of people from any cultural background. However, there is still a need to establish, conceptually as well as empirically, which those common principles are" (p. 322). An increasing number of normative studies internationally have found significant variations in local norms compared to norms in the United States (see Andronikof-Sanglade, 2000; Ephraim, 2000; Vinet, 2000; Pires, 2000). Considering these findings, Dana (1997) stated that "It seems more reasonable to suggest that cross-cultural construct validation of the RCS has not been demonstrated and that these scattered studies indicate that representative norms for each country are imperative as a basis for describing differences in constructs that can be subsequently examined" (Dana, 1997, p. 131). (Dana, 2000b, provides a more detailed critique of the cultural influences on the RCS.)

Conclusion

The central problem with standardized testing is that it assumes that there is a standard human being; fortunately, there is not. Although standardized tests can be helpful in understanding the specifics of individuals' abilities, they also hold the potential to do much damage. People of ethnic and other minority identities have often been hurt by the misuse of such tests. It is essential that psychologists be aware of the cultural biases inherent in standardized tests of intelligence, personality, and mental status so as to avoid misdiagnosing clients-which brings us to the topic of the next chapter, namely, cultural concerns in diagnosis.

KEY IDEAS 7.

Suggestions for Making Standardized Tests More Culturally Responsive

1. Begin with a thorough history, both personal and cultural.
2. When available and appropriate, arrange a preassessment meeting with the client's interpreter or cultural liaison.
   a. Develop a list of questions and confirmed answers that tap the skills and knowledge relevant to the client's experience and context.
3. Choose tests that match the referral question for the client.
4. Explore possible reasons for a client's test performance.
5. Push the limits of standardized tests:
   a. Ask the client to look at each item again and describe in detail what she or he sees.
   b. Ask the client to answer each item again, this time without time limits.
   c. If retesting is unlikely, tell the client the correct answer, then ask and watch if they see it or can point it out.
   d. Ask the client why they think they had trouble with an item or subtest.
   e. Ask the item in the client's native language (only if you are fluent).
6. Think ideographically-that is, whenever possible, compare clients' test performance and behaviors against their own past performance, rather than against others.
7. Avoid the use of standardized personality tests for diagnostic purposes with clients of minority identities.

Making Sense and Moving On: Culturally Responsive Diagnosis and the *DSM-IV*

8

> We organize suffering into categories to help cope with it, but often these categories themselves canceal some forms of suffering, even contribute to them. This latter experience leads some to suspect that suffering is never entirely reducible to any determinate set of categories. (Connolly, 1996, p. 251)

While working on a geropsychiatry unit, I was asked by a physician to evaluate a 63-year-old Mexican American man who had no physical or emotional complaints. Mr. García had been born in the United States, obtained a 9th-grade education, and spoke English with an accent. In the early 1960s, he began working as a custodian for a large corporation. He was well liked and a hard worker, and over the years he was promoted to a supervisory position, which required that he keep track of equipment. However, during the past 5 years, he had begun losing requests and forgetting orders. He had also been "talked to" for some odd behaviors, such as taking his shirt off on the work floor (he said he was hot). As a result, his responsibilities had gradually been reduced to sweeping floors and other cleaning tasks.

While Mr. García was not concerned about his work situation or health, his wife was deeply distressed. She reported that he did things that scared her—nothing abusive, but things like driving through red lights and draping a blanket over an electric heater. She had tried everything she could think of to help her husband, including rearranging things in the house and talking to his supervisors, family members, and friends. But no one had a reasonable explanation for why Mr. García was acting the way he was. She went to her priest, who prayed with her, and finally to the doctor, who conducted a thorough medical exam. Because the physician could find no physical reasons for the changes in Mr. García, he recommended a neuropsychological assessment.

Following a lengthy assessment, which included consultation with the physician, interviews with Mr. and Mrs. García, reports from a work supervisor, and neuropsychological testing, I concluded that Mr. García had a moderate dementia probably due to Alzheimer's disease. Normally, I dread having to share this information with patients and their families. But because of the extent of Mr. García's impairments, I figured that he would not be disturbed by this information, and in fact, he was not.

Mrs. García, I felt, would be a different matter. I assumed that she would be crestfallen and probably angry at me, the bearer of bad news. To my surprise, she did not become upset, but rather expressed relief and appreciation. As she explained, she was exhausted from trying to figure out her husband's strange behaviors and personality changes. At least now she knew that she was not imagining things or overreacting. Although she was realistically sad about what lay ahead, she was also ready to hear about available resources and to begin planning for the future.

As this case illustrates, much of the power of a diagnosis comes from the meaning it gives to a confusing situation. Ideally, this new understanding leads to specific actions that can eliminate the problem or reduce its harmful effects. Even when this is not possible, an accurate diagnosis may suggest new ways of thinking about the problem and coping with it. For example, although nothing could be done to reverse the Alzheimer's disease, as a result of learning that this was the primary problem, Mrs. García stopped questioning and blaming herself. Concomitantly, Mr. García left his job, which he was no longer able to perform anyway, obtained disability benefits, and began attending a day program that provided social interaction for him and a break for Mrs. García.

Toward the goal of establishing a shared understanding of mental syndromes and disorders, the American Psychiatric Association (1994) developed the *Diagnostic and Statistical Manual of Mental Disorders* (the current edition is known as the *DSM-IV*), the most widely used diagnostic system in North America. The widespread use of the *DSM-IV* does not mean that it is the most sensitive, most accurate, or only approach to diagnosis. Numerous more theoretically coherent alternatives have been proposed (see Follette, 1996, who introduced a special section of the *Journal of Consulting and Clinical Psychology* on alternatives to the *DSM* system). However, today there are few settings in which therapists can practice without a knowledge of the *DSM-IV.*

Because of its widespread use, this chapter offers practical suggestions for making culturally responsive diagnoses while also using the *DSM-IV*. First, a critique of the cross-cultural strengths and weaknesses of the *DSM-IV* is provided, with attention to its five new formats for addressing cultural concerns. Next, specific guidelines for making a culturally responsive diagnosis are outlined, including the use of a sixth Cultural Axis. Finally, a case example illustrating these suggestions describes a recently married Tunisian couple who present with marital distress and the wife's symptoms of depression following her recent immigration to the United States.

Using the DSM-IV *Across Cultures: Strengths and Weaknesses*

In response to criticisms of ethnocentrism in earlier editions of the *DSM*, the National Institute of Mental Health appointed a Work Group on Culture and Diagnosis in 1991 "to advise the DSM-IV Task Force on how to make culture more central to DSM-IV" (Lewis-Fernández, 1996, p. 133). Over the next three years, this group, composed of about 100 clinicians and social scientists, conducted extensive literature reviews and wrote detailed proposals for culturally related modifications to the new version (Kirmayer, 1998).

Unfortunately, though, as one member explained later,

> many of the substantive recommendations made by the task force—the wording of particular symptom criteria, variations in duration criteria, the inclusion of new or revised categories (a mixed anxiety-depression category, culturally distinctive forms of dissociative disorders, neurasthenia as seen and diagnosed in many Asian cultures), significant revisions of the definition of personality disorders—were not incorporated into the body of the manual, in spite of strong empirical data from the cross-cultural research literature. (Good, 1996, p. 128)

Furthermore, the recommendations that were followed do not challenge the ethnocentric assumptions underlying the *DSM-IV* (Kirmayer, 1998). The additions to the *DSM-IV* that address cultural concerns occur primarily in five formats:

1. specific culture, age, and gender features for many diagnoses,
2. an expanded Axis IV: psychosocial and environmental problems,
3. three new V codes, (Identity Problem; Religious or spiritual Problem; and Acculturation Problem).
4. an outline for cultural formulation, and
5. a glossary of culture-bound syndromes (American Psychiatric Association, 1994).

Let's look at the strengths and weaknesses of each of these additions.

SPECIFIC CULTURE, AGE, AND GENDER FEATURES

The first new inclusion involves the addition of a section entitled "Specific Culture, Age, and Gender Features" for many diagnoses. Of the approximately 400 disorders included in the *DSM-IV*, 79 include such a section (Smart & Smart, 1997). (See Paniagua, 1998, for a thorough listing of these disorders and their *DSM-IV* summaries regarding cultural variations; also included is a list of the disorders for which the *DSM-IV* does not provide cultural variations or examples.)

Unfortunately, the thoroughness and usefulness of these cultural sections vary greatly. On the more helpful end of the continuum is a paragraph-long discussion under "Schizophrenia and Related Psychotic Disorders" of the ways in which the symptoms, course, and outcome of schizophrenia vary across cultures. Although no specific cultures are mentioned, therapists are cautioned to consider cultural norms before deciding what constitutes a delusion or hallucination and to take into account linguistic variations and language abilities when assessing a client's thought processes, affect, and behavior. A paragraph of similar length and usefulness is included under "Mood Disorders."

However, under most of the other diagnostic categories, information on cultural features consists of only one or two sentences. Take the example of "Attention-Deficit/Hyperactivity Disorder." The *DSM-IV's* only comment regarding cultural influences relevant to this diagnosis is the following: "Attention-Deficit/Hyperactivity Disorder is known to occur in various cultures, with variations in reported prevalence among Western countries probably arising more from different diagnostic practices than from differences in clinical presentation" (American Psychiatric Association, 1994, p. 81). Unfortunately, the vagueness of this comment regarding "specific" cultural features is characteristic of the descriptions for many other diagnostic categories.

The age-related information under "Specific Culture, Age, and Gender Features" is similarly inconsistent and sparse with regard to children and adolescents. Although the Child Committee of the Culture and Diagnosis Work Group made several recommendations for addressing culture in the introductory section to "Childhood Disorders," none were included (Canino, Canino, & Arroyo, 1998). Under specific disorders, some recommendations were followed. With regard to "Mental Retardation," mention is made of the need to use tests "in which the individual's relevant characteristics are represented in the standardization sample of the test or by employing an examiner who is familiar with aspects of the individual's ethnic or cultural background" (American Psychiatric Association, 1994, p. 44). Clinicians are also advised, in evaluating behaviors for the diagnosis of "Conduct Disorder," to consider the possibility that the disruptive behaviors may be protective in the child's environment (Canino et al., 1998).

However, with regard to children of diverse identities, the DSM-IV assumes that children of similar ages have similar educational opportunities. More specifically, "the disorders related to reading, mathematics, and written expression are all based on an expectation related to 'age-appropriate education'" (Yamamoto, Silva, Ferrari, & Nukariya, 1997, p. 47). But school systems and ethnic minority communities often have fewer resources and opportunities for students. This assumption that a particular grade level is equivalent to particular learning experiences may lead to the overdiagnosis of developmental disorders in children of color (Yamamoto et al., 1997).

EXPANDED AXIS IV: PSYCHOSOCIAL AND ENVIRONMENTAL PROBLEMS

The second addition to the *DSM-IV* consists of changing the former "Axis IV Severity of Psychosocial Stressors" rating scale to a nonrated list of "Psychosocial and Environmental Problems" in the client's life. The main categories of these problems are similar to those listed in the *DSM-III-R*. However, within the categories, more specific examples relating to minority populations are included, such as discrimination, acculturation difficulties, homelessness, extreme poverty, inadequate health care services or insurance, being the victim of a crime, and war. These additions are noteworthy because they draw attention to such stressors in an integrated and central way (i.e., within the multiaxial diagnosis, and not as an appendix or add-on). Unfortunately, this axis, in the absence of one that emphasizes cultural strengths and supports, may reinforce the tendency to think about cultural influences only in terms of problems.

THREE NEW V CODES

The third cultural component added to the *DSM-IV* involves three new V codes under "Other conditions that may be the focus of clinical attention." The first, "Identity Problem," refers to situations in which the focus is "uncertainty about multiple issues relating to identity such as long-term goals, career choice, friendship patterns, sexual orientation and behavior, moral values, and group loyalties" (American Psychiatric Association, 1994, p. 685). The second code is for a "Religious or Spiritual Problem"; examples include "distressing experiences that involve loss or questioning of faith, problems associated with conversion to a new faith, or questioning of spiritual values that may not necessarily be related to an organized church or religious institution" (p. 685). Finally, an "Acculturation Problem" is described simply as one involving "adjustment to a different culture (e.g., following migration)" (p. 685).

These new V codes are important because they provide a way to diagnose problems that commonly affect clients of minority group membership (and many majority members) without pathologizing the individual. For example, identity problems may arise for individuals of diverse identities as a normal part of their development and lives (e.g., for a bicultural adolescent pulled by two opposing peer groups; for a man struggling to integrate a new identity as a person with a disability; for a person deciding to "come out" as gay, lesbian, or bisexual). Similarly, problems related to one's spiritual growth or religious involvement often reflect normal developmental processes and transitions. And finally, the conceptualization of acculturation difficulties as normal under certain circumstances (e.g., migration) is more accurate and generally more helpful to clients who are attempting to adjust to a new culture.

OUTLINE FOR CULTURAL FORMULATION

The fourth addition to the *DSM-IV* is an "Outline for Cultural Formulation," which names and briefly describes five cultural influences to be considered in assessment. These include

1. cultural identity of the individual, or the person's cultural reference groups, language abilities, and, when relevant, degree of involvement with culture of origin and host culture;
2. cultural explanations of the individual's illness, or predominant idioms of distress and local illness categories used by the client's family or culture; the meaning and severity of symptoms in relation to norms of the client's reference groups; perceived causes and explanatory models; and preferences for and experiences with professional and popular forms of health care;
3. cultural factors related to psychosocial environment and levels of functioning, including culturally relevant interpretations of social stressors, available supports, and levels of functioning and disability;

4. cultural elements of the relationship between the individual and the clinician, such as differences in culture and social status and problems these differences may cause in diagnosis and treatment; and

5. overall cultural assessment for diagnosis and care, which identifies how cultural considerations influence diagnosis and care. (Summarized from American Psychiatric Association, 1994, pp. 843-844)

This outline represents an important contribution to the *DSM* system, in that it calls attention to cultural influences on clients and on the therapeutic relationship (Kirmayer, 1998). But the outline contains no culture-specific information and is best thought of as a guide. The degree to which it is helpful will be determined by the therapist's cross-cultural knowledge base and experience (i.e., by one's ability to "fill in the blanks").

Unfortunately, because it appears as an appendix at the end of the manual, the outline is much less likely to be used or even seen (Hughes, 1998). Toward the goal of integrating cultural considerations into the diagnostic process, it would have been much more useful to include the outline at the beginning of the *DSM-IV* (a recommendation made by the Work Group; see Lewis-Fernández, 1996), with information on its use in relation to each of the axes.

GLOSSARY OF CULTURE-BOUND SYNDROMES

Within the same appendix and immediately following the outline is a fifth new section called the "Glossary of Culture-Bound Syndromes." The term culture-bound syndrome refers to "recurrent, locality-specific patterns of aberrant behavior and troubling experience that may or may not be linked to a particular DSM-IV diagnostic category" (American Psychiatric Association, 1994, p. 844). Culture-bound syndromes are also described within the DSM-IV as "folk categories"; brief descriptions of 25 such categories are included.

The *DSM-IV's* inclusion of culture-bound syndromes is surprising given long-standing criticisms of the concept by cross-cultural psychiatrists, psychologists, and anthropologists (see Langness, 1976, and Lebra, 1976). The term is problematic because it suggests that only certain disorders are affected or shaped by culture, namely, those found in "non-Western" cultures. But in fact, no psychiatric disorder can be understood apart from the culture in which it occurs (Marsella, 1980; Marsella & Yamada, 2000). It is misleading to think, for example, that the symptoms of recurrent depression in a Euroamerican woman are any less linked to cultural influences than the symptoms of *nervios* in a Latina client. As Hughes (1998) pointed out,

> the entire diagnostic process is a culturally determined activity, and "culture" is just as much a factor in shaping particular patterns of symptomatology in the Western societies as it is everywhere else. In this light, it may be suggested that all diagnostic categories need to have a section addressing their cultural content in Western, as well as other, societies. . . . [This] would overturn the equating of "cultural factors" with "other sorts of people" and "exotica," and bring the concept of "culture" into the mainstream of the diagnostic process. (p. 420)

Although the glossary was no doubt intended to educate therapists about syndromes found in minority cultures, its format and placement reinforce the idea that culture affects only minority groups (Smart & Smart, 1997). A more realistic approach would have been to integrate these syndromes into the multiaxial system. For example, the *DSM-IV* states that the culture-bound syndrome *shenjing shuairuo* is characterized by "physical and mental fatigue, dizziness, headaches, other pains, concentration difficulties, sleep disturbance, and memory loss," along with other symptoms that "in many cases . . . would meet the criteria for a DSM-IV Mood or Anxiety Disorder" (p. 848). Why then wasn't it included in the "Mood or Anxiety Disorders" section? Similarly, why not include *nervios* and *ataque de nervios* under "Anxiety Disorders," *taijin kyofusho* under "Phobias," and so on? Even those syndromes that would not technically be considered mental disorders (e.g., "brain fag" or fatigue in West African students who have studied too much) could have been included within the V codes.

Not surprisingly, there appears to be little use of the culture-bound diagnoses in mainstream mental health agencies and hospitals. This disinterest may be due to the fact that the *DSM-IV* makes no mention of how culture-bound syndromes are to be listed in a multiaxial diagnosis. Moreover, their exclusion from the commonly reimbursable Axis I and II sections decreases the likelihood that managed care companies will pay for their treatment (Paniagua, 1998).

SUMMARY

The *DSM-IV*'s cross-cultural additions represent about as much movement backward as forward. Certainly, the expanded Axis IV, the inclusion of specific cultural features for some diagnoses, and the three new V codes are positive, particularly in that they are integrated into the overall system. However, the inconsistent attention to cultural influences under "Specific Culture, Age, and Gender Features" is an area that clearly needs greater consistency and detail. In addition, the appendix format of the "Outline for Cultural Formulation" means that clinicians can easily ignore this framework. And finally, adoption of the concept of culture-bound syndromes reinforces the idea that certain disorders are shaped by certain cultures (i.e., certain minority cultures) whereas others are not (i.e., those of the dominant culture).

At a more fundamental level, Manson and Kleinman (1998) pointed to several patterns in the types of changes made to the DSM-IV:

(a) social context was systematically de-emphasized or eliminated;

(b) cultural variation was minimized or off-set by reference to "significant" or "enormous" individual variation;

(c) specifics were deleted or minimized and recast in more general terms;

(d) material that directly challenged essential elements of the criteria was either ignored or acknowledged in passing as merely variation in degree of emphasis rather than kind. (p. 383)

Clearly, the *DSM-IV* is a culturally constructed enterprise, but it is also a fact of life for many therapists (Kirmayer, 1998). Despite my reservations regarding the *DSM-IV,* I too am required to use it to do work that I think has positive results overall. The challenge has been to find ways to use it that meet clients' needs, but at the same time do not compromise my integrity or that of clients.

Making a Culturally Responsive Diagnosis

Building on the guidelines in chapter 6 for conducting a culturally responsive assessment, there are a number of additional steps that therapists can take to increase the probability of making a culturally responsive diagnosis. The first of these is to add a sixth axis that highlights cultural influences on the client. The idea of a sixth Cultural Axis was one of the original suggestions proposed by the Work Group on Culture and Diagnosis. However, it was eventually rejected in favor of the "Outline for Cultural Formulation" with the intention that this framework would be placed at the beginning of the manual, which did not happen (Lewis-Fernández, 1996).

One of the Work Group's primary concerns about an Axis VI was that it might "just add a sixth list of essentializing descriptors" (Lewis-Fernández, 1996, p.135). I share this concern, and certainly the Axis VI as I describe it below has the potential to be misused in this way. However, the uninformed application of any procedure or tool is always a problem. Because I have found the ADDRESSING acronym helpful in calling attention to cultural influences in any diagnosis, I use it as an Axis VI, as described below. But I want to emphasize that this approach assumes that the therapist is engaged in the cultural self-assessment and ongoing learning process described earlier in this book.

First, I list the Axes the way that they are listed in most intake reports—vertically on the left side of the page (see Table 8.1). However, the first axis I fill in is the cultural Axis VI: ADDRESSING Influences. I do this by listing the ADDRESSING acronym vertically next to Axis VI. Then, next to each of the influences I note the salient cultural influences and identities for that client. At the time, I am listing only those influences and identities of which I am aware; later, as I learn more about the client and her or his culture, I can add in information that is visible to anyone looking at the diagnosis.

Because information needs to be abbreviated in this format, you may be unsure of what to include next to each ADDRESSING category. As a guide, I suggest returning to the questions outlined in Exhibits 4.1 and 4.2 on understanding clients' identities.

Second, I fill in Axis IV: Psychosocial and Environmental Problems. Because I have just listed cultural influences on Axis VI, many of which may be strengths, it does not seem so skewed to focus here on the problems related to clients' sociocultural contexts. To be sure that I have thought to include or ask about all relevant stressors, I again use the ADDRESSING acronym as a reminder of problems that may be related to clients' age or generation, visible or nonvisible disability, religious upbringing or current identity, ethnic identity, socioeconomic status, and so on.

After filling in the Axis VI: ADDRESSING Influences and Axis IV: Psychosocial and Environmental Problems, the third axis I complete is Axis III: General Medical Conditions.

Completing these three axes first gives me a fuller picture of the client's context, decreasing the likelihood of making an inaccurate diagnosis on Axis I or II.

In making an Axis I or II diagnosis, it is important to recognize the legitimacy of the client's conceptualization of the problem and, whenever possible, to look for links between it and *DSM-IV* categories. For example, if a Latina client prefers to conceptualize her problem as *"nervios"* related to stressors at work, then this is probably a good starting point for the initial diagnosis. (Exceptions will include situations in which the client is clearly out of touch with reality.) If you must use a *DSM-IV* diagnosis, then look for diagnoses that most closely correspond to the client's description of her or his symptoms. To use the same example, *nervios* might be alternatively conceptualized as an "Anxiety, Mood, or Adjustment Disorder" or, if acculturation is an issue, a V code of "Acculturation Problem."

Equally important is the ability to explain the meaning of your diagnosis in language that the client understands. Although the use of theoretical language may increase the therapist's understanding, it will not necessarily help the client's (Holiman & Lauver, 1987). Moreover, it assumes a conceptualization of the problem that the client may not share.

With regard to Axis II, be cautious about diagnosing "Personality Disorders." The diagnosis of a personality disorder requires knowledge of "an enduring pattern of inner experience and behavior that deviates markedly from the expectations of the individual's culture and is manifested in at least two of the following areas: cognition, affectivity, interpersonal functioning, or impulse control" (American Psychiatric Association, 1994, p. 630). This pattern is "inflexible and pervasive across a broad range of personal and social situations" and leads to "clinically significant distress or impairment in social, occupational, or other important areas of functioning." Moreover, its onset can be traced "at least to adolescence or early adulthood" (p. 630).

It is important to remember that personality is in itself a cultural construct. As Dana (1998) noted, personality conceptualizations in the field of psychological assessment have historically "relied on Euro-American personality theories," with the more popular originating in psychoanalytic theory and positing "a human developmental process that has not been demonstrated to be universal" (p. 7). Because a personality disorder "reflects difficulties in how an individual behaves and is perceived to behave by others in the social field" (Alarcón & Foulks, 1995, p. 6), the specific criteria constituting a personality disorder will vary depending on the interpersonal skills and attitudes valued by a culture at any given point in time (Alarcón, 1997).

Consider, for example, the attitudes and behaviors constituting a "Paranoid Personality Disorder" as defined by the DSM-IV: "a pervasive distrust and suspiciousness of others such that their motives are interpreted as malevolent, beginning by early adulthood and present in a variety of contexts, as indicated by four (or more) of the following criteria" (p. 637). These criteria include (among others) preoccupation with "unjustified doubts" about the trustworthiness of others, a reluctance to confide in others because of "unwarranted fear" that information may be used against one, and a tendency to perceive attacks on one's character or reputation that are not apparent to others.

Without a consideration of cultural influences, these criteria seem reasonable. But who decides whether or not a client's suspiciousness, doubts, and fears are justified or unwarranted? Suspiciousness and paranoia have been described as a realistic reaction to oppression among African Americans (Grier & Cobbs, 1968) and among immigrant and refugee groups (Westermeyer, 1987). Even the *DSM-IV* notes that such attitudes and behaviors may be normal in anyone persistently exposed to oppressive conditions (e.g., members of ethnic and other minority groups, immigrants, and refugees) (p. 636).

To illustrate how dominant cultural values (particularly masculine-biased assumptions) regarding personality traits and styles have affected *DSM* categories, Kaplan (1983) noted that despite the existence of a "Dependent Personality Disorder" (disproportionately diagnosed in women), there is no such thing as an "Independent Personality Disorder"; apparently one can be too dependent, but never too independent. Similarly, the *DSM-IV* does not have a diagnosis for individuals who are racist, misogynistic, or homophobic (McGoldrick, 1998). Although such beliefs and behaviors are considered offensive, undesirable, and even dangerous, they are generally not seen as evidence of any mental disorder by mainstream culture.

To accurately diagnose a personality disorder, the therapist needs to know the client's culture well enough to judge whether the client's behavior represents a marked deviation from it. However, because personality disorders by definition involve disturbed interpersonal functioning and often misperceptions about the actions of others, it is important that therapists also seek information from people who have known the client for many years in a variety of situations. Because such information is rarely available in an initial assessment, the diagnosis of a personality disorder will often be premature.

Finally, the last suggestion in making a culturally responsive diagnosis is to move beyond the *DSM's* focus on individualistic diagnoses to think systemically and consider relational disorders (Kaslow, 1993). This is no easy task because, as Kirmayer (1998) explained, diagnosis is in itself an "essentializing" process; the DSM-IV reinforces the focus on "decontextualized entities whose characteristics can be studied independently of the particulars of a person's life and social circumstances" (p. 342).

While the DSM-IV includes categories of "Relational Problems" "Parent-Child"; "Partner"; "Sibling"; "Related to a Mental Disorder or General Medical Condition"; and "NOS," or not otherwise specified), these diagnoses are all listed as V codes (i.e., "Other Conditions that may be a Focus of Attention"). "Relational Problems" may be listed on Axis I if they are the focus of clinical attention; however, because they are placed in an appendix at the end of the *DSM-IV,* the implication is that these diagnoses are of secondary importance. Given this bias, the therapist will need to work hard to maintain a systemic perspective.

One additional dilemma for systemically oriented therapists concerns reimbursement; many insurance and managed care companies do not reimburse for V codes. When this is the case, it may be necessary to diagnose one individual, assuming that her or his symptoms also match a *DSM-IV* diagnosis, while continuing to conceptualize the primary problem as an interpersonal one. (More on the practical considerations of this issue are discussed in the case example below.)

In summary, I believe that it is possible, although not ideal, to make a culturally responsive diagnosis using the *DSM-IV.* Such an approach is strengthened by completion of the ADDRESSING Axis VI first, Psychosocial and Environmental Problems on Axis IV second, and General Medical Conditions on Axis III third. Recognition of the legitimacy of clients' conceptualizations is essential, and therapists are encouraged to connect these conceptualizations to DSM-IV categories. Using diagnostic language that is clear and comprehensible to clients, being cautious about the diagnosis of personality disorders, and thinking systemically about clients' presenting problems will also help to increase the usefulness of one's diagnosis.

Case Example: Mouna and Majid

To give an idea of how these suggestions may work in practice, the following case illustrates a therapist's diagnostic process with a couple. At the time of the initial assessment, the therapist, a Euroamerican woman in her early 50s, had little knowledge of the clients' cultures. However, she was committed to the learning process and was able to use the suggestions regarding diagnosis outlined in this chapter to make a helpful and culturally responsive diagnosis.

Majid, a 34-year-old Tunisian man, brought his wife Mouna, a 27-year-old Tunisian woman, to his female physician for an appointment. In fluent English with an Arabic accent, Majid explained to the physician that during the past 5 months, Mouna had lost weight, was "sleeping too much," and cried every day. Mouna did not speak English, but through Majid's interpretation she appeared to confirm his description. The physician knew that Majid and Mouna had recently been married and that Mouna had moved to the United States to live with Majid 8 months earlier. Following a medical check-up, which ruled out any hormonal, neurological, or nutritional deficiencies that might have contributed to Mouna's fatigue and weight loss, the physician referred the couple to a psychologist who specialized in women's issues and couples therapy.

At the initial assessment session, the psychologist greeted Mouna and Majid warmly and introduced herself as "Dr. Kate Smith." They chatted briefly, with Majid interpreting for Mouna, about the difference between the weather in northeastern United States and Tunisia. Kate observed to herself that Mouna appeared very dressed up, with carefully done makeup, a stylish short haircut, and noticeable perfume. Mouna was alert and her affect seemed sad, but she smiled at appropriate times and, despite the language difference, always looked directly at Kate when Kate spoke. Majid was dressed neatly, although more casually. He showed a full range of affect but appeared tense. The couple seemed comfortable interacting with each other; for example, twice Mouna spoke sharply to Majid, and he responded with an irritated look.

Kate began the assessment by asking Majid to explain why they had come in to see her. Majid said that he did not think that they needed a psychologist, but that the doctor couldn't find anything wrong with Mouna and told them they ought to see her. Kate sensed some embarrassment on his part. She said that she hoped she could be helpful and that she would like to start by hearing a bit more about their concerns. As Majid repeated the information he had told the physician, Kate periodically made eye contact with Mouna.

After about 15 minutes of talking with Majid, Kate asked him if he would interpret a few questions for her directly to Mouna. He agreed, and through this process, Kate learned that before marrying Majid, Mouna had lived with her parents and two brothers in the capital city of Tunis. Through a meeting arranged by family members, she was introduced to Majid on one of his visits home; they corresponded for a year and then married. Mouna immediately left her work in a hospital and moved to the United States with Majid. During their first few months together, she was happy with her new life, but then she began to miss her family, her friends, and her home. She also began to worry about not being able to have children, because after 8 months of marriage she had not yet become pregnant. When asked what she wanted, she said that she wished to return to Tunisia with Majid, but in the same sentence she acknowledged that she knew he couldn't leave his work.

Due to the interpretation process, obtaining the above information took the full 90 minutes scheduled. Although she did not complete her assessment, Kate considered the meeting successful because Mouna brightened a little when questioned directly about her thoughts and feelings, and Majid appeared less tense than when he had arrived. When asked, both Mouna and Majid agreed to return for a second assessment session.

CONSULTATION TIME

At this point, Kate was well aware of her own limitations in working with Mouna and Majid. Although she had some experience working with people who had immigrated from South America and Europe, she had no personal or professional experience with Tunisians or Arab people. She was familiar with some of the values and behaviors more common in Mediterranean cultures (e.g., the emphasis on family, the value placed on motherhood, and expectations of marriage and children for both men and women; see Barakat, 1993; Halila, 1984; Toubia, 1988).

After listening to Majid, Kate realized that she held some assumptions about Arab and Muslim men's attitudes toward women. For example, she was surprised by the sincerity of Majid's concern for Mouna and by their apparent comfort level with one another. In thinking about her surprise, she realized that she had assumed that given their arranged marriage, the couple would be quite formal with one another, and that Majid would care about Mouna's health only insofar as it affected his needs. But this was clearly not the case. Kate realized that changing her biases would require work outside the therapy session.

Before their next session, Kate went to the library and read about Tunisia. She learned that Tunisia is a North African country of approximately 10 million people who are predominantly Arab and Muslim. The country was colonized by France (technically a protectorate) until it gained independence in 1956. Tunisia has a high literacy rate and mandatory schooling for boys and girls, and French is a commonly spoken second language. During the past 40 years, Tunisia has become a leader in the Arab world on the subject of women's rights, with minimum ages set for marriage, consent of both women and men required for marriage, the legalization of abortion and divorce initiated by women, and family planning services offering free contraceptives across the country. The Tunisian government sends university students abroad for graduate study in particular fields. Although most go to France, some are sent to the United States every year, and many of these individuals become permanent residents (condensed from Hays & Zouari, 1995, and Primedia, 2000).

Kate also spoke with an Arab American therapist, who advised her that she should have arranged for an interpreter before their first session. Kate telephoned Majid to talk with him about this, but he reacted defensively. Kate realized that he took her suggestion to mean that he was not sufficiently fluent in English or that he could not represent Mouna's views fairly. Kate explained that neither was the case, but rather that she wanted Majid to feel free to express his own concerns without the pressure of needing to attend to Mouna's needs simultaneously. Majid finally agreed to an interpreter on one condition— that he know the name of the person beforehand to be sure that they were not in the same social circle, the Tunisian community in their city being relatively small. A Lebanese woman who spoke Arabic and occasionally did interpretation for a large hospital was agreed upon.

Before their next assessment session, Kate talked with the interpreter on the telephone and described her impressions of Mouna and Majid. She noted that she thought Mouna's "very dressed up appearance" was strange, given that she had come from home. The interpreter explained that it is not unusual for Arab women to dress up when going out. Kate also talked with the interpreter about Mouna's and Majid's arranged marriage. The interpreter sensed some judgmentalism on Kate's part and explained that arranged marriages are still common in Tunisia and that they help to ensure that families as well as individuals are well matched. She added that divorce is relatively uncommon. Her comments challenged Kate to think further about her assumptions regarding arranged marriages.

SECOND ASSESSMENT SESSION

Following Kate's introduction of the interpreter, who was about 50 years old and preferred to be addressed as Mrs. Salem, the four engaged in some social conversation. Mrs. Salem shared that she was married to a Lebanese man with whom she had immigrated to the United States as an adult. She was familiar with the Tunisian dialect of Arabic, something Kate had not thought to ask about, because she had worked in a Tunisian-owned travel agency for many years. She had also been trained as a peer counselor and worked as a volunteer at the local mental health center. Kate then reiterated their commitment to confidentiality, primarily to reassure Majid; she and Mrs. Salem had already discussed this prior to the session. The assessment resumed, with an emphasis on completing the histories of Mouna and Majid.

Mouna's History

Mouna was born and grew up in the same house in Tunis, along with her parents, two older brothers, and paternal grandmother. Her father was a university professor and her mother an elementary school principal. Her two older brothers (ages 28 and 30) left home in their early 20s to attend university in Paris. Mouna wanted to join them but said that her parents worried too much about her safety to allow her to move to France. While living at home, Mouna completed a master's degree in biology at the University of Tunis and then obtained a position as a research assistant in a hospital, where she worked for a year before marrying Majid.

Mouna described her family as very close, noting her parents' pride in her educational accomplishments. Because everyone except her grandmother spoke French fluently, the family's language was a mixture of Tunisian and French. Although they observed religious holidays and never drank alcohol in their home, Mouna's family members were not practicing Muslims (i.e., they did not perform the prayers five times a day, nor did they intentionally follow a religious diet). Mouna referred to her family and herself as "Tunisoise" (pronounced too-neez-wahz), the feminine form of a term used to describe the well-educated middle and upper middle class of the capital city.

To better understand the meaning of Mouna's identity, Kate asked Mouna to describe her life as a young woman in a Tunisoise family. Mouna responded by describing her typical day as "busy and mostly happy." After waking early to help her mother prepare a breakfast of bread, olive oil, and coffee for the family, Mouna would then get dressed and go to work. She enjoyed the walk to the hospital and being part of the hustle and bustle of the city. She liked her work, too, where she had many women friends. She would return home to have lunch with her family (the largest meal of the day, prepared by the maid), then take a nap and talk a little with her mother before returning to the hospital to complete her work there. In the evenings after dinner, she and her mother frequently entertained at home or visited female friends and relatives, while Mouna's father and brothers went to the café to see their male friends.

In response to Kate's questions about Mouna's experience in the United States, Mouna said that during her first few months, she continued to awaken early to prepare Majid's breakfast and sit with him while he ate. However, getting up in the morning became increasingly difficult for her, and she eventually stopped. She tended to wake up closer to noon now and described her only activities as cleaning the house, watching television (although she understood almost nothing said), and preparing dinner, beginning in the late afternoon. She didn't like going outside alone, so she mostly stayed in the apartment. Although she looked forward to Majid's return all day, she felt angry when he arrived home, especially when he didn't want to take her out. She did admit that he drove her to English classes two nights each week, went out with her most Saturdays and Sundays, and had arranged several dinners with couples who were his friends.

Majid's History

Majid reported that he, too, grew up in a close family. His grandparents on both sides were poor but very religious. His father attended Quranic school and eventually bought and ran his own small grocery store, which provided a modest income for the family. Majid's mother completed elementary school and worked in the home preparing meals, maintaining the household, and caring for Majid and his older brother and younger sister. Majid's parents were both practicing Muslims, and he himself practiced the prayers and followed the required diet until he left home.

Majid's parents held high expectations of him, and at school he was known for his intelligence and hard work. He won a government scholarship to a U.S. university, where he completed a master's degree in electrical engineering. He subsequently obtained work as an engineer in a medium-sized company, which allowed him to obtain permanent residence status in the United States. He worked for four years, saving money for a dowry and a nice apartment, and then began looking for a wife. He stated that his family was very proud of him but also disappointed and angry that he did not return home after university.

Majid described his early years in the United States as "hard" but added that "everybody has to go through the same thing when they move here." He considered the key element in his adjustment to be his focus on learning English, noting that "once you speak English, you can do almost anything." When pressed by Kate to think of other things that had helped him to adjust, he recalled learning to cook some Tunisian dishes, playing Tunisian music, and finding a café frequented by North Africans. In addition, a "turning point" occurred when his brother came to visit; Majid said that showing his brother around the city made Majid realize how much he liked living in the United States. Although Majid intended to return to Tunisia to retire, he did not want to live and work there now, because he said that even during visits, he became impatient with "the slow pace" and could no longer stand the heat in summer.

When asked about his marriage, Majid said that he thought he and Mouna had a good relationship and that the problem was just her homesickness. He had tried everything he could to help her: He took her out as much as possible and encouraged her to take more English classes. He was starting to worry about their ability to have a baby, and he was beginning to think that she might have some sort of physical problem.

UNDERSTANDING THE CLIENTS' IDENTITIES

As Kate listened and recorded information about Mouna's and Majid's lives, she began forming hypotheses about their identities and the salient cultural influences in their lives. She used the ADDRESSING framework to help her organize this information and to be sure that she was not ignoring potential influences.

Mouna's Identity

For Mouna, Kate asked herself which of the ADDRESSING factors Mouna had mentioned and which she had not. (See Axis VI in Table 8.1.) While influences related to age and generation, nationality, religion, and social status were all stated by Mouna, those related to disability, ethnicity, sexual orientation, gender, and Indigenous heritage were not. Kate was guided by her own general knowledge, sensitivity, and intuition to ask about some of these factors and to refrain from asking about others. As a part of her history taking, she did ask more detailed questions about Mouna's religious upbringing. But she did not ask about Mouna's ethnicity (because she already knew that Mouna was ethnically Tunisian Arab); gender (which she hypothesized was self-evident); disability or Indigenous heritage (because these did not appear to be relevant); or sexual orientation (which she knew was a topic too sensitive to explore with an apparently heterosexual couple in an initial assessment).

To gain a better understanding of the meaning of the cultural influences salient in Mouna's life, Kate sought information about Tunisian cultural norms in the following three ways. First, she asked Mouna about her friends' situations. For example, with regard to

Mouna's wish to study in France, Kate learned that in Mouna's social circle, her parents' insistence that she stay in Tunisia was considered well intentioned and reasonably protective, rather than sexist or punishing. Second, Kate listened for differences between Mouna's and Majid's descriptions of their situations (e.g., hearing Majid's description of his Muslim upbringing alerted Kate to the differences in practices among Muslims and, more importantly, between Mouna's family and Majid's). Third, between and after sessions, Kate consulted with Mrs. Salem.

By the end of the second session, it was clear that Mouna's personal norms regarding women's roles and behaviors corresponded closely to those of the dominant Tunisian class. Kate hypothesized that Mouna's attitudes and worldview would soon be challenged by her new cultural context. However, she understood that although she was there to help this couple consider possible new behaviors and views, she would need to be careful not to impose her own beliefs regarding relationships and men's and women's roles.

TABLE 8.1.

Diagnosis Example: Mouna

DSM-IV Axis	Details
Axis I	309.0 Adjustment Disorder with Depressed Mood V62.4 Acculturation Problem V61.1 Partner Relational Problem
Axis II	V71.09 No Disorder
[a]Axis III	None
[b]Axis IV	Problems with Primary Support: loss of primary support group secondary to immigration Problems related to Social Environment: inadequate support for new role as wife, completely new social and cultural environment, language barrier Occupational: loss of previous work due to immigration Other: family pressure to become pregnant
Axis V	GAF = 75 (current) GAF = 90 (highest level in past year)
[c]Axis VI	Age and generational influences: 27 years old; born in 1973 (17 years after Tunisian independence). Mouna was the second generation of girls to enter school after it became mandatory. She is the youngest child and only daughter in a *Tunisoise* (upper-middle-class, urban) family. **Developmental and acquired** **Disabilities:** None reported or apparent.

Table 8.1. Continued

CAxis VI (cont.)	Religion and spiritual orientation: Parents both Muslim, but nonpracticing; Mouna's personal beliefs are Muslim, but she has a secular lifestyle.
	Ethnicity: Mother and father both of Arab/Tunisian heritage; family/Tunisoise heritage. First language Tunisian Arabic; however, French also spoken in the home. Mouna does not yet speak English.
	Socioeconomic status: Parents both university educated and of upper-middle-class backgrounds.
	Sexual orientation: Probably heterosexual.
	Indigenous heritage: None.
	National origin: Tunisian; recent immigrant, living as a permanent resident in United States.
	Gender: Female, youngest child and only daughter in family of origin. Newly married with no children, but has expectations of motherhood as central to her life and identity as a woman.

^aComplete this Axis third.
^bComplete this Axis second.
^cComplete this Axis first.

Majid's Identity

Although Majid's identity was as firmly connected to his culture and family of origin as was Mouna's, the meaning of this connection was quite different. Majid was not from a Tunisoise family; the lower social class and religious practice of his family set them apart from Tunisian society's more secular ideal during the 1960s and 1970s, just after independence was obtained from France (information that Mrs. Salem provided). Even before he moved to the United States, Majid had felt "different."

Through his family, Majid had developed a deep sense of himself as a religious and spiritual person. Although nearly all of the Muslims he met growing up were Tunisian, his parents taught him to think about Muslims around the world as one community. After arriving in the United States, he attended a mosque for a few years and was delighted to meet Muslims who were Cambodian, Indonesian, Nigerian, and African American.

Majid identified himself primarily as a Tunisian man; however, during his 14-year residence in the United States, he had learned that most Americans know little if anything about Tunisia. Thus, when describing himself to Kate, he added information that he would not have added for a Tunisian listener (e.g., that he was Arab and Muslim). Although he did not specifically refer to himself as a member of an ethnic minority culture in the United States, his experiences had led him to identify with diverse people of color rather than with the Euroamerican majority.

With regard to his expectations and beliefs about marriage and the influence of gender, Majid's point of reference was a mélange of Tunisian, Muslim, and American influences. He described his belief in the equality of men and women and in his marriage as an egalitarian relationship in which he and Mouna should "support each other to be good people and to do our best." From his years of living alone, he was used to cooking and cleaning up after himself, although Mouna always made dinners now. He wanted Mouna to make friends and return to working outside the home again, even after having children, if that would make her happy. He assumed that he would be the primary breadwinner but imagined that once Mouna was fluent in English, she would manage their money, as his mother had in his family. Since their marriage, he had tried to make important decisions in collaboration with Mouna (e.g., about decorating the apartment, where to go on outings, planning for the future), and he expected that she would start driving once her English was sufficient to pass the driver's test. Table 8.2 summarizes the salient ADDRESSING influences in Majid's life.

TABLE 8.2.

Cultural Influences in Majid's Life

Cultural Influences	Details
Age and generational influences	34 years old; born in 1966; middle child of three. Majid was in the second generation of boys educated after independence, for whom expectations of success were extremely high. His generation expected to live a secular lifestyle, but Majid was not brought up this way.
Developmental and acquired Disabilities	None reported or apparent.
Religion and spiritual orientation	Parents both practicing Muslims. Majid has a deep sense of himself as a religious and spiritual person, although not currently practicing.
Ethnicity	Mother and father both Arab/Tunisian. Arabic is spoken in their home; Majid is fluent in French and English too.
Socioeconomic status	Parents had elementary school educations and were working poor; family lived in Tunis but were not *Tunisoise.*
Sexual orientation	Probably heterosexual.
Indigenous heritage	None.
National origin	Tunisian; living as a permanent resident in the United States; has considered obtaining U.S. citizenship as well.
Gender	Male, middle child but youngest son. Newly married with a strong desire to be a "good husband" (meaning in an egalitarian, mutually supportive relationship); no children but has expectations of fatherhood as central to his life and identity as a man.

CASE CONCEPTUALIZATION AND DIAGNOSIS

With this understanding of the salient cultural influences on Mouna and Majid, Kate was in a position to consider what would be the most accurate and useful conceptualization and diagnosis for their case. Fortunately, she was knowledgeable enough about the stressors involved in immigration to realize that Mouna's depressive symptoms (crying, weight loss, excessive sleeping, sad mood and affect) are common responses to the enormous changes involved in such a transition. But thinking systemically, Kate also recognized the adjustment difficulties that Majid was experiencing as a result of the marriage and his new role as a husband. And from Mrs. Salem, she learned that a huge missing piece in the adjustment of both Mouna and Majid was the social support from extended families that they would have received as a newly married couple in Tunisia.

Majid's distress did not meet criteria for a *DSM-IV* diagnosis. For Mouna, the V code Acculturation Problem was clearly justified, but the question remained whether this would be a primary, sole, or secondary diagnosis. Mouna's symptoms suggested the possibility of a Major Depressive Episode or Adjustment Disorder with Depressed Mood. Kate ruled out the first diagnosis because Mouna met only four of the five required symptoms, but the decision to rule out an Adjustment Disorder was more complex.

Diagnosis of an Adjustment Disorder requires "the development of emotional or behavioral symptoms" in response to a stressor or stressors that have occurred in the previous three months (American Psychiatric Association, 1994, p. 626). The symptoms or behaviors must be "in excess of what would be expected from exposure to the stressor" or result in "a significant impairment in social or occupational (academic) functioning" (p. 626). Immigration qualifies as a stressor (or more accurately, a collection of stressors), and Mouna's symptoms had begun within three months after her move. However, her distress was not in excess of what one would expect in the face of such a transition.

The difficult question was deciding whether or not her symptoms were significantly impairing her social, occupational, or academic functioning. Mouna was not impaired in her ability to relate to people or to form new relationships; she simply lacked opportunities and was limited by the language barrier. She continued to carry out most of her household responsibilities, although she no longer cooked breakfast. And she attended her English classes, although she reported some difficulty with studying due to a decreased ability to concentrate.

With this information in mind, Kate chose to conceptualize the case as one in which extraordinary stressors were affecting both Mouna and Majid individually and in their relationship as a couple. Mouna was clearly more expressive of her distress and thus more easily seen as "the patient." Her symptoms were marginally diagnosable as an Adjustment Disorder. In an ideal world, Kate noted to herself, she would not diagnose Mouna so as to avoid pathologizing her. However, in their current situation, the managed care company would pay only for treatment of a Clinical or Personality Disorder (i.e., not for a V code such as Acculturation or Partner Relational Problem). In addition, Kate suspected that Mouna and Majid would not return if their insurance did not cover the therapy. (See Eisman et al., 2000, and Cooper & Gottlieb, 2000, regarding reimbursement and ethical issues related to managed care).

CONSIDERING CLIENTS' VIEWS

Toward the end of their second assessment session, Kate reviewed with Mouna and Majid the social and cultural stressors involved in immigration and talked about common responses to those stressors. She also said that beginning a new marriage is stressful, although she did not elaborate on this point because she did not feel informed enough about what Tunisian newlyweds experience and expect. Finally, she noted the unique aspects of Mouna's adjustment—as a Tunisian woman—to life in a U.S. city. For example, she mentioned the need for Mouna to develop a level of caution about going out alone that acknowledged real dangers but was not unreasonably limiting. Kate concluded that she saw their difficulties as due primarily to the normal stressors related to immigration (for Mouna, but also affecting Majid) and to beginning a new relationship (for them both); in addition, these stressors were being compounded by the lack of family support in their current environment.

Majid and Mouna appeared relieved by Kate's summary. They agreed that they would be willing to discuss the possibility of counseling. Kate then explained that their insurance would cover only the diagnosis and treatment of one person. She described two solutions to this dilemma: (a) They could pay themselves for couples therapy, or (b) because Mouna could technically be diagnosed with an Adjustment Disorder, Kate could make this diagnosis and be paid by the managed care company. In the latter case, the stated goal would be to facilitate Mouna's adjustment to a new country, life, and marriage, but couples counseling could be the method chosen to address this goal and their relationship. Mouna and Majid chose the latter option and returned for couples counseling.

CASE EXAMPLE CONCLUSION

Kate was not the ideal therapist in this case. She did not speak her clients' language, she had only a general familiarity with Arab cultures, and she held some prejudices about Arab and Muslim men. In addition, she made some significant mistakes. For one, she neglected to obtain an interpreter before the first session, an oversight that might have ended the chance of therapy with some clients. She also forgot to ask about the Lebanese interpreter's familiarity with Tunisian Arabic; fortunately, the interpreter was aware enough to have thought about dialectic differences.

However, Kate was committed to providing culturally responsive services to Mouna and Majid. She did her homework in learning about her clients' cultures (i.e., going to the library, consulting with an Arab American therapist, and obtaining the help of an interpreter). She was also careful to obtain a detailed history, including information about each person's cultural context and identity. And she paid attention to differences between Mouna's and Majid's stories as cues about what was normative in their families' contexts.

With regard to the diagnosis, Kate started with the cultural Axis VI and considered the salience of each of the ADDRESSING influences in Mouna's and Majid's lives. While she recognized that Mouna's symptoms met criteria for Adjustment Disorder, she was quick to see the larger context, including contradictory pressures (e.g., that the diagnosis of Mouna would reinforce the idea that Mouna was the problem, but that finances were also a concern for the couple). She included both Mouna and Majid in the diagnostic process, using straightforward language and a systemic perspective that acknowledged the impact on both Mouna and Majid of Mouna's recent immigration, their newly married status, and decreased social support.

In sum, Kate's diagnosis was not ideal, but it was ethical, culturally responsive, and likely to lead to help for this couple. Of course, completion of an initial assessment and diagnosis does not end the need to attend to cultural issues. As the next chapter illustrates, culturally responsive assessment and diagnosis simply pave the way for more effective interventions.

KEY IDEAS 8.

Making a Culturally Responsive Diagnosis

1. Start with new cultural Axis VI: ADDRESSING Influences, to describe identities, contexts, and strengths.

2. Next, complete Axis IV: Psychosocial and Environmental Problems, using the ADDRESSING acronym as a reminder of problems that may be related to clients' age or generation, visible or nonvisible disability, religious upbringing and current identity, ethnic identity, socioeconomic status, and so on.

3. Third, complete Axis III: General Medical Conditions.

4. Consider the client's conceptualization of the problem. Recognize the legitimacy of this conceptualization and look for links between it and *DSM-IV* categories.

5. Be able to explain the meaning of your diagnosis in language that the client understands.

6. Be cautious about diagnosing personality disorders.

7. Move beyond the *DSM-IV* focus on individualistic diagnoses to think systemically and consider relational disorders.

V | CULTURALLY RESPONSIVE PRACTICE

How to Help Best: Culturally Responsive Therapy | 9

When I was living in North Africa, a man I knew well (who knew that I was a psychologist) asked if he could talk with me about a problem he was having. He was experiencing anxiety related to worries about money and his work. He had always been an intense person, and these were ongoing worries, but suddenly he found that he was unable to swallow. He would put food or drink in his mouth but couldn't get it to go down. As a result, he had lost quite a bit of weight, and he was extremely uncomfortable because it was summer, and the heat made him unbearably thirsty. He was a school teacher, so during the summer, he also had more free time to sit and worry. He did not want to talk about his feelings in any depth, and I was not in a position to be of any help professionally. However, I listened, encouraged him to believe this was a problem that could be solved, and suggested that he see his doctor (there were no psychologists in his country at the time).

Several months later, when I was back in the United States, I learned that although the problems in his life were still there, he was no longer having difficulty swallowing, and his anxiety had decreased. He had gone to see a doctor, but this was not what helped. What made the difference was that he began practicing the religious requirements of Islam. The most essential of these requirements are commonly called the "five pillars of Islam" and include

1. the *Shahadah*, a profession of faith in the one God and Mohammed as his prophet;
2. prayer;
3. fasting during the holy month of Ramadan, which celebrates Mohammed's initial revelation from God and his journey from Mecca to Medina;
4. giving alms to the poor; and
5. the pilgrimage to Mecca, made toward the end of one's life if at all possible (Abudabbeh, 1996; Fernea & Bezirgan, 1977; H. Smith, 1991).

Of these requirements, the prayers require the greatest commitment over time. In Muslim countries, the call to prayer is made from the mosques (more recently, over loudspeakers) at regular intervals five times each day. In response to the call, devout believers stop what they are doing and perform special washing rituals, which clean one's body and also symbolically purify the soul. The prayer

> begins in dignified, upright posture but climaxes when the supplicant has sunk to his or her knees with forehead touching the floor. This is the prayer's holiest moment for it carries a twofold symbolism. On the one hand, the body is in a fetal position, ready to be reborn. At the same time it is crouched in the smallest possible space, signifying human nothingness in the face of the divine. (H. Smith, 1991, p. 246)

The act of praying in the direction of Mecca, along with the knowledge that Muslims around the world are also turned toward Mecca saying the same prayers at similar intervals, "creates a sense of participating in a worldwide fellowship, even when one prays in solitude" (Smith, 1991, p. 246).

With regard to this man and his anxiety, one could view his healing from a strictly behavioral perspective; his religious practice, particularly the prayers, may have provided the structure needed to keep the anxiety down and take the focus off himself. However, it is just as possible that he found spiritual comfort, peace, and even enlightenment through his religious efforts. In any case, the practice worked for him.

In many cultures, psychotherapy is a treatment of last resort because it is unavailable, or because shame prevents people from accessing services, or because there are other treatments that are more effective. For these reasons, it is essential that therapists who work cross culturally be eclectic in their approaches. This chapter describes an eclectic perspective on cross-cultural practice, beginning with a brief discussion of multicultural therapy and its unique characteristics. Next, four categories of therapeutic work are described: (a) culturally related strategies and therapies, (b) adaptations of mainstream approaches in psychotherapy with diverse minority groups, (c) nonverbal expressive therapies, and (d) systems-level interventions. These categories are not mutually exclusive; however, they do provide some organization to the enormous number of interventions a therapist may consider. To avoid writing a chapter the size of an encyclopedia, I will describe just a few examples in relation to each category. Finally, considerations in developing a treatment plan are discussed.

Eclecticism and Multicultural Therapy

Researchers note that eclecticism can take two forms. The first involves an integration of diverse theories of psychotherapy into one "transtheoretical model" (see Prochaska & Norcross, 1994). The second, known as "technical eclecticism," describes the increasingly common practice of systematically choosing and using a wide range of interventions and procedures (Lazarus & Beutler, 1993). It seems to me that multicultural therapy (MCT) is more an example of the latter; while there are theoretical premises unique to MCT (e.g., that cultural differences between therapist and client affect therapy), it is far from an integrated, transtheoretical model.

This is probably because unlike the major schools (e.g., psychoanalysis, behavioral, cognitive-behavioral, family systems, and humanistic/existential therapies), which begin by describing how therapy is done, MCT begins from the question, With whom is it done? Although MCT certainly involves a paradigm shift in that it calls into question the usefulness of all preceding theories, the diversity and complexity of clients' identities rule out the possibility of easy prescriptions (e.g., "With a client of culture A, you use X technique, with a client of culture B, you use Y technique.")

But MCT does offer a perspective that opens up an enormous set of questions and considerations that may otherwise be ignored. These new considerations point to the inadequacy of any sole conceptualization, approach, or strategy. MCT requires therapists to think about therapy in new ways and to intervene in ways that may not fit mainstream conceptualizations but that will benefit people of both minority and dominant groups. Let's look first at some approaches that emanate from minority cultures themselves.

Culturally Related Strategies and Therapies

In my experience, when people begin learning about multicultural therapy, they often expect suggestions from this first category. However, to date, empirically validated studies of culturally related strategies and therapies are sparse. Studies that do exist are mainly descriptions from the author's experiences in that culture (Jilek, 1994). I deliberately avoid the use of the term "culture-specific" therapies, because it would be nearly impossible to demonstrate that any one approach truly is specific to only one culture. In any case, below are a few examples.

STORYTELLING

In the movie *Smoke Signals* (Rosenfelt & Estes, 1998) (based on Sherman Alexie's (1993) book *The Lone Ranger and Tonto Fistfight in Heaven*), a handsome but angry young man named Victor lives with his mother on the Coeur d'Alene reservation. Victor has painful childhood memories of his father's drinking. He pretends not to care that his father left them when Victor was a boy. But one day, when Victor is in his 20s, his mother gets a telephone call. The woman on the other end says that Victor's father has died and that she has his things if someone wants to come to Arizona to get them.

There is no question that Victor will go; the problem is how. They have no money and no car. Then a nerdy young man named Thomas offers his pot of savings on one condition: Victor has to take Thomas with him. Thomas is like a pesky younger brother to Victor; his constant talking, upbeat attitude, pigtails, and goofy grin all annoy Victor to no end. Neither of them has ever been off the reservation, and Victor does not want his first trip complicated by having to deal with Thomas.

Later, as Victor's mother is cooking fry bread in the kitchen, Victor explains his disinterest in Thomas's offer. In response, Victor's mother asks Victor if he knows how she learned to make such good fry bread. He replies that he knows she makes it all by herself.

She smiles and then goes on to tell him about all the people who have helped in making her fry bread delicious—her grandmother who taught her how to make it, and *her* grandmother who passed down the recipe, and all the people who have eaten it over the years and said, "Arlene, there's too much flour" or "Arlene, you should knead your dough more." And, she adds, "I watch that Julia Child. She's a good cook too, but she gets lots of help." The point is not lost on Victor, who eventually accepts (albeit begrudgingly) Thomas's offer.

The interaction between Victor and his mother is a good example of one of the most common forms of verbal learning in Indigenous (and some non-Indigenous) cultures (Brendtro, Brokenleg, & Van Bockern, 1998). Storytelling is also an important mechanism for passing knowledge on to others across generations (Acklin et al., 1999; Herring, 1999). Used as a helping strategy, storytelling does not directly advise the listener, but rather tells a story via a metaphor that offers a social message. The listener is then free to draw a conclusion if she or he is ready to do so (Swinomish Tribal Community, 1991).

RELIGION

Despite the clear benefits of religious coping activities (e.g., prayer, confession, seeking strength and comfort from God or a religious community), the field of psychology has been slow to recognize religion as a source of help (Tix & Frazier, 1998). How can religion be a therapy? Well, first think about how you would define a system of therapy. It would probably offer (a) a framework for understanding human experience, (b) guidelines for personal development and the maintenance of social relationships, and (c) a method for addressing human suffering. By these criteria, Buddhism, Islam, Judaism, Christianity, and Hinduism would certainly qualify.

But religion offers something beyond the frameworks, guidelines, and methods of psychotherapy. As Pargament (1996) noted, "What makes religion unique is its focus on the sacred" (p. 216). When one's usual way of understanding the world becomes inadequate, religion offers the opportunity for transformation or transcendence. Religion also offers models (e.g., Gautama Buddha, Moses, Mohammed, Jesus Christ) for the transformative process (Pargament, 1996, p. 225). And as the example of the North African man illustrates, religious practice is often a more comprehensive and culturally responsive intervention than psychotherapy.

There are also therapies indigenous to particular cultures that share religious assumptions while not being religions per se. D. K. Reynolds (1980) described five therapies indigenous to Japan (*morita, naikan, shadan, seiza,* and Zen). The goals in these therapies are to refocus attention away from self and everyday self-consciousness and to slow the pace of thought, which in turn will deepen it (Reynolds, 1980, p. 103). Like Buddhism, these therapies emphasize the acceptance of suffering as "an integral part of life to be accommodated rather than eliminated" (Bradshaw, 1994, p. 105). In contrast to mainstream psychotherapies, talking is discouraged; instead, clients are placed in quiet isolation (with some guidance provided by the therapist) to facilitate the development of the "natural inner strength," which can lead to "a more enlightened understanding" of oneself (Reynolds, 1980, p. 104).

Based on Buddhist practice, the specific strategy of "mindfulness meditation," in which one's attention is directed to the present moment, has been used as a stress-reduction technique, for pain control, and as an integral part of psychotherapy to bring up material for therapeutic sessions (see DeSilva, 1993). Perhaps even more important than the behavioral and cognitive changes that can be facilitated with these approaches is the shift in consciousness that can occur. The practices of "stopping," calming oneself via conscious breathing, and simply "being" in the present moment can bring

> enlightenment, awareness, understanding, care, compassion, liberation, transformation, and healing. If we practice mindfulness, we get in touch with the refreshing and joyful aspects of life in us and around us, the things we're not able to touch when we live in forgetfulness. Mindfulness makes things like our eyes, our heart, our non-toothache, the beautiful moon, and the trees deeper and more beautiful. If we touch these wonderful things with mindfulness, they will reveal their full splendor. When we touch our pain with mindfulness, we will begin to transform it. (Hahn, 1992, p. 29)

Christianity also offers a broad range of healing practices, including the rituals of prayer, testimony or "witnessing," sacrifice, and reliving experience (Tseng, 1999). African American churches (and those of other ethnic groups and denominations) often serve multiple purposes, offering an extended family with opportunities for involvement in church-related social services, leadership development, and role models for young people (Boyd-Franklin, 1989). In addition, African American churches offer a message of hope and support for members' painful experiences of racism and discrimination (Boyd-Franklin, 1989).

ALCOHOLICS ANONYMOUS

Alcoholics Anonymous (AA) is a worldwide movement of self-help groups aimed at helping people who are alcoholic to stop drinking. Related groups include Adult Children of Alcoholics (ACOA) and Narcotics Anonymous (NA). There are no fees, and meetings are open to anyone who has a desire to stop using alcohol or other drugs (Lewis, Dana, & Blevins, 1994). The format and structure of AA groups vary, but in general, meetings begin with a formal statement of the purposes of AA, followed by a reading of the Twelve Steps, a set of guidelines for recovery that read as follows:

Step 1: [We] admitted we were powerless over alcohol [drugs]—that our lives had become unmanageable.

Step 2: Came to believe that a Power greater than ourselves could restore us to sanity.

Step 3: Made a decision to turn our will and our lives over to the care of God as we understood Him.

Step 4: Made a searching and fearless moral inventory of ourselves.

Step 5: Admitted to God, to ourselves, and to another human being the exact nature of our wrongs.

Step 6: Were entirely ready to have God remove all these defects of character.

Step 7: Humbly asked Him to remove our shortcomings.

Step 8: Made a list of all persons we have harmed and became willing to make amends to them all.

Step 9: Made direct amends to such people wherever possible, except when to do so would injure them or others.

Step 10: Continued to take personal inventory and when we were wrong, promptly admitted it.

Step 11: Sought through prayer and meditation to improve our conscious contact with God as we understood Him, praying only for knowledge of His will for us and the power to carry that out.

Step 12: Having had a spiritual awakening as the result of these Steps, we tried to carry this message to alcoholics [drug abusers] and practice these principles in all our affairs. (quoted in Lewis et al., 1994, pp. 119–120)

AA is an important community-based resource that provides social and spiritual support to participants (Fukuyama & Sevig, 1999). However, it originates in Euroamerican culture and contains practices and assumptions that may be inappropriate or uncomfortable for many people (Tseng, 1999). Clients of minority identities may feel uncomfortable in AA groups in which the realities of racism, sexism, heterosexism, and so forth are ignored (Comas-Díaz & Greene, 1994a).

In referring clients to AA groups, it is important to be familiar with the group-specific adaptations of African Americans, women, American Indians, and gay and lesbian groups (Hopson, 1996). In American Indian AA groups, the expectation of anonymity is often rejected, participation is open to anyone in the community, and meetings are less structured in terms of procedures and arrival and departure times; in addition, potlatches may be held to celebrate anniversaries of sobriety (Jilek, 1994). The membership of Men in Recovery consists primarily of African American men; this group objects to the ideas of admitting one's powerlessness and "surrendering," which are seen as detrimental to African American men (Hopson, 1996). Similarly, Women for Sobriety reject the concept of dependency and instead stress "healthy self-esteem, autonomy, and individual responsibility" for women in recovery (Hopson, 1996, p. 538). In general, with clients who do not identify completely with the AA philosophy but may benefit from the support of a group committed to abstinence, it can be helpful to remind them that they may take what is helpful from AA traditions and overlook the parts that don't work for them (Herman, 1997).

TRADITIONAL HEALERS AND HEALING PRACTICES

In discussing culturally related strategies and therapies, it is important to recognize the role of traditional healers. In the not-too-distant past, traditional healers were viewed by the North American medical establishment as necessary only until a sufficient number of health care professionals could be trained to meet the needs of everyone. However, during the past two decades, interest in traditional or natural healers has increased (see Marsella, Kaplan, & Suárez, in press, for a list of 27 healing systems or therapies including acupuncture, ayurvedic medicine, *curanderos, ho'oponopono, morita, naikan,* t'ai chi ch'uan, yoga, and Zen). Traditional healers are now the helpers of choice for many people of both minority and dominant cultures, particularly for problems that have a psychological or psychosocial aspect (Jilek, 1994).

For example, for many people of Central and Latin American cultures, *curanderos* (male healers) and *curanderas* (female healers) are sought out for help with a variety of illnesses, but most especially those "with psychological components , such as *susto* (fright), *mal de ojo* (evil eye), *empacho* (indigestion), or *envidia* (envy)" (Falicov, 1996, p. 173). They may also be consulted for such problems as depression, impotence, alcoholism, and menstrual cramps (Falicov, 1998). Among Mexicans and Mexican Americans, such healers are primarily women and use practices derived from Catholicism, ancient Mayan and Aztec cultures, and herbology (Novas, 1994). With regard to serious health problems, *curanderos* and *curanderas* are generally not seen as competition for medical providers. On the contrary, in California and the southwestern United States, their services are included in some innovative health care programs as complementary options that broaden the range of care available to clients (Falicov, 1998; Novas, 1994).

When clients wish to use a traditional healer, it is important to consider coordination of services (Marsella & Yamada, 2000). In some institutions, there may already be a formal relationship in place; for example, Koss, 1980, described a program that engaged spiritist healers, mental health workers, and medical professionals in Puerto Rico. When such a relationship does not exist, the therapist can obtain permission from clients to talk with other health care providers, including traditional healers. Then it is up to the therapist to give the healer a call and even arrange a meeting if this seems appropriate. For therapists who are skeptical of such approaches, it may be helpful to remember how negative the dominant cultural attitudes were only a few years ago toward chiropractic medicine, massage therapy, and acupuncture. Work with a traditional healer can be viewed as an opportunity to learn information that is not taught in mainstream institutions.

However, it is important to note that in some cultures, some types of information are intended only for selected individuals. For example, among American Indians, the degree of openness about spiritual knowledge and practices varies widely; that is, information may be considered public or highly personal depending on the particular individual, group, or type of information (Swinomish Tribal Community, 1991). The need for spiritual privacy can have a strong cultural basis related to the desire to

(a) preserve one's special relationship to a spiritual being;
(b) avoid loss of spiritual power;
(c) avoid potential misuse of spiritual knowledge;
(d) avoid ridicule or persecution from non-Indians; and/or
(e) demonstrate respect. (Swinomish Tribal Community, 1991, p. 131)

The use of spiritual rituals, concepts, or symbols by non-Indians (and even by certain Indian people) may be considered sacrilegious. Therapists are advised to be cautious as they are learning about Indian people's spirituality. The best approach is a "quiet and non-intrusive interest" with few questions, allowing the individual to share when and what he or she chooses (Swinomish Tribal Community, 1991, p. 132). For additional reviews of traditional healing systems and therapies, see Das (1987), Jilek (1994), and Tseng (2000).

Adaptation of Mainstream Approaches With Minority Groups

You might think that there would be many empirical studies of adapted therapies, but at this point there are not. In 1995 I did a literature search for applications of cognitive-behavior therapy with people of ethnic minority cultures and found so few that I expanded the search to include all minority groups identified by the ADDRESSING framework (Hays, 1995). At about the same time, Iwamasa and Smith (1996) found that only 1.31% of the articles published in three leading behavioral journals focused on ethnic minority groups in the United States. And this does not mean that these studies were adapted to minority groups; in many cases, such approaches were simply used with clients of minority groups, with little or no attention given to their special needs.

Although the number of articles is growing, I know of no book on cognitive-behavioral therapy with clients from minority cultures. I have found books on behavior therapy with African Americans (Turner & Jones, 1982), women (Blechman, 1984), and older people (Hussian, 1981, 1985). And there is at least one book on psychodynamic practice with multicultural populations (Berzoff, Flanagan, & Hertz, 1996) and one on existential therapy with clients of diverse cultures (a casebook by Vontress, Johnson, & Epp, 1999). I have not yet seen any books on person-centered therapy with people of minority identities.

Drawing from these resources, let's consider a few examples of mainstream adaptations. One is an adaptation of Lazarus's (1997) multimodal therapy to the example of a Mexican American man who was experiencing anxiety related to his difficulties obtaining financial help from an unresponsive monolingual agency (Ponterotto, 1987). Multimodal therapy involves the assessment of a client's functioning in seven modalities that form the acronym BASIC-ID (**B**ehavior, **A**ffect, **S**ensations, **I**magery, **C**ognition, **I**nterpersonal relationships, and **D**rugs including biological functioning). Ponterotto's modification consisted of adding the category "Interaction with an oppressive environment" to the Interpersonal relationships modality. This addition led to the suggestion that the therapist might help the client develop a plan to pressure the agency to hire a bilingual employee from the Spanish-speaking community, a form of social action beyond the usual intrapsychic focus of cognitive-behavioral therapy.

When I use the multimodal approach, I integrate cultural considerations, both strengths and oppressive influences, into every modality. For example, I consider the following:

- *Behavior:* cultural influences, norms, and expectations regarding clients' behaviors;
- *Affect:* cultural differences in the expression of affect and feeling;
- *Sensations:* cultural influences on how one experiences or conceptualizes physiological phenomena;
- *Imagery:* culturally related images and the impact of oppression on self-image;
- *Cognition:* culturally related beliefs, values, attitudes, and statements about self and others;
- *Interpersonal relationships:* cultural norms regarding relationships and cultural identities of and influences on partner, friends, family, and networks; and
- *Drugs:* culture-specific conceptualizations of illness, health, approaches to health care, and alcohol/drug use.

Another adaptation of a mainstream theory was described by LaFromboise and Rowe (1983) in their work with American Indian clients. Using the concept of bicultural competence, these researchers emphasized the need for their clients to understand and develop a broad range of communication skills for use with both Indian people and Euroamericans. Interventions were designed in the form of social skills training groups that paralleled traditional Indian approaches (e.g., role modeling, apprenticeship training, and group consensus). The Indian community selected situations targeted for change in consultation with tribal leaders, groups, and agencies.

Wood and Mallinckrodt (1990) offered suggestions for adapting assertiveness skills training with people of color. To illustrate the cultural assumptions embedded in most assertiveness programs, they described a scenario in which an African American man is waiting in a movie line and a White man cuts in front of him. Although in some parts of the United States it would be considered appropriately assertive for the African American to say, "Excuse me, I believe that the end of the line begins behind me," in other areas or situations, such a statement from an African American man could be perceived as aggressive and challenging, and his safety might even be endangered by this response (Wood & Mallinckrodt, 1990, p. 6). The authors noted that what has traditionally been called assertiveness in the field of psychology are those behaviors valued by and for the dominant culture, but not necessarily by and for minority groups. Therapists are advised to help clients develop as wide a repertoire of responses as possible, but because the client is the best judge of what is right and safe, she or he is the one who should decide what constitutes appropriately assertive behavior in a given situation.

An interesting adaptation of rational emotive behavior therapy (RET) with fundamentalist Christian clients illustrates how therapists may use clients' culture-specific beliefs to facilitate change (Johnson & Ridley, 1992). Christian Rational Emotive Therapy (CRET) is unique in three ways. First of all, therapists encourage clients to challenge their irrational beliefs by using biblical verses that define "ultimate truth." For example, to dispute the belief that "I must be thoroughly competent, adequate, and achieving in all possible respects if I am to consider myself worthwhile," therapists counter with Isaiah 64:6, "All of us have become like one who is unclean and all our righteous acts are like filthy rags" (Johnson & Ridley, 1992, p. 225). The second unique component of CRET is an emphasis on prayer and Christian content throughout the therapeutic work. And the third is the use of prayer at the end of each session, "asking for Christ's empowerment in overcoming IBs [irrational beliefs]" (Johnson & Ridley, 1992, p. 225).

In a comparison of two groups of depressed Christian clients, one of which received standard RET and the other CRET, the authors found that both therapies reduced clients' self-reported depression and automatic negative thoughts, but CRET also reduced clients' irrational beliefs. Obviously, a therapist would need to be a Christian or very knowledgeable about and comfortable with the client's religion to adapt rational emotive behavior therapy in this way. Whether or not this is the case, the larger point is that therapists work with, not against, the client's core values.

While the psychodynamic theories are less technique oriented, a number of related concepts can be adapted for use with clients of minority identities. In chapter 4, I discussed cross-cultural applications of the concepts of transference and countertransference. In addition, the idea of the unconscious can be helpful in learning and teaching about privilege and oppression. I have found that people seem to have less difficulty accepting the idea that they hold prejudices if these prejudices are conceptualized as unconscious. Once they acknowledge the existence of unconscious assumptions, they are more likely to engage in the process of change.

Similarly, the concept of splitting, which has been viewed primarily as a pathological defense mechanism, may be conceptualized as a functional response for individuals who hold bicultural or multicultural identities. Although it is usually defined as a process of separating the good from the bad, splitting can be seen more generally as a way of organizing chaos or separating out something that it is threatening from that which is not (Flanagan, 1996). For bicultural people, maintenance of "the integrity of dual selves" may be essential to their biculturalism (Chin, 1994, pp. 213–214). Splitting can help clients maintain this integrity by decreasing the intrapsychic conflict created by dominant and minority cultures' insistence on monocultural identifications.

Finally, there are a number of studies documenting the adaptation of mainstream theories with nonethnic minority groups (reviewed in Hays, 1995). For example, cognitive therapy has been successfully used to help gay men change internalized heterosexist beliefs and thoughts (Kuehlwein, 1992). RET (recently relabeled REBT by Ellis, 1997, to emphasize the role of behavior) was used by Wolfe (1992) with a lesbian client to help her cope with parental and societal discrimination; RET group therapy was a strong component of this approach. And Ellis himself described the use of REBT in coping, at the age of 82, with his own physical disabilities.

Nonverbal Expressive Therapies

All of the major psychological theories listed above are heavily language dependent. This reliance on verbal skills as the dominant mode of expression places many people at a disadvantage, including people who speak English as a second language, individuals born with certain developmental disabilities, or those who have experienced a stroke or who have some other form of brain impairment. In addition, individuals who speak English as a first language and have no impairments may vary in their verbal facility.

Solutions to the language-centered bias of psychotherapy may be found in the use of nonverbal interventions such as art, music, body movement, play, and horticultural therapies (e.g., see Hanser, 1999; Hiscox, 1995; Hiscox & Calish, 1998; Hoshino, in press; Itai & McCrae, 1994; Kenny, 1989; McNiff, 1986; Wadeson, 1980). Such nonverbal modalities can facilitate interaction and elicit responses where verbal modalities fail. For example, with clients for whom direct eye contact is uncomfortable or inappropriate from their cultural frame of reference, nonverbal therapies may be more effective because they give clients something to look at and something to do with their hands. A specific instance was described by Itai and McCrae in a study of horticultural therapy, in which clinicians used gardening to engage Japanese American elders.

Another advantage to creative modalities is that the therapist's appreciation of a client's art may have positive effects on the client and on the therapeutic relationship. Wadeson (1980) noted,

Many people with whom I have worked, particularly hospitalized, depressed patients, have been convinced on entering art therapy that their art work was meaningless and inadequate (which is how they saw themselves). As a result of my interest in their art expressions they soon became interested in them themselves. (p. 38)

With children, play therapy can be especially therapeutic, because it provides a space in which children can re-enact and dramatize problems or conflicts and practice possible solutions. The therapist facilitates this process by establishing a safe environment, giving her or his undivided attention to the child during play, and occasionally making well-timed interpretations or suggestions that help the child's understanding and development of new skills (Swinomish Tribal Community, 1991). These are good ideas for work with children of any culture.

Some challenges specific to nonverbal expressive therapies may not be apparent to therapists who are less familiar with them. In art therapy, a common pitfall for therapists is the overinterpretation or misinterpretation of clients' drawings (e.g., assuming that a drawing of an empty house means loneliness) (Wadeson, 1980). Cultural differences between therapists and clients increase this potential. To avoid the problem, it is better to let clients interpret their own work.

Therapists are also encouraged to exercise care in their use of clients' artwork. Hammond and Gantt (1998) recommended that artwork be viewed as equivalent to verbal communication and subject to the same protections of confidentiality. For example, clients' artwork should not be displayed without their permission, and therapists need to take special care in their inclusion of clients' artwork in clinical records, where it could be misinterpreted or "susceptible to inappropriate exposure" by others (Hammond & Gantt, 1998, p. 273).

Because older clients (and I would add some younger ones) may feel frustrated by, overwhelmed by, or inhibited about art activities, Weiss (1999) advised therapists to give clients an explanation of the types of art media available, demonstrate their use, and offer a varied selection (e.g., colored pencils, fine-tip felt-tip pens, pastels, acrylics or oils). Different media have varying degrees of flexibility and ease of use and thus elicit different emotions (e.g., consider the difference between clay and pencil drawing) (Weiss, 1999).

Herring (1999) provided a detailed description of the variety of creative arts used in American Indian cultures. In their book *Integrating Spirituality into Multicultural Counseling*, Fukuyama and Sevig (1999) also described a number of methods for engaging people in the creative process both inside and outside therapy sessions. Weiss (1999) offered specific art exercises for work with older adults (e.g., "Symbol of My Life," "Making Your Own World," "Tree of Life," and "Draw Your Future"; pp. 193–195); many of these exercises may be helpful with people of other age groups. And Hoshino (in press) described the use of the ADDRESSING framework in art therapy with families of minority cultures. In sum, if you intend to use creative modalities in your work with clients, I advise obtaining additional training in the particular expressive therapy you want to use.

Systems-Level Interventions

Another type of eclecticism in cross-cultural approaches involves the use of systems-level interventions. Systems therapists have consistently emphasized the advantages of involving families in therapy. More information is available for assessments, changes are more likely to be maintained, and in many cultures family involvement or approval may be essential, even for work with individuals. Although the ADDRESSING framework assumes a systemic perspective, it may be helpful to highlight some particular applications with families, couples, and groups.

FAMILY THERAPY

Until recently, family systems theorists focused almost exclusively on the Euroamerican family ideal (i.e., two young or middle-aged heterosexual parents and their children). This narrow definition of the family has been challenged for its ethnocentric biases and gendered assumptions by both multicultural and feminist therapists (Boyd-Franklin, 1989; M. K. Ho, 1987; Hong, 1988; McGoldrick, Anderson, & Walsh, 1989; McGoldrick, Giordano, & Pearce, 1996). These researchers have encouraged a more inclusive definition of family that includes gay, lesbian, and heterosexual couples; single parents; grandparents; relatives; and even non-kin family members.

"Intergenerational family therapy" is one of many terms used to describe therapy in which the extended family is the focus of treatment (Greene, 1986). One key aspect of intergenerational family therapy is that older family members are seen not simply as resources for the nuclear family, but rather as central figures with desires and goals of their own (Duffy, 1986). Because this approach is more inclusive, it offers a model for working with diverse kinds of families.

Duffy (1986) provided several suggestions for therapists conducting intergenerational family therapy. Noting that the size of extended families and the number of coexisting generations are growing as people live longer, Duffy challenged the idea that family therapy must involve the physical presence of every family member. Telephone conference calls, letters, and audiotapes can be used to include members who are unable to attend therapy sessions. Home visits may allow some family members to participate more easily (e.g., elders, those with disabilities), and special scheduling may facilitate the involvement of members who live out of town. For example, meetings may be scheduled in 1- to $1^1/_2$-hour sessions on three consecutive days, an arrangement that is less exhausting than a 3- or 4-hour session and allows the family informal "processing time" between sessions.

With Asian American families, S. C. Kim (1985) used a combination of strategic (Haley, 1963) and structural (Minuchin, 1974) family therapies. Several of the key components of this adaptation are as follows. The therapist carefully assesses the power structure of the family system and does not overtly challenge the leadership of those in authority. To enhance the therapist's ability to offer well-informed, empathic statements about the family's situation, she or he obtains as much information as possible about the family before the initial assessment through prior records and outside reading and consultation about clinical, social, cultural, and immigration issues relevant to the family; this knowledge base increases the therapist's credibility as well. The directive, problem-focused (rather than person-focused) approach provides clients with a sense that practical suggestions will be aimed at changing the situation as quickly as possible. Although insights and emotional expressiveness may result from these situational changes, they are not the primary focus.

Kim's strategic-structural adaptation is flexible in who is included. The whole family, subsystems, or significant others may be scheduled depending on the particular issues involved. Similarly, Hong (1988) conceptualized the role of the therapist as similar to that of a family doctor who sees individuals and family subsystems on an as-needed basis for whatever problems may arise. Because the therapist is considered the family's care provider, the need to establish trust with every new family member is decreased. In addition, this approach is more cost-effective than that of assigning a different therapist to each individual or family subsystem.

Network therapy is another adaptation of the systems approach to the situation of American Indians (Attneave, 1969). The client's natural supports, including family, friends, and community members, are brought together, usually in someone's home, for the purposes of problem solving and supporting the client. The counselor acts primarily as a catalyst to mobilize the natural support process. Because whole networks are engaged, up to 70 people may be involved at any one time (LaFromboise, Trimble, & Mohatt, 1993).

While the preceding therapies are Euroamerican inventions adapted to minority cultures, *ho'oponopono* is a systems therapy developed by Native Hawaiians that has been adapted to the mental health setting. *Ho'oponopono* is a formally organized family meeting in which relationships are "set right" through a process of "prayer, discussion, confession, repentance, mutual restitution, and forgiveness" (Pukui, Haertig, & Lee, 1972, p. 60). In response to a problem, the family gathers together in a spirit of honesty and sincerity (Rezentes, 1996). A healer or family elder leads the meeting and guides discussions, questions participants, and controls disruptive emotions. In addition, the "setting right" of the problem involves:

- Honest confession to the gods (or God) and to each other of wrong-doing, grievances, grudges, and resentments.
- Immediate restitution or arrangements to make restitution as soon as possible.
- Mutual forgiveness and releasing from the guilts, grudges, and tensions occasioned by the wrong-doing (*hala*). This repenting-forgiving-releasing is embodied in the twin terms, *mihi* and *kala*.
- Closing prayer.
- Nearly always, the leader called for the periods of silence called *ho'omalu*. *Ho'omalu* was invoked to calm tempers, encourage self-inquiry into actions, motives and feelings, or simply for rest during an all-day *ho'oponopono*. And once a dispute was settled, the leader decreed *ho'omalu* for the whole subject, both immediately and long after *ho'oponopono* ended. (Pukui et al., 1972, p. 62)

Although it would be inappropriate for a therapist to lead a *ho'oponopono* unless he or she has been trained to do so, the therapist may work with a family elder or healer to arrange it. Also, *ho'oponopono* may be effectively used as a formalized part of a treatment program. For example, Gaughen and Gaughen (1996) reported that *ho'oponopono* is an integral component of the family and group therapy approach used at *Ho'omau Ke Ola*, a substance abuse program on the island of Oahu. In this program, emphasis is placed on the value of *lokahi*, in which everything is perceived to be interconnected and one, and a sense of balance is sought between "the person (*kanaka*), family (*'ohana*), nature (*'aina*) and spiritual world (*akua*)" (Gaughen & Gaughen, 1996, p. 34).

COUPLES THERAPY

Keeping in mind all of the ADDRESSING influences and identities that two individuals may hold, it is not surprising that couples' conflicts often emerge in relation to differences in worldviews and values. Understanding the origins of these differences as individual, familial, or cultural is often key in helping clients to accept and make changes. For example, recognizing that a particular behavior has come from a client's family or cultural upbringing may decrease an individual's sense of guilt and thus allow him or her to consciously decide whether he or she wants to continue the behavior. Similarly, recognizing cultural influences on a partner's views can facilitate the development of understanding and the acceptance of differences.

Consider the situation of a 28-year-old Indonesian man married for 3 years to a 28-year-old Euroamerican woman. Amin left his family in Indonesia to attend university, where he met his wife, Liz, who graduated at the same time. Both biologists, they decided to forgo having children for 5 years and live in a small one-bedroom apartment to save money. Conflict arose when Amin's family decided to send his younger sister to university with the expectation that she would live with Amin and Liz. To Liz, it seemed that the decision had been made without her consent. Amin, however, could not understand Liz's resistance—it was his sister who would be living with them, not a complete stranger; furthermore, if she did not live with them, she would not be able to leave their parents' home.

In a counseling session with the couple, it became clear that Liz and Amin both placed a high value on family relationships. However, Liz's family and culture emphasized independence, self-sufficiency, and plenty of physical space as necessary ingredients for a well-functioning family. In contrast, Amin's family placed more value on physical proximity and interdependence; young adult Indonesians commonly live at home until they marry (Piercy, Soekandar, & Limansubroto, 1996).

As Falicov (1995) noted, intermarried couples may either focus on and thus overemphasize their differences, or minimize these differences and fail to see the impact of culture on their interactions. For Amin and Liz, recognizing the differences in their values was the first step toward a resolution. Next, exploring the influence of culture on these values helped Liz and Amin to step back from their assumptions about what "should be" or "must be." What seemed like enormous differences in their viewpoints were reconceptualized as only different degrees of emphasis. Liz also valued interdependence—just a little less than Amin. Similarly, Amin liked having his own physical space, but he didn't need as much as Liz. This reconceptualization helped the couple to come up with new ideas for solutions and eventually decide on a compromise. Because it would cost extra for his sister to live with them, Amin asked his parents for a monthly allowance for her living expenses, and they readily agreed. This extra money allowed them to rent a nicer two-bedroom apartment, which gave the sister her own room and satisfied Liz's need for space.

Although value differences are an obvious source of conflict for cross-cultural couples, they can be especially problematic for families with a recent history of immigration. Intergenerational conflict often occurs as older members support traditional values, language, and behaviors, but younger members are pulled toward more current expressions of their own culture or the dominant culture. In a creative approach to helping families cope with this type of cultural transition, Landau (1982) used a brief, strategic intervention known as link therapy to involve extended families who could not or would not attend therapy together.

In an initial family session (often a home visit), one family member was chosen to take the role of the link therapist. In families with patriarchal traditions, this person was usually a man of some seniority. The therapist then trained and coached the link therapist in individual sessions to return to the family and facilitate the resolution of conflicts. Because the link therapist had a strong impact on the direction of change (i.e., toward reinforcing traditions or overturning them), Landau advised against choosing individuals with extreme views in either direction. She found that the most effective resolutions seemed to occur with family members who, at the initiation of therapy, had not yet resolved their own position about the importance of maintaining family traditions.

Whether link therapy is used or not, it is important that therapists be clear about their own leanings and willing to share this information with families in transition. More specifically, therapists will want to let clients know when their values may conflict with client goals. For example, if you do couples therapy, it may be necessary to tell couples at the outset whether you place more emphasis on the satisfaction of each individual or the preservation of a relationship. This type of self-disclosure needs to be handled cautiously, though, because too much sharing can shift the focus to the therapist's unresolved value conflicts. When in doubt, consult with someone who shares or knows well the client's value system.

ADDRESSING POWER AND ABUSE

Until now, I have taken the position that therapists need to be able to accept and work with the value systems of their clients—the view promoted by the multicultural counseling field in general. For example, therapists working in families with clearly defined hierarchies may need to address elders first (i.e., parents before their children) and show respect for family members who hold more authority (S. C. Kim, 1985; Murgatroyd, 1996). Such a stance does not require that therapists completely agree with their clients; value differences can have a positive effect of opening up a wider range of options for the client's consideration. However, it does mean that therapists may have to settle for the small changes desired by clients rather than fundamental structural changes in clients' relationships.

As a feminist, this is a difficult statement for me to make, because it suggests support for relationships defined by patriarchal assumptions. As L. S. Brown (1994) noted, feminist therapy aims to change patriarchal assumptions, beliefs, and structures that cause distress in people's lives: "It attends as well to prescribed 'normal' patterns of being with which people may be comfortable but which are ultimately destructive to their integrity" (p. 19).

The practical application of these ideas can be difficult, to say the least. B. L. C. Kim (1996) provided a concrete example in the case of a couple consisting of an Asian woman (Korean, Filipina, or Japanese) and an American man working on a U.S. military base near their home. The woman is likely to hold a low-status, low-paying job in comparison to the man, whose position, while not necessarily high status in the United States, is associated with the most powerful military presence in the world. In addition, the woman may have experienced abuse, neglect, poverty, or economic exploitation (although the man may have also). In this context, "sexist expectations and cultural colonialism" create a special form of racism in which "the husband's superior and dominant position in such a couple's relationship is affirmed and reinforced" (B. L. C. Kim, 1996):

> For a woman who comes to such a marriage with low socioeconomic status and low self-esteem, her dignity and identity are further diminished. Moreover, the arduous tasks of learning English and becoming acculturated to the American lifestyle are placed upon the wife, whereas the husband is nearly always exempted from learning his wife's language and culture. . . . The clear message to the wife is that her own heritage of language and culture is unworthy of her husband's attention or respect. (p. 311)

From a feminist perspective, the therapist's work with couples whose power is so imbalanced would be to help them recognize the imbalance and then consider the advantages but also the costs of maintaining such a relationship, with the ultimate goal being to help the couple become more egalitarian in their interactions (Sims, 1996). But obviously the couple may not share the values embedded in this goal. As B. L. C. Kim (1996) noted in relation to couples in the situation described above,

> Very often the partners are quite satisfied with small changes in the relationship, along with clarification of misunderstandings and miscommunications. Many wives are happy when their husbands move from the role of dictator to that of benevolent though still domineering husband. Nearly three-quarters of the couples I have seen have terminated therapy at this point. Only about one-fifth are motivated to go on with treatment and seek further growth. (p. 317)

The question then becomes: Is it possible to help people work toward "better" relationships when their definition of *better* is different from yours? Obviously, I believe this is possible, or I would be looking for another line of work. At the same time, I recognize that therapists vary in what they are willing (or not willing) to help clients do (e.g., some feminist therapists may believe that it compromises their ethics to work with couples who prefer a power differential in their relationship). However, I also think that it is important to consider how our own cultural heritage and context influence our sense of what is ethical.

There is one exception to my suggestion that therapists try to avoid imposing their values on the client, and that is when there is a risk of harm to the client or someone else. Such a statement might seem obvious, but there seems to be a perception among many Euroamericans that minority groups, particularly those with patriarchal traditions (e.g., Latino, Asian, Arab, Muslim), condone domestic violence. But one could make the same observation regarding Euroamerican culture, which also has patriarchal traditions and a high rate of violence against women (American Psychological Association, 1996). Although patriarchal relationships tend to increase the likelihood of violence, just because a culture is patriarchically organized does not mean that violence is normative or that a given family will view it as such.

The American Psychological Association's Task Force on Violence and the Family defined domestic violence as "a pattern of abusive behaviors including a wide range of physical, sexual, and psychological maltreatment used by one person in an intimate relationship against another to gain power unfairly or maintain that person's misuse of power, control, and authority" (Walker, 1999, p. 23). In therapeutic settings, domestic violence is largely a hidden problem; clients rarely come to therapy stating that they are being abused or abusing someone else. Rather, they bring other problems that are often related to, caused by, or exacerbated by abuse.

For this reason, therapists need to be sensitized to the signs and symptoms of abuse. One of the best ways for female therapists to gain this sensitivity is to work or volunteer in a shelter for abused women and children. For male therapists, such work is usually less possible; however, a knowledge base may be obtained through volunteer work with a women's resource center, reading, and consultation. (For information on programs across many cultures, see the 1999 special edition of *American Psychologist*, (Walker) Vol. 54, titled "International Perspectives on Domestic Violence.")

Culture should never be used as an excuse for violence, but the ways in which a therapist addresses it may vary depending on the culture (C. K. Ho, 1990). For example, community and family elders may be helpful in cases of domestic violence in Asian and Asian American communities. By giving the woman permission from a position of authority to escape the dangerous situation, elders can help to bypass the problem of a woman's loyalty to an abusive husband (C. K. Ho, 1990, p. 146).

Although research on power in relationships has traditionally focused on heterosexual couples, power differentials related to gender role socialization may be equally influential for gay and lesbian partners. As Farley (1992) noted, with gay men, therapists should consider how each partner defines masculinity, including how they view competition and aggression within relationships. Because men are more often socialized to fear a loss of control or power, holding back from a commitment to intimacy may be an issue for gay (male) couples. In contrast, because women are more often socialized to make relationships their center, bonding in lesbian couples may result in "fusion, with the struggle becoming one of individuation" (Farley, 1992, p. 235).

When power differences related to culture are added in, lesbian and gay couples often face the additional problem of limited social support (Pearlman, 1996). For instance, for a Euroamerican/Latina lesbian couple, a predominantly White lesbian community may be less than welcoming to the Latina, whereas both partners' families and ethnic cultures may not validate their relationship because they are both women.

With clients of all cultural heritages, a key step is to look for the ways in which power is organized in the family. Although one might be inclined to assume a patriarchal organization, the variation between and within cultures is so great that it is safer to start with well-informed questions. These questions may be generated using the ADDRESSING framework. Power may be distributed or accorded by

■ **A**ge or generational status (e.g., couples with a large age difference),
■ Developmental or acquired **D**isabilities (Is power withheld on this basis?)
■ **R**eligious commitment or leadership,
■ **E**thnic or **I**ndigenous heritage (Who holds the dominant cultural identity in bi- or multicultural couples and families? Are there differences in status related to skin color or other ethnically related characteristics?),
■ **S**ocioeconomic status (i.e., Who makes the money or holds the highest status by income, education, or occupation?),
■ **S**exual orientation (Does one family member receive less social support or status base on his or her sexual orientation?)
■ **N**ational origin (Who is a citizen or holds a work visa? Who speaks English most fluently?), and
■ **G**ender.

With some families, therapists may be able to ask and discuss these questions directly. However, with others, such an approach would be much too threatening; in these cases, the questions are best used to raise therapists' awareness of possibilities. Whenever a therapist suspects that violence may be occurring, the first priority is always to ensure the safety of the abused individual. Couples counseling is not an appropriate modality when violence between partners is ongoing, because "the dynamics of abusive relationships preclude the feasibility" of a safe therapeutic setting for both individuals (Farley, 1992, p. 241).

GROUP THERAPY

Group therapy is another systemic intervention that can be helpful in creating an environment in which clients can learn from others, practice new behaviors, and obtain support. Multicultural groups have the added advantage of increasing members' opportunities for growth through interactions with people of diverse backgrounds. When problem solving is a focus, diverse groups offer a broader information base and a wider range of potential solutions for group members.

Of course, diversity has its down side, namely the conflict that invariably occurs with differences. The best preparation for conflict is the careful screening and orientation of group members before the group begins (Corey, 1995). The goal of this preparatory work is not to form a homogeneous group, but rather to ensure that participants will be able to engage with and learn from one another.

Because groups can easily replicate oppressive conditions in the larger society, therapists must pay special attention to the needs of individuals in the minority in a group. For example, consider the special issues involved in referring a gay African American man to a predominantly White gay and lesbian group. Before referring the client, the counselor would need to find out whether the group therapist is knowledgeable about and sensitive to African American culture. As Gutiérrez and Dworkin (1992) noted, "Otherwise the referral could backfire if [the client] experiences insensitivity from the other group members and/or the facilitator" (p. 149).

As with individual and family therapy, awareness of one's own values is essential in group work. Dominant cultural values permeate assumptions about how a healthy group member "should be." For example, "active participants" are often expected to speak openly about their families, state their desires and viewpoints directly, and express their emotions freely. But as mentioned earlier, many cultures emphasize the importance of protecting the family's reputation, expressing one's desires indirectly to avoid offending others, and maintaining control of one's emotions as a sign of maturity (S. C. Kim, 1985; D. W. Sue & D. Sue, 1999). Clients' reluctance to speak up may also reflect a realistic suspiciousness acquired from a lifetime of experiences as a member of a minority group.

Group therapy may also be problematic in rural areas or within close-knit minority groups, because confidentiality is difficult to ensure (Schank & Skovholt, 1997). For example, R. Y. Shapiro (1996) described the particular challenges in conducting group therapy with Orthodox Jewish patients in New York, including the impossibility of anonymity, patients' discomfort with mixed-gender groups, and cultural restrictions regarding language and the appropriateness of certain topics (in Tseng, 1999, p. 164). One way around the limitations of small communities is to offer time-limited educational or experiential classes or workshops that provide information and allow a structured format for discussion—and indirectly involve social support (LaFromboise, Berman, & Sohi, 1994).

SOCIOCULTURAL AND POLITICAL ACTION

Systems-level interventions need not stop at the level of families or therapeutic groups (Ponterotto, 1987). Often, clients' problems involve nonfamily systems, for example, work environments, social services, medical facilities, or the courts (Aponte, 1994). When this is the case, it important that therapists be willing to intervene in ways that help and empower clients. For example, with a non-English-speaking client who feels too intimidated to ask his physician for information, it may be appropriate for the therapist to call the physician (with a release from the patient) and discuss the need for the client to obtain an interpreter and additional information.

Many members of minority groups do not seek help from mainstream agencies or institutions because they perceive such entities as representing the dominant culture (Boyd-Franklin, 1989). In general, this is an accurate perception. Studies show that people of color, older people, and those of lower socioeconomic status are less likely to receive therapy and, when they do, are more likely to be assigned to less experienced therapists and to terminate earlier (Butler, Lewis, & Sunderland, 1998; Jones, 1974; Snowden & Cheung, 1990; S. Sue, Fujino, Hu, Takeuchi, & Zane, 1991). In addition, mental health services may be so foreign to some people as to not even be considered an option. For example, Iwamasa (1997) noted, "we will be waiting a long time if we expect Japanese Americans to initiate behavior therapy" (p. 352).

The key to changing this situation lies in finding out where and how minority groups obtain help or are likely to accept help and then working with these individuals and groups to provide more culturally appropriate services. The focus of this work is on outreach (i.e., the agency or clinician reaching out to the minority community) and collaborative learning (between therapists and community helpers and activists).

In addition, the mental health of communities at large may be improved through broader social action (Constantine, 1999). As community psychologists have noted for many years, psychotherapy is a relatively slow way to create change, because it addresses problems only "after the fact." Moreover, it is a "modulative" (as opposed to a generative) approach; individuals are helped to adapt to the larger social environment, but not vice versa (Moghaddam, 1990, p. 22, based on the ideas of Laing, 1965, and Szasz, 1961). To truly decrease the incidence of mental illness and milder forms of psychopathology, societies need to change environments themselves to eliminate the causes of these problems, which may include poverty, lack of educational and economic opportunities, poor nutrition, and inadequate health care (Albee, 1981; Levine, 1998).

Years of work with individuals and families has led many therapists to realize that political action is an important part of the social changes needed to prevent mental illness. The type of action chosen by a therapist will depend on his or her experience and concerns. For example, a therapist frustrated by the limitations of being a professional for Child Protective Services may become involved in lobbying for increased legal protections for children. A psychologist who works with crime victims may work to pass a law that obliges offenders to compensate those who have lost property or a loved one. A school counselor who works with the children of Latino migrant workers may become involved in protests against inhumane housing and working conditions in the farming business. Such activities can have the added advantage of energizing therapists who feel discouraged by the slow pace of psychotherapeutic change.

Developing a Treatment Plan

A final suggestion concerns the development of a treatment plan. It is essential that therapists work collaboratively with clients to set goals and decide on interventions. (Of course there are exceptions, for example, when a client's ability to choose is severely impaired.) Such collaboration makes sense when one recognizes that clients know more about their particular contexts and needs than a therapist ever can, especially a therapist who differs culturally from the client. It also means that there will be times when clients choose goals that do not fit with the therapist's expectations or preferences.

COLLABORATIVE GOAL SETTING

Take the case of a middle-class Greek American woman who came to therapy "for help in making my daughter behave." The mother had been separated from her husband for 10 years but never legally divorced, and she and their sole daughter lived together. The daughter was making good grades at the community college she was attending but wanted to do things that the mother did not like (e.g., go to movies with friends at night, wear baggy pants). When the daughter tried to explain her desires and reason with her mother, the mother would interpret this as "talking back" and become furious and shout at her daughter.

The therapist realized that the mother's behavior was understandable in relation to some childrearing practices and views in Greek culture (e.g., the questioning of authority and disobedience being seen as disrespectful) (Tsemberis & Orfanos, 1996). With further discussion, it became clear that the mother was unwilling to change her conceptualization of the problem, and through a telephone call, the therapist learned that the father would not become involved in what he perceived as a "mother-daughter problem."

The therapist's initial inclination was to help the daughter become more independent and eventually move out on her own. However, neither the mother nor the daughter were interested in this solution. Thus, the therapist worked with the daughter to help her find more effective ways to interact with her mother. Through therapy, the daughter came to realize that when she spent more time with her mother, her mother was more likely to let her go out or bring friends home. The two continued to have disagreements about clothes, but the conflicts over the daughter's socializing subsided, at least to a more acceptable level for the pair. In sum, by joining with the clients in pursuing their goals, the therapist was able to help them both.

At the same time, there may be situations in which behaviorally oriented goals are inappropriate. For example, some Indian people come to counseling primarily for support and want someone who will listen and provide encouragement, reassurance, practical suggestions, and caring but realistic feedback; for these individuals, behavioral goals or homework assignments are generally not appropriate (Swinomish Tribal Community, 1991, p. 226). Similarly, with clients experiencing grief over the death of a loved one, the most helpful approach may be supportive counseling that provides a safe place to cry and reassurance that the experience of bereavement is a normal process. (For information on what constitutes normal bereavement in diverse minority cultures, see Shapiro, 1995, and Irish, Lundquist, & Nelsen, 1993).

USE OF MEDICATION

When a client's treatment plan involves medication, there are several points a therapist will want to remember. First, ethnic and age-related differences in drug metabolism mean that appropriate dosage levels may vary significantly for elders and people of ethnic minority identities (Lin, Poland, Chang, & Chang, 1995; Lin, Poland, & Nakasaki, 1993). In addition, older people of any culture are more likely than younger people to be taking medications prescribed by different health care providers who are not coordinating with one another. For this reason, asking about prescriptions and nonprescription treatments and self-medication (e.g., the use of Chinese medicine among Asian clients) is important (Lai & Yue, 1990). Whenever I see an older client for the first time, I ask them to put all of their medications in a bag and bring the bag to the assessment session to decrease the likelihood of misunderstandings regarding what they are taking.

Of equal concern are cultural differences in expectations. People of Asian, Central American, and Arab heritage are likely to expect medication and may feel that they are not being taken seriously if one is not prescribed (Gleave & Manes, 1990; Paniagua, 1998). Among American Indian clients, a more common view is that medication is not healthy, whereas many African Americans see medication as too impersonal (Paniagua, 1998). Given the range of cross-cultural and intracultural variations, I suggest talking with clients about their expectations and what medications can and cannot to do for them. (Some clinicians advise the use of placebos, but in general I don't feel comfortable with this.)

When medications are necessary, compliance may be complicated by the belief that "Western medicine" is too strong, particularly among people of Chinese, Southeast Asian, Indian, Pakistani, and other South Asian countries (Assanand, Dias, Richardson, & Waxler-Morrison, 1990; Lai & Yue, 1990; Richardson, 1990). There is some basis for this view in the cross-cultural differences in metabolism. It is not uncommon for people who hold this belief to reduce prescribed dosages themselves or take the medication only until the symptoms disappear (Lai & Yue, 1990).

Clients may also hold particular assumptions that work against the use of medications. For example, Falicov (1998) described the case of a nine-year-old Latino boy who was diagnosed with attention deficit disorder and prescribed Ritalin. His parents were reluctant to give him the medication because they feared that it would "begin a drug addiction and a life in the streets," as they had seen daily among youngsters in their neighborhood (Falicov, 1998, p. 142). For all of these reasons, it is important to provide a careful explanation of the need for clients to take medications as instructed. When possible, enlisting family support for the prescribed regimen may increase the likelihood of compliance. Sometimes therapists and clients disagree about the need for medication. When this happens, it is important to remember that ultimately, the client is the one who has to live with the results of her or his decision. (For a detailed consideration of cross-cultural ethical issues involved with medications, see Fadiman's 1997 book *The Spirit Catches You and You Fall Down*).

Conclusion

Whether one's interventions are at the level of individuals, couples, families, groups, or institutions, culturally responsive therapy involves a systemic perspective that recognizes the impact of diverse cultural influences on clients' lives. With this perspective, eclecticism is essential; the wider the repertoire a therapist holds, the more able she or he will be to work effectively with each client. Culturally related therapies, adaptations of mainstream approaches, nonverbal expressive therapies, and systems-level interventions offer enough ideas to keep therapists busy learning for a long time.

KEY IDEAS 9.

Implementing Culturally Responsive Interventions

1. Develop knowledge of culturally related therapies and strategies.

2. Consider religion as a potential source of strength and support.

3. Adapt mainstream approaches (e.g., psychodynamic, humanistic/existential, behavioral, cognitive-behavioral, family systems therapies) to the cultural context of the client.

4. Become familiar with nonverbal expressive therapies, and obtain additional training when appropriate.

5. Use family systems interventions whenever possible.

6. Conceptualize "family" broadly to include gay and lesbian parents, single parents, elders, relatives, and non-kin family members.

7. Be willing to see individual members or subsystems of the family on an as-needed basis.

8. Recognize power differentials related to each of the ADDRESSING domains.

9. Use group therapy to create a multicultural environment in which clients can learn from others, practice behaviors, and obtain support.

10. Intervene at sociocultural, institutional, and political levels when appropriate and possible.

11. Set goals, develop treatment plans, and choose interventions in collaboration with clients.

12. When medications are prescribed, be aware of ethnic and age-related differences in metabolism and cultural expectations regarding medications.

Practice Doesn't Make Perfect, But It Sure Does Help: A Final Case Example

10

The following case pulls together the main suggestions I've made for understanding clients' identities, establishing a respectful relationship, conducting a culturally responsive assessment, making a culturally responsive diagnosis, and implementing culturally responsive therapies at both the individual and systemic levels. As you read the case, note how the therapist demonstrates ways that these suggestions can be implemented.

The therapist in this case was Robert, a 33-year-old, bicultural geropsychologist. Robert's mother was Euroamerican and his father African American, and he grew up with close connections to both of his parents' families. Robert was working in a mental health center located in an ethnically diverse, urban community.

Referral

Robert received a telephone call from a woman who introduced herself as Janet and said that she was calling about her mother. Janet told Robert that her mother, Mrs. Penn, was 73 years old, widowed for 7 years, retired, and living with Janet in the latter's home along with Janet's husband, their recently divorced 25-year-old daughter, and the daughter's 2-year-old daughter. Although Mrs. Penn had lived in her own home most of her life, Janet said that about 2 years earlier her mother had experienced a stroke and had moved in with Janet and her husband. Janet stated that Mrs. Penn had gradually recovered most of her physical and mental abilities since the stroke, but still experienced some weakness in her left leg.

Janet's present concerns had developed over the past few months. Her mother had begun sleeping more than usual, and Mrs. Penn's unwillingness to follow a diet despite her diagnosis of diabetes, had resulted in several trips to the hospital when she became sick from eating too many sweet foods. Janet told the therapist that she was feeling very frustrated with her mother because "she doesn't do anything anymore. She doesn't see friends or want to go to church. She doesn't help with dinner or dishes, or even make her bed, and she'll only take a bath after I nag her for a week." She added, "I have to work all day, so I can't stay home and take care of her, but I could never put Mother in a nursing home. I don't know what to do."

Robert responded to Janet's story by suggesting that she and her mother come in for an assessment within the next week. He told Janet that he would like to talk with both her and her mother, and that the meeting would take approximately an hour and a half. He asked that they bring with them the name, address, and telephone number of Mrs. Penn's physician, a bag with all of Mrs. Penn's current medications in it, and reading glasses or hearing aid if she used either.

Initial Assessment

Janet and Mrs. Penn arrived 15 minutes early for their appointment with the requested information and items. Robert greeted them warmly, showed them to his office, and asked if they would like a cup of tea or coffee. He noticed that Mrs. Penn, an African American woman, appeared to be about 20 pounds overweight and that her clothes were wrinkled and worn. He also noticed a slight smell of body odor and recalled Janet's comment about Mrs. Penn's resistance to baths. Mrs. Penn declined the cup of tea or coffee, chose to keep her coat on, and clutched her purse to her stomach throughout the session. Her demeanor was subdued. She did not seem distracted, and she answered questions when asked but volunteered no information. In contrast, Janet, an African American woman in her early 50s, was well-dressed, of medium weight, and talkative; as she spoke, she rolled and unrolled a tissue in her hands.

After a few minutes of social conversation about their neighborhoods, Robert explained to Mrs. Penn that Janet had called him because she was concerned about her (Mrs. Penn's) health. He said that he had told Janet that if her mother were willing, it would be a good idea for them to come in together to talk about how things were going at home. He then outlined the kinds of questions he would like to ask them so that he could have an accurate picture of their situation. As he talked, Janet seemed to relax a little, but Mrs. Penn's facial expression remained somewhat flattened.

Robert began by looking at Mrs. Penn's bottles of medications, which included insulin pills and two antidepressants. Janet said that her mother had not liked taking the antidepressants, and did so irregularly, finally stopping completely several months earlier. Robert tried to ask Mrs. Penn questions about her health, but in the pause before Mrs. Penn answered, Janet frequently answered for her. Robert suggested that it would be helpful for him to gain an understanding of each person's concerns by meeting separately with each of them for about 30 minutes; then they could all meet together at the end for a final discussion. Neither Mrs. Penn or Janet seemed bothered by this plan.

Robert met first with Mrs. Penn. He asked if anything about her health was bothering her, to which she replied, "I just don't feel good." In response to more specific questions, Mrs. Penn denied any disturbing thoughts or perceptions, but admitted being hungry often and sleeping "a lot, except for last night, because I was worried about what this meeting would be about." She said that she had noticed her memory "wasn't as good as it used to be." She denied hearing difficulties but said that she needed glasses to read.

Putting aside any mental status tests until he felt some rapport develop between them, Robert told Mrs. Penn that he would like to hear more about her life, both before and after moving in with her daughter. In response to specific questions, Mrs. Penn said that she was born in Tennessee in 1927, that her father had worked doing odd jobs and her mother as a housekeeper, and that they were poor. Her parents had three girls; Mrs. Penn was the youngest.

When Mrs. Penn was 14, her mother died of tuberculosis, and shortly thereafter, her father took his daughters to Los Angeles to live closer to their relatives. Mrs. Penn graduated from high school a year early because she was such a good student. She married the year of her graduation, but her husband was drafted and then killed in "the War," Mrs. Penn said, "before he could see his baby Janet." Mrs. Penn then moved back into her father's home and, with the help of her sisters, managed to care for Janet and work full-time for an office cleaning business, where she met her second husband. With him, she had a daughter, Laura. When Laura began school, Mrs. Penn obtained a job as a receptionist at a branch of the Department of Social and Health Services, where she was promoted to secretary and then administrative assistant, and she worked until her retirement at age 65. She and her second husband had been married for almost 45 years when he died of a heart attack. Mrs. Penn's sisters were both living in another state, and Mrs. Penn talked to them about twice a month, but they always called her.

The chronological ordering of Mrs. Penn's story was provided by the order of Robert's questions. Robert noticed that the only date given by Mrs. Penn was her birth year. When tactfully pressed about the years of her high school graduation; the births of her children, grandchildren, and great-grandchildren; and her first and second marriages, Mrs. Penn gave general or vague answers such as "sometime in the '40s" or "oh, too long ago." Considering her exceptional high school performance and responsible work history, Robert thought that these were all pieces of information she should know.

During the interview with Mrs. Penn, Robert sketched a timeline containing significant events in the lives of Mrs. Penn and her family. He later filled in the dates Janet provided and added sociocultural influences and events that had occurred during Mrs. Penn's lifetime (see Figure 10.1). The latter included the Great Depression; segregation; World War II; school desegregation; the Civil Rights movement; the assassination of Martin Luther King, Jr.; and in Los Angeles specifically, the Watts riots and later, the violence related to the Rodney King incident.

FIGURE 10.1.

Mrs. Penn's Timeline

						Civil		Watts				
Great	Segregation			War		School	Rights	Antiwar	riots	Dr. King		
Depression	in TN	WWII		ends		desegreg.	Act	protests	(LA)	Assassinated		LA riots
1929		1940–44		1945		1954	1964		1965	1968		1992

1927	1930's	1941	1944	1948	1949			1967	1969	1975	1985	1993	1998
born	Childhood	Mom died	HS grad	Re-	Laura		Began	Daughters	Father	1st	Twins	2nd	1st great
	in TN	Family	Married	married	born		work	left home	died	grandchild	born	husband	grandchild
		moved					at DSHS			born		died	born
		to LA	1st husband died										CVA
			Janet born										Moved to
												Retired	Janet's

Despite the hardships related to the time periods in which Mrs. Penn had lived, she showed no emotion when talking about her life. Robert hypothesized that Mrs. Penn's unemotional presentation was due to some stoicism or resignation in her approach to life. When he asked if she felt sad about some of the events in her life, she said, "I learned early on that life is hard, and you better not get too happy, or you'll just get slapped down." When he asked if she had ever "thought of ending it all," she said that she had thought about it after her mother died but not since, then added, "But if I were going to do it, it would be stupid to tell you, now, wouldn't it?"

Subsequently, in the interview with Mrs. Penn's daughter, Janet talked about feeling overwhelmed by her responsibilities. "I come home from work, the phone is ringing, dinner needs fixing, the baby is crying, and my husband wants to talk to me. Then on top of it, when Mother goes to visit my sister Laura for the weekend, Laura lets her do whatever she wants; she doesn't make Mother take a bath and lets her eat sweets, knowing that she has diabetes. And all Mother can say when she gets home is what a good time she has at Laura's and how much she wishes she could stay there longer."

At the end of the individual sessions, Robert met and talked with Janet and Mrs. Penn together about his beginning understanding of their situation. He noted that the first question that needed to be addressed concerned Mrs. Penn's memory difficulties. He explained that the difficulties described by Janet, along with Mrs. Penn's inability to recall some of the things he had asked her, suggested the need for further evaluation. He said that a thorough medical examination and a neuropsychological assessment would help to clarify whether there really was a memory problem that needed to be addressed. He explained what a neuropsychological assessment involves and added that often what appears to be a memory problem may be something else—for example, focusing too much on one's memory, feeling depressed, or just not seeing the point in remembering some things.

Robert went on to say that something he was concerned about was how tired Janet seemed, at which point her eyes filled with tears. From his reading of a book written for caregivers (Carter, 1994), he was aware of the pressures on caregivers and particularly of the difficulties faced by daughters caring for their parents (Hinrichsen, 1991). He said that he felt concerned that Janet was trying to do too much. Out of respect for the family's value expressed by Janet on the telephone that Mrs. Penn's place was with her family, he did not mention the idea of an alternative living arrangement for Mrs. Penn. Nor did he press the idea of a caregivers support group after Janet responded that "It would just be one more thing to do." Instead, he suggested that they might want to look as a family at some ways to lessen Janet's load. Both Mrs. Penn and Janet seemed open to this, and so he suggested that they schedule a meeting in 2 weeks to discuss the results of Mrs. Penn's medical exam and neuropsychological assessment, and then afterwards, set up a family meeting. Janet agreed, and Mrs. Penn nodded that she would participate. (See Belgrave, 1998, regarding the extended family as a resource with African American clients.)

Case Formulation and Diagnosis

Following the medical examination, which found nothing new, and the neuropsychological assessment, which found mild impairments in concentration, short-term memory, insight, judgment, and initiation, Robert recognized that there were several possible explanations for Mrs. Penn's presentation and Janet's complaints. Beginning with the DSM-IV format, he listed the salient ADDRESSING influences in Mrs. Penn's life on the new Cultural Axis VI (Table 10.1). He also made an ADDRESSING outline for Mrs. Penn's family (Table 10.2). He then noted the following events under Axis IV: Psychosocial and Environmental Problems: the loss of her own home and previous independence, the move to her daughter's home, the loss of daily contact with her friends and church, and the absence of meaningful activity such as work. On Axis III he noted Mrs. Penn's diabetes and stroke.

Next, on Axis I, Robert recorded: Relational Problem related to a Mental Disorder or General Medical Condition (V61.9), referring to the strained relationship between Mrs. Penn and Janet. Diagnosing Mrs. Penn's behavioral and cognitive deficits was more complicated. Clearly, Mrs. Penn's functioning was moderately impaired compared with her pre-stroke baseline, when she was retired but ran her own household, and maintained a moderately active social life. Although Robert believed that the cumulative effects of stressors over the past few years were contributing to her current difficulties, he did not diagnose an Adjustment Disorder, because the most recent behavioral symptoms had not begun within three months of the stressors.

Similarly, he did not diagnose Dysthymia, because Mrs. Penn's attitude toward life seemed an appropriate adaptation given the hardships she had experienced since a young age. Robert decided to diagnose Mrs. Penn with a Major Depressive Disorder, based on the family's report that her poor self-care and apathetic behavior had begun or increased in the past few months, and on his own knowledge that depression can cause the kind of concentration and memory problems she was having. Robert was aware that Depression should not be diagnosed if the symptoms are related to a medical condition; however, the relationship in this case was not clear (and it was a greater risk to not treat for Depression—see National Institute of Health Consensus Development Panel on Depression in Late Life, 1992).

At the same time, Robert recognized that Mrs. Penn's impaired judgment and insight were not well-explained by this diagnosis. Because he did not feel comfortable in diagnosing a Vascular Dementia at this point, he noted on Axis I "the presence of mild to moderate cognitive impairments, which may be related to effects of the depression, cerebrovascular disease, stroke, and/or diabetes." Before diagnosing a Vascular Dementia, it seemed prudent to see if counseling, family interventions, and antidepressant medication could lift

TABLE 10.1.	

Mrs. Penn's Diagnosis

DSM-IV Axis	Diagnosis as Formulated by Robert
Axis I	296.32 Major Depressive Disorder, recurrent, moderate V61.9 Relational Problem related to a Mental Disorder or General Medical Condition (daughter's complaints) Mild to moderate cognitive impairments with etiology unclear (possibly related to depression, cerebrovascular disease, stroke, and/or diabetes).
Axis II	V71.09 No Disorder
[a]Axis III	Insulin-dependent diabetes mellitus; CVA (stroke) 2 years ago with residual left leg weakness and possible cognitive impairments
[b]Axis IV	Problems with Primary Support (adjustment to daughter's home) Problems related to Social Environment (loss of daily contact with church, neighbors, and friends; loss of own home and previous independence; no meaningful activity/work)
Axis V	GAF = 50 (current) GAF = 85 (estimated baseline prior to 2 years ago)
[c]Axis VI	Age and /generational influences: Grew up as an African American in the South (Tennessee) during the Depression, severe poverty, oppressive conditions. Attended segregated schools. Developmental and acquired Disabilities: Stroke 2 years ago, with recovery except for residual left leg weakness and possible cognitive impairments. Religion and spiritual orientation: Parents both Christians. Mrs. Penn was an active member of a Baptist church until her stroke and subsequent move to Janet's house. Ethnicity: Both parents African American. Socioeconomic status: Grew up with severe poverty. As an adult, with her second husband, had a lower middle-class income. Currently living on family income, including own pension and Social Security. Sexual orientation: Heterosexual. Indigenous heritage: None. National origin: Born and reared in United States; English is first language. Gender: Woman, youngest child in a family of three daughters. Mother died when Mrs. Penn was 14. Married twice, two daughters. Role as the family's grandmother involved "active authority" (therapist's words) before the stroke and move to Janet's, but not since.

[a]Complete this Axis third.   [b]Complete this Axis second.   [c]Complete this Axis first.

TABLE 10.2.	
ADDRESSING Outline for the Family	
Cultural Influences	**Mrs. Penn's Family**
Age and /generational influences	Four-generation African American family, lifetimes spanning 1920's to 2000.
Developmental and acquired **D**isabilities	Only family member with disability is Mrs. Penn (left leg weakness and cognitive impairments related to stroke).
Religion and spiritual orientation	Christian. Mrs. Penn grew up and brought up her daughters in a non-denominational African American church. As adults, she and Janet attended a Baptist church. No other family involvement or interest.
Ethnicity	African American.
Socioeconomic status	Current household middle-class with three incomes: Janet's, Jim's, and Mrs. Penn's pension and supplemental security income. Laura and her children are lower socioeconomic status and live in a poor neighborhood.
Sexual orientation	Adults are heterosexual.
Indigenous heritage	Native American grandfather on Jim's side of the family, but little connection to this heritage.
National origin	Born and reared in United States.
Gender	Household includes three adult women, one adult man, and a baby girl. Extended family is larger, including Mrs. Penn's younger daughter, her two boys, and Mrs. Penn's two sisters. Gender roles are relatively fluid; Jim shares cleaning responsibilities with Janet and their daughter and watches his granddaughter when the women go out; Laura expects her boys to help with dinner, cleaning, and laundry.Women are expected to work outside the home; —Mrs. Penn, Janet, and Laura do so; Janet's daughter is looking for a job.

the depression, in which case the cognitive impairments might improve; if they did not, at least Mrs. Penn might feel better.

During the second assessment meeting with Mrs. Penn and Janet, Robert recommended that Mrs. Penn begin anti-depressant medication again and return weekly for half-hour meetings for the next 6 months. Although within himself he was pessimistic about Mrs. Penn complying with the medication recommendation (given her history of non-compliance with anti-depressants and her diet) he hoped that closer monitoring via counseling sessions might reinforce its importance. At the same time, he felt a positive connection with Mrs. Penn, who seemed, even with her subdued manner, to enjoy the extra attention. Robert expected that as their rapport continued to grow, she might benefit from talking about her life, current difficulties, and strengths.

Individual Therapy With Mrs. Penn

Robert had recently learned about a therapeutic approach known as life review therapy, through which older clients are helped to look back on their lives, remember, and talk about events and relationships (Lewis & Butler, 1974). One goal of this reminiscing is for clients to become more accepting of their decisions, because the choices they made in the past led to the experiences that have shaped who they are in the present. The process of integrating one's past experiences with the present can be facilitated by creating a book filled with photographs, drawings, news clippings, pressed flowers, writings, and poems, along with any other forms of documentation that the client considers meaningful (Butler, Lewis, & Sunderland, 1998).

Robert was interested in trying this collaborative intervention with Mrs. Penn. He believed that it would provide some structure to his sessions with her, and he saw it as a way to affirm her life. He also saw the benefits to her family, for whom this documentation might provide a deeper appreciation of Mrs. Penn and a reminder of their family's history to pass on to younger generations. Mrs. Penn and Janet appeared only mildly interested in the idea, but said they would be willing to try it.

Over the next few weeks, Mrs. Penn did engage in the verbal review of her life. However, she never brought in pictures or any other mementoes, despite Robert's reminders. After 4 weeks, Robert realized that Mrs. Penn either did not want to or simply could not do such a project, given her cognitive deficits and apathy. Expecting Janet to bring in items would simply add to Janet's workload.

Recognizing that the impetus for the project was coming from his assumption that the family would value it as much as he did, Robert let go of the documentation piece of this particular intervention. However, he continued the life review process verbally with Mrs. Penn, whose mood seemed to lift slightly by the end of the second month (possibly also due in part to the antidepressants, which she was taking more regularly). However, no improvement occurred in her "resigned" attitude, her activity level, or her memory difficulties. Robert now believed that these problems were due to an inseparable combination of previous personality tendencies, stressful life events, and a mild dementia related to the stroke.

Intergenerational Family Therapy

Recognizing that Janet's needs had not yet been addressed, Robert worked with Janet to schedule and invite all members to the family meeting they had discussed. This meeting turned into three sessions, which were attended by Mrs. Penn, Janet and her husband Jim, their daughter Clarisse and the daughter's child, Mrs. Penn's younger daughter Laura, and Laura's twin 15-year-old sons. Mrs. Penn's sisters couldn't attend, but Janet and Laura both promised to talk with them about the sessions. (See Figure 10.2 for a genogram.)

Members took turns expressing their concern about Mrs. Penn and Janet, but the support for Janet was particularly striking, as her family sympathetically noted that "she

FIGURE 10.2.

Genogram: Mrs. Penn & Family

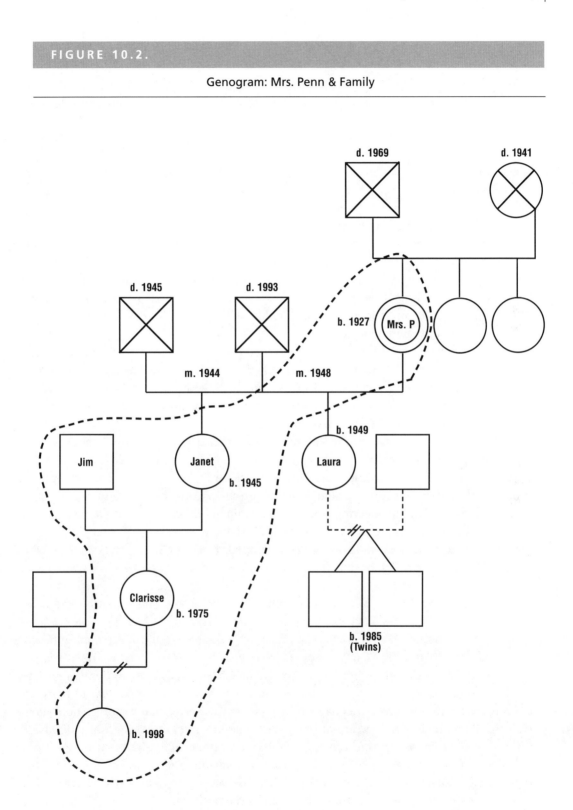

tries to take on everything." Each person subsequently volunteered for a small task that Janet had previously assumed (e.g., taking Mrs. Penn to have her eyes and glasses checked, picking up medications at the pharmacy, making sure that there were fresh vegetables cut up for snacks). Robert was impressed by the family's willingness to "come through" for Janet, and his statements to this effect clearly pleased the family.

One deeply meaningful experience occurred for Janet during the second session, when Laura explained her lesser involvement in Mrs. Penn's care: "When Mother is with me, she always talks about Janet, how responsible Janet is, how great it is living with Janet, and how well Janet takes care of her. So I just always figured Janet didn't need my help. I know Janet gets mad at me for letting Mother eat candy and not take baths, but I want Mother to enjoy her time with me, too."

Janet was clearly surprised by this revelation, which indicated that Mrs. Penn was saying things to one about the other that made both Laura and Janet feel as though they could never do enough. Janet then shared how their mother referred to Laura as "her baby," talked about how nice Laura was to her, and said, "Laura lets me eat what I want." At this point, Mrs. Penn appeared uncomfortable, but she could not or would not engage in a discussion of her behavior.

However, the shared information clearly decreased the tension between Laura and Janet. Later, Janet reported that she and Laura began talking on the telephone more often. She described their conversations about Mrs. Penn as having shifted to "comparing notes instead of competing." The improvement in their relationship was a significant move forward in the family's functioning overall.

Unfortunately, the family's practical support for Janet lasted only about 2 months, after which time, individuals, with the exception of her husband Jim, began forgetting their commitments or simply letting Janet take the tasks on again. Rather than lament the "irresponsibility" of her family members, Robert chose to reframe the situation more positively. In an individual meeting with Janet, he told her that although it seemed difficult for the family to maintain their extra efforts, it was good to know that they could be there for her in a crisis, as they had clearly demonstrated. But now it was up to Janet, who admitted to being more responsible than was always necessary, to figure out a way to take on less in her day-to-day life.

Recognizing Janet's time and financial constraints, he recommended that he and Janet meet individually for 8 sessions to talk about her needs during the 45 minutes following his 30-minute sessions with Mrs. Penn. Because meeting with Janet on this subject could ethically be framed as part of helping Mrs. Penn, her time could be billed under Mrs. Penn's insurance.

Two main themes emerged in therapy with Janet. The first concerned her tendency to "take on too much." Janet came to understand her behavior in the context of her own upbringing; her mother and father had worked hard and expected her to share in household responsibilities, including the care of her younger sister. Janet and Robert also discussed how her tendencies were reinforced as an adult, for example, at work. As the only African American woman in her office, she knew that she was often seen, as she put it, "as the representative Black woman." She believed that she had had to work twice as hard as her White counterparts to reach and keep her managerial position.

Robert affirmed her experiences but also challenged Janet's often unrealistic standards for herself, as well as her assumption that she "must *always* be responsible and hard-working" to avoid disappointing others. As she learned to recognize the automatic thoughts that were contributing to overwhelming feelings of anxiety and guilt, she was able to change these cognitions to more helpful ones (see A. T. Beck, Rush, Shaw, & Emery, 1979; J. S. Beck, 1995.)

The second theme involved Janet's sense of herself as a spiritual person. She told Robert that during the past few years, she felt like she had "lost that part of myself." She'd become so busy that it was easier to sleep on Sundays than go to church, and she no longer prayed. Using cognitive–behavioral strategies here also, Janet was able to let go of the guilt she felt. But Robert helped her go a bit further by asking her several questions about her spirituality, which included

   a. What are your three greatest sources of strength?
   b. When you want to feel comforted, where do you go, or whom do you see?
   c. In one sentence, how would you describe the purpose of your life?
   d. How would you respond to someone who said, "Do you believe in God?"
   e. Do you believe in any kind of existence after this life? (Smith, 1995, p. 179)

These questions led Janet to talk about what her "soul needed," which included "more quiet time, in a park or by some trees, and to start praying again." She also said that she would like to find a book from which she could read an encouraging idea every morning. She had done this in the past and had liked carrying the hopeful idea or thought with her throughout the day.

Over the next few weeks, Janet talked with Robert about the importance of these needs and how she might begin to meet them. With his encouragement, she began attending church again, taking her mother with her, and the two of them would go to the park for a little while afterward. Janet also began getting up half an hour earlier to read one passage a day from a prayer book. At the end of 3 months, her schedule had not changed dramatically, but she felt more in control and hopeful about the future.

Conclusion

As the situation of Mrs. Penn and her family illustrates, culturally responsive therapy can be a complex endeavor. Clearly, Robert's previous knowledge of African American culture and his professional experience with elders, (including those with disabilities,) enabled him to establish rapport, ask relevant questions, and obtain the necessary information. In turn, his assessment and diagnosis laid the groundwork for culturally responsive interventions. His familiarity with different theories and therapies enabled him to choose what would work best for his individual clients and their family system (i.e., life review, cognitive–behavioral and family systems therapies, and even a spiritual orientation). Finally, his collaborative and flexible approach facilitated therapy, particularly when something did not work (e.g., the documentation piece of the life review). In sum, Robert's assessment, diagnosis, and interventions were culturally responsive and, even more importantly, helpful.

Conclusion: Addressing the Other in Each of Us

11

"The challenges are great, our knowledge is quite limited. In every situation, we have as much to learn and receive from others as we have to share with them."
                                                        —Kenneth Maton (2000, p. 50)

The day after I began thinking about this final chapter, I was on a flight to Alaska. As the plane was taking off, I heard an angry voice and leaned forward to see what was going on. In the seats directly in front of me were an (apparently) Euroamerican couple in their early 60s who looked like they were from the Midwest. (Earlier, I had heard them say that this was their first visit to Alaska.) The wife was sitting by the window, and her husband was in the middle seat. Next to him, in the aisle seat, was a stylishly dressed young woman whom I guessed to be American Indian, from Los Angeles or San Francisco. This woman was angrily saying to the man, "No, that's wrong. It's just wrong." I couldn't hear the man, but hypothesized that he had just made some well-intentioned comment about American Indian people that had offended her. They kept talking, and I heard her say something about "fishing rights . . . the American people don't know what really goes on." I hypothesized further that she was a newly appointed professor (i.e., not burned out) of American Indian studies at the University of California. At some point, the wife pretended to be taking a nap, but occasionally she would lean forward to add some benign comment like, "Well, you know, there's just good and bad in all cultures."

Now, what subsequently amazed me about this interaction was not what they were talking about, but rather, that these two people were talking at all. Although I was uncomfortable with the angry tone in the woman's voice, I identified more with her. As the conversation continued, I thought to myself, "Why is she putting so much energy into educating this one guy?" After his initial comment, I would have said something polite to indicate my disagreement, and then started reading a book. But she stayed in there, and

189

so did he, and to his credit, I never heard him get defensive in response to her anger. By the end of the flight, something had shifted, and they were laughing and sharing details about their children. When we landed, they gave each other their names, shook hands, and wished each other a good stay.

While admiring these two people, I thought to myself, yes, this is what it's all about— that two people who have extremely different upbringings, identities, and views of the world can come together, interact, learn from each other, and even appreciate one another.

A Word About Conflict

The difficult thing about the field of multicultural studies (in psychology, counseling, social work, or any other discipline) is the conflict that so naturally arises. Diversity brings multiple perspectives, and multiple perspectives often lead to conflict. I suspect that this is one of the reasons why people who are not professionally engaged in this work tend to avoid the topics of racism, sexism, homophobia, and so on. Because one can so easily offend another person, even by one's choice of terms, the simplest solution often appears to be avoidance.

But as therapists, we do not have the option of ignoring cultural influences. If we are to work effectively with people of diverse identities, we must learn to deal with difference and conflict in ways that do not simply reinforce dominant power structures, but rather, empower and show respect for one another. In the preceding chapters, I have explained most of what I know about this work. The only additional point I would make here is to reiterate the role of mistakes. Just as conflict is inherent in this work, so too are mistakes. The challenge is to be accepting of our fallible selves and others, but at the same time continually to be looking for biases that limit our thinking and work with clients, colleagues, and students.

Education and Training

The field of psychology has traditionally been a conservative one, supporting and supported by the values and beliefs of dominant cultural groups in the United States and Europe. The impact of Euroamerican culture is most obvious in the cultural backgrounds of psychotherapists. Not only are the vast majority of psychologists in the United States of Euroamerican heritage (Hammond & Yung, 1993), but even casual observation suggests that they are also predominantly middle-class, heterosexual, and without physical disability. And although this figure applies only to the United States, the dominance of one particular group in U.S. psychology has global implications: The questions, knowledge base, and reference points for research, education, and clinical practice are inevitably limited.

In the United States, graduate student populations are diversifying too slowly to change this imbalance in the near future. At the last census, people of color constituted

25% of the U.S. population, and this proportion was estimated to rise to about 30% by the 2000 Census (Ijima Hall, 1987). In contrast, less than 20% of graduate students in psychology are people of color; even more disturbing is the finding that in 1996 and 1997, the number of African and Latino Americans entering graduate programs in psychology dropped by 30% and 23%, respectively (Sleek, 1998).

In addition, education and training programs continue to reflect dominant cultural interests, both in the cultural homogeneity of faculty and in graduate psychology curricula. According to data collected by the American Psychological Association's Research Office, only about 9% of full-time faculty in graduate psychology programs are members of ethnic minority groups (Sleek, 1998). Although increasing attention is being given to multicultural curriculum development, most psychology departments and training programs still have a long way to go before achieving the integration of multicultural content into the core curriculum (Aponte & Aponte, 2000; D. W. Sue & D. Sue, 1999).

One of the challenges facing faculty who wish to develop an integrated curriculum is the continued lack of empirical research with people of minority identities (Ijima Hall, 1987). Research is needed that goes beyond the simplistic identification of participants' racial characteristics, to include and help us understand people who hold diverse, bicultural, and multicultural identities (e.g., see Root, 1996). Such work needs to include studies of culturally related therapies and cultural adaptations of mainstream theories (Wohl & Aponte, 2000). Moreover, it would need to offer a more global perspective. Due to the disproportionate number of publication outlets for U.S. psychologists and to the dominance of the English language in the field, "American psychology" is still, as Kagitcibasi (interviewed in Sunar, 1996) noted, "to a large extent self-contained, serving as its own reference group. So for most practical purposes, it is not open to knowledge arising elsewhere. Yet, it is exported to the world" (p. 140).

Of course, all of these problems are interactive. It is difficult to attract students of minority identities when they do not see people of their cultures reflected in the curriculum, in the student body, or among faculty and supervisors. Even when students of minority identities can be recruited, it is difficult to teach students what they need to know without a research base that includes people of diverse identities. And it is difficult to develop an empirical research base that is more inclusive and globally relevant, when a diversity of perspectives is lacking among researchers.

The encouraging part of all this is that change is happening. The number of multicultural textbooks listed in chapter 1 is a good indication of the enormous increase in interest in cultural concerns among counselors, psychologists, and social workers. The creation of organizational structures, policies, and clinical guidelines regarding cross-cultural practice by such powerful organizations as the American Psychological Association and the American Counseling Association is having an impact on recruitment practices, research publications, and graduate training (Aponte & Aponte, 2000). And as evident in the growing number of psychologists conducting research worldwide, there seems to be increasing interest in global perspectives within the field (Rosenweig, 1999).

A Summary of the ADDRESSING Framework

If there is a central point to this book, it is this: To work effectively with people of diverse identities, we must first be willing to critically examine our own value systems, beliefs, and sociocultural contexts. To understand the impact of culture on our clients and in our work, we must also understand the impact of culture on ourselves. Although in this book I have chosen to focus on practitioners, its content is equally relevant to researchers, educators, and supervisors.

The ADDRESSING framework facilitates therapists' engagement in their own cultural self-assessment by providing a broad outline of influences and related identities that therapists can use to explore their own biases. As chapters 2 and 3 explained, a therapist's cultural self-assessment is facilitated by humility, compassion, and critical thinking skills. Equally key is an understanding of the relationship of privilege to culture, and the ways in which privilege separates those who hold it from those who do not. The self-knowledge that comes with such learning is essential for understanding the dynamics in cross-cultural therapeutic relationships and in developing the ability to comfortably discuss such dynamics with clients, when appropriate. A healthy sense of humor, with awareness of the ways in which humor differs across cultures, also helps.

Although parts of the self-assessment process may occur during sessions with clients, the bulk of this work takes place outside the therapy setting. The therapist will want to engage in individually- oriented work (e.g., introspection, self-questioning, reading, some forms of research) but also seek out ways to learn from people of diverse identities. Becoming involved in culturally related community activities, reading and viewing diverse media, and developing peer-level intimate relationships offer opportunities for such interpersonal learning.

Once engaged in this ongoing self-assessment process, the next step for therapists involves learning about and understanding the diverse identities that clients hold. Here again, the ADDRESSING outline can be a helpful reminder of influences and identities to be considered, including bicultural and multicultural identities. Although information about the person-specific meanings of identity will usually come from the client, it is the therapist's responsibility to obtain knowledge of the culture-specific meanings of a client's identity outside the therapy setting.

Knowledge of clients' salient identities gives the therapist clues about how clients see the world, what they value, how they may behave in certain situations, and how they are treated by others. Such knowledge can guide the therapist in developing respectful, therapeutic relationships. Critical thinking about your own assumptions is essential in this regard, because even if you do not know the specific meanings of clients' physical gestures, eye contact, nonverbal cues, and other culturally influenced forms of communication, simply staying aware of the diversity of meanings across cultures can help you avoid inaccurate assumptions. Minimizing and explaining professional terminology, and questioning the meanings of terms used by you and the client can also help to decrease misunderstandings.

During the assessment itself, therapists can take several practical steps to increase understanding and accuracy. These include seeking out and using multiple sources of information, considering sociocultural historical events that may have affected clients during particular developmental periods in their lives, and actively looking for culturally related strengths at the individual, interpersonal, and environmental levels. Therapists will also want to ask about clients' conceptualizations of their situation, and about health care (including self-care) practices, staying aware of the diversity of beliefs across cultures and time regarding illness, health, and disability.

The use of standardized tests for assessment purposes requires careful consideration of the role of cultural bias. Whenever possible, it can be helpful to think about clients' performance ideographically, keeping in mind the difference between academic knowledge and tacit knowledge (i.e., knowledge required in clients' everyday life functioning), and comparing clients' test performance against their own past performance, rather than against the performance of others. With clients who speak English as a second language, the interpreter or cultural liaison can be a valuable source of information to aid in the development of questions that tap the skills and knowledge relevant to clients' experience and contexts.

When standardized tests must be used, the relevance of responses will be greatly enhanced by an exploration of the reasons for clients' poor test performance. Testing the limits is one of the primary methods used in this exploration; clients may be asked to look at an item again, describe what they see, answer an item without time limits, or even explain why they think they had difficulty with an item or test. Although standardized tests of personality may be helpful in raising questions and ideas for clients' consideration, their use with clients of minority identities for diagnostic purposes is problematic; careful consideration of Eurocentric biases embedded in these tests is essential.

In making a culturally responsive diagnosis, it can be helpful to add a Cultural Axis VI: ADDRESSING Influences and to list cultural influences and identities related to each of the ADDRESSING categories. Completing the cultural Axis VI first, Axis IV: Psychosocial and Environmental Problems second, and Axis III: General Medical Conditions third, facilitates a more systemic understanding of clients' presenting problems, decreasing the likelihood of an inaccurate diagnosis on Axis I and Axis II. Looking for links between clients' conceptualizations of their problems and *DSM–IV* categories, as well as explaining the meaning of one's diagnosis in language that the client understands, will enhance therapeutic work later on.

Choosing the most culturally responsive intervention requires familiarity with a broad range of culturally related helping strategies, adaptations of mainstream psychotherapies, nonverbal expressive modalities, and systems-level interventions. Choice of intervention may be facilitated by a broader conceptualization of family, a willingness to see individual members and subsystems of the family on an as-needed basis, and skill in setting goals, developing treatment plans, and deciding on interventions collaboratively with clients. When medications are a part of the intervention, it is important to stay aware of ethnic and age-related differences in metabolism and of different cultural expectations regarding the prescription and use of medicines.

The systemic perspective inherent in culturally responsive work may lead therapists to intervene at sociocultural, institutional, community, and political levels—sometimes in relation to specific clients, and other times not. Group therapy with clients of diverse majority and minority identities can be a powerful systems-level intervention, because diverse groups offer a wider range of solutions and interpersonal learning opportunities. Throughout their work with individuals, couples, families, groups, and institutions, therapists are encouraged to stay aware of power differentials between therapist and clients, and between clients and others. The ADDRESSING framework can be a helpful reminder of the various domains in which these power differences may occur.

Conclusion

I'd like to end with a story that relates to the title of this chapter. My mother grew up during the Depression and World War II. Her father was a Presbyterian minister who believed in equal opportunity, although I doubt that the term had yet been coined. The family was of Scotch–Irish, Christian descent; however, my mother believed that this was only part of her heritage. She is tall and has relatively dark skin, black hair, high cheek bones, and deep-set eyes. People sometimes think that she is part American Indian.

Once, after going to the movies, she and her father were talking about Indian people, and he said to her, "You know, you have some Indian blood in you." Another time, when they were living in the South and talking about "Negro" people, her father said, "You know, you probably have some Negro blood in you, too." And still another memory she has is of her father coming home from the war; they were talking about the horrible things being done to Jewish people, and he said, "You know, your ancestors were also Jewish." My mother took all of these comments literally (reinforced by an awareness of her appearance), and until her late teens, she truly believed that she was related to all of these groups. When she would see, read, or hear about some injustice that had occurred to someone of these cultures, she felt a strong sense of connection and empathy that has shaped her work and life.

Of course, in the broadest sense, my mother is related to each of these groups, and so are we all. The Other is in each of us, and we're all in this together. Maybe if we could believe and act on this idea more consistently, social justice would become the norm in this world.

KEY IDEAS 10.

Summary of Suggestions for Culturally Responsive Practice

1. Engage in your own ongoing cultural self-assessment through individually-oriented work (e.g., introspection, self-questioning, reading, some forms of research) and interpersonal learning (e.g., community activities, diverse media, peer-level relationships).

2. Use the ADDRESSING framework to consider the influence of culture and related areas of privilege on your identity, beliefs, and behaviors.

3. Use the ADDRESSING framework to consider cultural influences on each client's identity, beliefs, and behaviors.

4. Actively engage outside the therapy setting in learning about clients' cultural histories, to better understand their personal histories.

5. Take the time to establish rapport in a culturally congruent way.

6. Think critically about your assumptions regarding the diverse meanings of physical gestures, eye contact, and other nonverbal and verbal forms of communication, to prevent inaccurate assumptions.

7. Consider the interaction of your own identity with that of each client.

8. Seek out and use multiple sources of information regarding clients (with appropriate releases of information) for assessment purposes.

9. Consider sociocultural historical events that may have affected clients during particular developmental periods in their lives.

10. Deliberately look for culturally related strengths and supports at the individual, interpersonal, and environmental levels.

11. Use standardized tests cautiously, with consideration of their inherent cultural biases.

12. Work with interpreters or cultural liaisons to develop questions that assess skills and knowledge relevant to clients' experiences and contexts.

13. Use the method of testing the limits to explore the reasons for clients' poor test performance.

14. Make a diagnosis that takes into account the client's conceptualization of the problem.

15. Move beyond the *DSM–IV* focus on individualistic diagnoses to think systemically and consider relational disorders.

16. When using the *DSM–IV*, complete the Cultural Axis VI: ADDRESSING Influences first, Axis IV: Psychosocial and Environmental Problems second, and Axis III: General Medical Conditions third.

17. Take an eclectic approach to therapy, recognizing the possible usefulness of culturally related strategies and therapies, mainstream therapies adapted to minority cultures, nonverbal expressive therapies, and systems-level interventions.

18. Set goals, develop treatment plans, and choose interventions collaboratively with clients.

19. Use the ADDRESSING framework as a reminder of the various domains in which power differences may exist in couples and family therapy.

20. Keep in mind culturally related expectations regarding medications and ethnic and age-related differences in metabolism.

References

Abudabbeh, N. (1996). Arab families. In M. McGoldrick, J. K. Pearce, & J. Giordano (Eds.), *Ethnicity and family therapy* (pp. 333–346). New York: Guilford Press.

Acklin, F., Newman, J., Arbon, V., Trindal, A., Brock, K., Bermingham, M., Thompson, C., & Koori Elders. (1999). Story-telling: Australian Indigenous women's means of health promotion. In R. Barnhardt (Ed.), *Indigenous education around the world: Workshop papers from the 1996 World Indigenous Peoples Conference: Education* (pp. 1–10). Fairbanks: University of Alaska–Fairbanks, Center for Cross-Cultural Studies.

Acosta, F. X., Yamamoto, J., Evans, L. A., & Wilcox, S. A. (1982). Effective psychotherapy for low-income and minority patients. In F. X. Acosta, J. Yamamoto, L. A. Evans, & S. A. Wilcox (Eds.), *Effective psychotherapy for low-income and minority patients* (pp. 1–29). New York: Plenum Press.

Adams, C. E., & Gilbert, J. M. (1998). Providing effective counseling services to Australia's ethnic minority groups. *Australian Social Work, 51,* 33–39.

Adams, H. (1995). *A tortured people: The politics of colonization.* Penticton, British Columbia, Canada: Theytus Books.

Adelson, N. (2000). Re-imagining Aboriginality: An Indigenous peoples' response to social suffering. *Transcultural Psychiatry, 37,* 11–34.

Akamatsu, N. N. (1998). The talking oppression blues. In M. McGoldrick (Ed.), *Re-Visioning family therapy: Race, culture, and gender in clinical practice* (pp. 129–143). New York: Guilford Press.

Alarcón, R. D. (1997). Personality disorders and culture: Conflict at the boundaries. *Transcultural Psychiatry, 34,* 453–461.

Alarcón, R. D., & Foulks, E. F. (1995). Personality disorders and culture: Contemporary clinical views (Part A). *Cultural Diversity and Mental Health, 1,* 3–18.

Albee, G. W. (1981). Politics, power, prevention, and social change. In J. M. Joffe & G. W. Albee (Eds.), *Prevention through political action and social change* (pp. 5–25). Hanover, NH: University of New England Press.

Alexie, S. (1993). *The Lone Ranger and Tonto fistfight in heaven.* New York: Harper Collins.

Allen, J. (1998). Personality assessment with American Indians and Alaskan Natives: Instrument considerations and service delivery style. *Journal of Personality Assessment, 70,* 17–42.

Allman, K. M. (1996). (Un)Natural boundaries: Mixed race, gender, and sexuality. In M. P. P. Root (Ed.), *The multiracial experience: Racial borders as the new frontier* (pp. 277–290). Thousand Oaks, CA: Sage.

Almeida, R. (1996). Hindu, Christian, and Muslim families. In M. McGoldrick, J. Giordano, & J. K.

Pearce (Eds.), *Ethnicity and family therapy* (pp. 395–426). New York: Guilford Press.

American Psychiatric Association. (1994). *The diagnostic and statistical manual of mental disorders, fourth edition (DSM-IV)*. Washington, DC: Author.

American Psychological Association. (1992). *Revised code of ethical principles*. Washington, DC: Author.

American Psychological Association. (1993). Guidelines for providers of psychological services to ethnic, linguistic, and culturally diverse populations. *American Psychologist, 48*, 45–48.

American Psychological Association. (1996). *APA presidential task force on violence and the family report*. Washington, DC: Author.

Anastasi, A. (1992). What counselors should know about the use and interpretation of psychological tests. *Journal of Counseling and Development, 70*, 610–615.

Anderson, J. M., Waxler-Morrison, N., Richardson, E., Herbert, C., & Murphy, M. (1990). Conclusion: Delivering culturally sensitive health care. In N. Waxler-Morrison, J. Anderson, & E. Richardson (Eds.), *Cross-cultural caring: A handbook for health professionals* (pp. 245–267). Vancouver, British Columbia, Canada: University of British Columbia Press.

Andronikof-Sanglade, A. (2000). Use of the Rorschach Comprehensive System in Europe: State of the art. In R. H. Dana (Ed.), *Handbook of cross-cultural and multicultural personality assessment* (pp. 329–344). Mahwah, NJ: Lawrence Erlbaum.

Anzaldua, G. (1987). *Borderlands/La Frontera: The new mestiza*. San Francisco, CA: Aunt Lute Books.

Aponte, H. J. (1994). *Bread and spirit: Therapy with the new poor*. New York: Norton.

Aponte, J. F., & Aponte, C. E. (2000). Educating and training professionals to work with ethnic populations in the twenty-first century. In J. F. Aponte & J. Wohl (Eds.), *Psychological intervention and cultural diversity* (pp. 250–267). Needham Heights, MA: Allyn & Bacon.

Aponte, J. F., Rivers, R. Y., & Wohl, J. (Eds.). (1995). *Psychological interventions and cultural diversity*. Needham Heights, MA: Allyn & Bacon.

Ardila, A., Rosselli, M., & Puente, A. E. (1994). *Neuropsychological evaluation of the Spanish speaker*. New York: Plenum Press.

Arredondo, P., Toporek, R., Brown, S. P., Jones, J., Locke, D. C., Sanchez, J., & Stadler, H. (1996). Operationalization of the multicultural counseling competencies. *Journal of Multicultural Counseling & Development, 24*, 42–78.

Arroyo, W. (1997). Children and families of Mexican descent. In G. Johnson-Powell & J. Yamamoto (Eds.), *Transcultural child development: Psychological assessment and treatment* (pp. 290–304). New York: John Wiley & Sons.

Assanand, S., Dias, M., Richardson, E., & Waxler-Morrison, N. (1990). The South Asians. In N. Waxler-Morrison, J. Anderson, & E. Richardson (Eds.), *Cross-cultural caring: A handbook for health professionals* (pp. 141–180). Vancouver, British Columbia, Canada: University of British Columbia Press.

Atkinson, D. R., Furlong, M. J., & Poston, W. C. (1986). Afro-American preferences for counselor characteristics. *Journal of Counseling Psychology, 33*, 326–330.

Atkinson, D. R., Poston, W. C., Furlong, M. J., & Mercado, P. (1989). Ethnic group preferences for counselor characteristics. *Journal of Counseling Psychology, 36,* 68–72.

Atkinson, D., Morten, G., & Sue, D. (Eds.). (1993). *Counseling American minorities: A cross-cultural perspective.* Dubuque, IA: William C. Brown.

Atkinson, D. R., Wampold, B. E., Lowe, S. M., Matthews, L., & Ahn, H. (1998). Asian American preferences for counselor characteristics: Application of the Bradley-Terry-Luce model to paired comparison data. *Counseling Psychologist, 26,* 101–123.

Attneave, C. L. (1969). Therapy in tribal settings and urban network intervention. *Family Process, 8,* 192–210.

Azar, B. (1999). Wider path to cultural understanding: Researchers move toward a multicultural, rather than a linear, model of acculturation. *APA Monitor, 30,* 14–15.

Barakat, H. (1993). *The Arab world: Society, culture, and state.* Berkeley: University of California Press.

Baruth, L., & Manning, M. (1991). *Multicultural counseling and psychotherapy.* New York: Merrill.

Bass, B. A., Wyatt, G. E., & Powell, G. J. (1982). *The Afro-American family: Assessment, treatment, and research issues.* New York: Grune & Stratton.

Beck, A. T., Rush, A. J., Shaw, B. F., & Emery, G. (1979). *Cognitive therapy of depression.* New York: Guilford Press.

Beck, J. S. (1995). *Cognitive therapy: Basics and beyond.* New York: Guilford Press.

Belgrave, F. Z. (1998). *Psychosocial aspects of chronic illness and disability among African Americans.* Westport, CT: Auburn House/Greenwood.

Bennett, S. K., & Bigfoot-Sipes, D. S. (1991). American Indian and White college student preferences for counselor characteristics. *Journal of Counseling Psychology, 36,* 68–72.

Bergin, A. E., Payne, I. R., & Richards, P. S. (1996). Values and psychotherapy. In E. Shafranske (Ed.), *Religion and the clinical practice of psychotherapy* (pp. 297–326). Washington, DC: American Psychological Association.

Bernal, G., & Shapiro, E. (1996). Cuban families. In M. McGoldrick, J. Giordano, & J. K. Pearce (Eds.), *Ethnicity and family therapy* (pp. 155–168). New York: Guilford Press.

Bernstein, R. (1993, May 2). A growing Islamic presence: Balancing sacred and secular. *New York Times,* p. 1.

Berry, J. W. (1997). Immigration, acculturation, and adaptation. *Applied Psychology, 46,* 5–68.

Berry, J. W., Poortinga, Y. H., Segall, M. H., & Dasen, P. R. (1992). *Cross-cultural psychology: Research and applications.* New York: Cambridge University Press.

Berzoff, J., Flanagan, L. M., & Hertz, P. (1996). *Inside out and outside in: Psychodynamic clinical theory and practice in contemporary multicultural contexts.* Northvale, NJ: Jason Aronson.

Betancourt, H., & López, S. R. (1993). The study of culture, ethnicity, and race in American psychology. *American Psychologist, 48,* 629–637.

Bibb, A., & Casimir, G. J. (1996). Haitian families. In M. McGoldrick, J. K. Pearce, & J. Giordano (Eds.), *Ethnicity and family therapy* (pp. 86–111). New York: Guilford Press.

Blechman, E. A. (1984). *Behavior modification with women.* New York: Guilford Press.

Blood, P., Tuttle, A., & Lakey, G. (1995). Understanding and fighting sexism:

A call to men. In M. L. Anderson (Ed.), *Race, class and gender: An anthology* (pp. 154–161). New York: Wadsworth.

Boden, R. (1992). Psychotherapy with physically disabled lesbians. In S. H. Dworkin & F. J. Gutiérrez (Eds.), *Counseling gay men and lesbians: Journey to the end of the rainbow* (pp. 157–174). Alexandria, VA: American Counseling Association.

Boyd-Franklin, N. (1989). *Black families in therapy.* New York: Guilford Press.

Bradford, D. T., & Munoz, A. (1993). Translation in bilingual psychotherapy. *Professional Psychology: Research and Practice, 24,* 52–61.

Bradshaw, C. (1994). Asian and Asian American women: Historical and political considerations in psychotherapy. In L. Comas-Díaz & B. Greene (Eds.), *Women of color: Integrating ethnic and gender identities in psychotherapy* (pp. 72–113). New York: Guilford Press.

Brendtro, L. K., Brokenleg, M., & Van Bockern, S. (1998). *Reclaiming youth at risk: Our hope for the future.* Bloomington, IN: National Educational Service.

Brink, T. (Ed.). (1986). *Clinical gerontology: A guide to assessment and intervention.* New York: Haworth Press.

Brookfield, S. (1987). *Developing critical thinkers.* San Francisco, CA: Jossey-Bass.

Brown, D. (1997). Implications of cultural values for cross-cultural consultations with families. *Journal of Counseling and Development, 76,* 29–35.

Brown, L. S. (1990). Taking account of gender in the clinical assessment interview. *Professional Psychology: Research and Practice, 21,* 12–17.

Brown, L. S. (1994). *Subversive dialogues.* New York: Basic Books.

Brown, L., & Root, M. P. P. (Eds.). (1990). *Diversity and complexity in feminist therapy.* New York: Harrington Park Press.

Burke, M. T., & Miranti, J. G. (Eds.). (1995). *Counseling: The spiritual dimension.* Alexandria, VA: American Counseling Association.

Burlingame, V. S. (1999). *Ethnogerocounseling: Counseling ethnic elders and their families.* New York: Springer.

Butcher, J. N., Dahlstrom, W. G., Graham, J. R., Tellegen, A., & Kaemmer, B. (1989). *Minnesota Multiphasic Personality Inventory-2 (MMPI-2): Manual for administration and scoring.* Minneapolis: University of Minnesota Press.

Butler, R. N., Lewis, M., & Sunderland, T. (1998). *Aging and mental health.* New York: Allyn & Bacon.

Campbell, A., Rorie, K., Dennis, G., Wood, D., Combs, S., Hearn, L., Davis, H., Brown, A., & Weir, R. (1996). Neuropsychological assessment of African Americans: Conceptual and methodological considerations. In R. L. Jones (Ed.), *Handbook of tests and measurements for Black populations* (75–84). Hampton, VA: Cobb & Henry.

Canadian Psychological Association. (1991). *Canadian code of ethics for psychologists.* Old Chelsea, Quebec, Canada: Author.

Canino, I., Canino, G., & Arroyo, W. (1998). Cultural considerations for childhood disorders: How much was included in DSM-IV? *Transcultural Psychiatry, 35,* 343–355.

Canino, I. A., & Spurlock, J. (1994). *Culturally diverse children and adolescents: Assessment, diagnosis, and treatment.* New York: Guilford Press.

Carter, R. (1994). *Helping yourself help others: A book for caregivers.* New York: Times Books.

Cass, V. C. (1979). Homosexual identity formation: A theoretical model. *Journal of Homosexuality, 4,* 219–235.

Cervantes, R. C., Padilla, A. M., & Salgado de Snyder, N. (1990). Reliability and validity of the Hispanic Stress Inventory. *Hispanic Journal of Behavioral Sciences, 12,* 76–82.

Chan, C. S. (1992). Cultural considerations in counseling Asian American lesbians and gay men. In S. H. Dworkin & F. J. Gutiérrez (Eds.), *Counseling gay men and lesbians: Journey to the end of the rainbow* (pp. 115–124). Alexandria, VA: American Counseling Association.

Chin, J. L. (1994). Psychodynamic approaches. In L. Comas-Díaz & B. Greene (Eds.), *Women of color: Integrating ethnic and gender identities in psychotherapy* (pp. 194–222). New York: Guilford Press.

Choney, S. K., Berryhill-Paapke, E., & Robbins, R. R. (1995). The acculturation of American Indians. In J. G. Ponterotto, J. M. Casas, L. A. Suzuki, & C. M. Alexander (Eds.), *Handbook of multicultural counseling* (pp. 73–92). Thousand Oaks, CA: Sage.

Coleman, H. L. K., Wampold, B. E., & Casali, S. L. (1995). Ethnic minorities' ratings of ethnically similar and European American counselors: A meta-analysis. *Journal of Counseling Psychology, 42,* 55–64.

Comas-Díaz, L., & Greene, B. (1994a). Overview: Gender and ethnicity in the healing process. In L. Comas-Díaz & B. Greene (Eds.), *Women of color: Integrating ethnic and gender identities in psychotherapy* (pp. 185–193). New York: Guilford Press.

Comas-Díaz, L., & Greene, B. (Eds.). (1994b). *Women of color: Integrating ethnic and gender identities in psychotherapy.* New York: Guilford Press.

Connolly, W. E. (1996). Suffering, justice, and the politics of becoming. *Culture, Medicine, and Psychiatry, 20,* 251–277.

Constantine, M. G. (1999). Racism's impact on counselors' professional and personal lives: A response to the personal narratives on racism. *Journal of Counseling and Development, 77,* 68–72.

Cooper, C. C., & Gottlieb, M. C. (2000). Ethical issues with managed care: Challenges facing counseling psychology. *Counseling Psychologist, 28,* 179–236.

Corey, G. (1995). *Theory and practice of group counseling.* Pacific Grove, CA: Brooks/Cole.

Costantino, G., Malgady, R. G. (2000). Multicultural and cross-cultural utility of the TEMAS (Tell-Me-A-Story) Test. In R. H. Dana (Ed.), *Handbook of cross-cultural and multicultural personality assessment* (pp. 481–513). Mahwah, NJ: Lawrence Erlbaum.

Costantino, G., Malgady, R. G., & Rogler, L. H. (1988). *TEMAS (Tell-Me-a-Story) manual.* Los Angeles: Western Psychological Services.

Costantino, G., Flanagan, R., & Malgady, R. (1995). The history of the Rorschach: Overcoming bias in multicultural projective assessment. *Rorschachiana: Yearbook of the International Rorschach Society, 20,* 148–171.

Costantino, G., Malgady, R., & Vasquez, C. (1981). A comparison of the Murray-TAT and a new thematic apperception test for urban Hispanic children. *Hispanic Journal of Behavioral Science, 3,* 291–300.

Cox, D. R. (1989). *Welfare practice in a multicultural society.* Sydney: Prentice-Hall of Australia.

Criddle, J. (1992). *Bamboo and butterflies: From refugee to citizen.* Dixon, CA: East/West Bridge.

Croteau, J. M. (1999). One struggle through individualism: Toward an antiracist White racial identity. *Journal of Counseling and Development, 77,* 30–32.

Cruikshank, J. (1990). *Life lived like a story: Life stories of three Yukon Native elders.* Lincoln: University of Nebraska Press.

Cuéllar, I. (1998). Cross-cultural clinical psychological assessment of Hispanic Americans. *Journal of Personality Assessment, 70,* 71–86.

Cuéllar, I. (2000). Acculturation as a moderator of personality and psychological assessment. In R. H. Dana (Ed.), *Handbook of cross-cultural and multicultural personality assessment* (pp. 113–129). Mahwah, NJ: Erlbaum.

Cummings, J. L., & Benson, D. F. (1992). *Dementia: A clinical approach.* (2nd Ed.). Boston: Butterworth-Heinemann.

Dana, R. H. (1993). *Multicultural assessment perspectives for professional psychology.* New York: Allyn & Bacon.

Dana, R. H. (1994). Testing and assessment ethics for all persons: Beginning and agenda. *Professional Psychology: Research and Practice, 25,* 349–354.

Dana, R. H. (1997). Multicultural assessment and cultural identity: An assessment-intervention model. *World Psychology, 3,* 121–141.

Dana, R. H. (1998). Cultural identity assessment of culturally diverse groups: 1997. *Journal of Personality Assessment, 70,* 1–16.

Dana, R. H. (1999). Cross-cultural–multicultural use of the Thematic Apperception Test. In L. Geiser & M. I. Stein (Eds.), *Evocative images: The Thematic Apperception Test and the art of projection* (pp. 177–190). Washington, DC: American Psychological Association.

Dana, R. H. (2000a). An assessment-intervention model for research and practice with multicultural populations. In R. H. Dana (Ed.), *Handbook of cross-cultural and multicultural personality assessment* (pp. 5–16). Mahwah, NJ: Lawrence Erlbaum.

Dana, R. H. (2000b). Culture and methodology in personality assessment. In I. Cuéllar & F. A. Paniagua (Eds.), *Handbook of multicultural mental health: Assessment and treatment of diverse populations.* (pp. 79–120). San Diego, CA: Academic Press.

Dana, R. H. (Ed.) (2000c). *Handbook of cross-cultural and multicultural personality assessment.* Mahwah, NJ: Lawrence Erlbaum.

D'Andrea, M. (1999, May). Alternative needed for the DSM-IV in a multicultural-postmodern society. *Counseling Today,* 44–46.

Darling, B. (1996). *Foundations of solution-focused therapy.* Unpublished manuscript, Antioch University, Seattle, WA.

Das, A. K. (1987). Indigenous models of therapy in traditional Asian societies. *Journal of Multicultural Counseling and Development, 15,* 25–37.

Dator, J. (1979). The futures of culture or cultures of the future. In A. J. Marsella, R. G. Tharp, & T. J. Ciborowski (Eds.), *Perspectives on cross-cultural psychology* (pp. 369–388). New York: Academic Press.

Davidson, G. (1995). Cognitive assessment of Indigenous Australians:

Towards a multiaxial model. *Australian Psychologist, 30*, 30–34.

Davis, H. (1993). *Counselling parents of children with chronic illness or disability.* Leicester, England: British Psychological Society.

Del Castillo, J. C. (1970). The influence of language upon symptomatology in foreign-born patients. *American Journal of Psychiatry, 127*, 242–244.

Department of Social and Health Services, State of Washington. (1999). *Language interpreter services and translations: Professional language certification examination manual (update: January 1999).* Olympia, WA: Author.

deShazer, S. (1985). *Keys to solution in brief therapy.* New York: Norton.

DeSilva, P. (1993). Buddhist psychology: A therapeutic perspective. In U. Kim & J. W. Berry (Eds.), *Indigenous psychologies* (pp. 221–239). Newbury Park, CA: Sage.

Dobson, K., & Dobson, D. (Eds.). (1993). *Professional psychology in Canada.* Seattle, WA: Hogrefe & Huber.

Downing, N. E., & Roush, K. L. (1985). From passive acceptance to active commitment: A model of feminist identity development of women. *Counseling Psychologist, 13*, 59–72.

Duffy, M. (1986). The techniques and contexts of multigenerational therapy. In T. Brink (Ed.), *Clinical gerontology: A guide to assessment and interventions* (pp. 347–362). New York: Haworth Press.

Duffy, M. (Ed.). (1999). *Handbook of counseling and psychotherapy with older adults.* New York: John Wiley & Sons.

Dworkin, S., & Gutiérrez, F. J. (Eds.). (1992). *Counseling gay men and lesbians: Journey to the end of the rainbow.* Alexandria, VA: American Counseling Association.

Ebigbo, P. O., Oluka, J. I., Ezenwa, M. O., Obidigbo, G. C., & Okwaraji, F. E. (1996). Clinical psychology in sub-Saharan Africa. *World Psychology, 2*, 87–100.

Eisman, E. J., Dies, R. R., Finn, S. E., Eyde, L. D., Kay, G.G., Kubiszyn, T. W., Meyer, G. J., & Moreland, K. L. (2000). Problems and limitations in using psychological assessment in the contemporary health care delivery system. *Professional Psychology: Research and Practice, 31*, 131–140.

El-Islam, F. (1982). Arabic cultural psychiatry. *Transcultural Psychiatric Research Review, 19*, 5–24.

Elliott, J. E., & Fleras, A. (1992). *Unequal relations: An introduction to race and ethnic dynamics in Canada.* Scarborough, Ontario: Prentice-Hall Canada.

Ellis, A. (1997). Using rational emotive behavior therapy techniques to cope with disability. *Professional Psychology: Research and Practice, 28*, 17–22.

Ephraim, D. (2000). Culturally relevant research and practice with the Rorschach Comprehensive System. In R. H. Dana (Ed.), *Handbook of cross-cultural and multicultural personality assessment* (pp. 303-328). Mahwah, NJ: Lawrence Erlbaum.

Escobar, J. I., Burman, A., Karno, M., Forsythe, A., Landsverk, J., & Golding, J. M. (1986). Use of the Mini-Mental State Examination (MMSE) in a community population of mixed ethnicity. *Journal of Nervous and Mental Disease, 174*, 607–614.

Fadiman, A. (1997). *The spirit catches you and you fall down.* New York: Farrar, Strauss & Giroux.

Falicov, C. J. (1995). Cross-cultural marriages. In N. S. Jacobson & A. S. Gurman (Eds.), *Clinical handbook of couple therapy* (pp. 231–246). New York: Guilford Press.

Falicov, C. J. (1996). Mexican families. In M. McGoldrick, J. K. Pearce, & J. Giordano (Eds.), *Ethnicity and family therapy* (pp. 169–182). New York: Guilford Press.

Falicov, C. J. (1998). *Latino families in therapy.* New York: Guilford Press.

Farley, N. (1992). Same-sex domestic violence. In S. H. Dworkin & F. J. Gutiérrez (Eds.), *Counseling gay men and lesbians: Journey to the end of the rainbow* (pp. 231–244). Alexandria, VA: American Counseling Association.

Fernea, E. W., & Bezirgan, B. Q. (1977). Introduction. In E. W. Fernea & B. Q. Bezirgan (Eds.), *Middle Eastern Muslim women* (pp. xvi–xxxvi). Austin: University of Texas Press.

Fiore, J., Coppel, D. B., Becker, J., & Cox, G. B. (1986). Social support as a multi-faceted concept: Examination of important dimensions for adjustment. *American Journal of Community Psychology, 14,* 93–111.

Fish, J. (1996). *Culture and therapy: An integrative approach.* Northvale, NJ: Jason Aronson.

Fiske, S. (1993). Controlling other people: The impact of power on stereotyping. *American Psychologist, 48,* 621–628.

Flanagan, L. M. (1996). Object relations theory. In J. Berzoff, L. M. Flanagan, & P. Hertz (Eds.), *Inside out and outside in: Psychodynamic clinical theory and practice in contemporary multicultural contexts* (pp. 127–171). Northvale, NJ: Jason Aronson.

Follette, W. C. (1996). Introduction to the special section on the development of theoretically coherent alternatives to the DSM system. *Journal of Consulting and Clinical Psychology, 64,* 1117–1119.

Folstein, M., Anthony, J. E., Parhad, I., Duffy, B., & Gruenberg, E. M. (1985). The meaning of cognitive impairment in the elderly. *Journal of the American Geriatrics Society, 33,* 228–235.

Fowers, B. J., Tredinnick, M., & Applegate, B. (1997). Individualism and counseling: An empirical examination of the prevalence of individualistic values in psychologists' responses to case vignettes. *Counseling and Values, 41,* 204–218.

Frager, R., & Fadiman, J. (1998). *Personality and personal growth.* New York: Longman.

Fukuyama, M. (1990). Taking a universal approach to multicultural counseling. *Counselor Education and Supervision, 30,* 6–17.

Fukuyama, M. A., & Sevig, T. D. (1999). *Integrating spirituality into multicultural counseling.* Thousand Oaks, CA: Sage.

Gaines, S. O., & Reed, E. S. (1995). Prejudice: From Allport to DuBois. *American Psychologist, 50,* 96–103.

Garcia-Preto, N. (1996). Latino families: An overview. In M. McGoldrick, J. K. Pearce, & J. Giordano (Eds.), *Ethnicity and family therapy* (pp. 141–154). New York: Guilford Press.

Gatz, M. (1994). Application of assessment to therapy and intervention with older adults. In M. Storandt & G. R. VandenBos (Eds.), *Neuropsychological assessment of dementia and depression in older adults: A clinician's guide* (pp. 155–176). Washington, DC: American Psychological Association.

Gaughen, K. J. S., & Gaughen, D. K. (1996). The Native Hawaiian (Kanaka Maoli) client. In P. B.

Pedersen & D. C. Locke (Eds.), *Cultural and diversity issues in counseling* (pp. 33–36). Greensboro, NC: School of Education, University of North Carolina at Greensboro. ERIC Counseling and Student Services Clearinghouse, ERIC no. ED400486.

Geisinger, K. (1992). *Psychological testing of Hispanics.* Washington, DC: American Psychological Association.

Gibbs, J. T., Huang, N., & Associates. (1989). *Children of color: Psychological interventions with minority youth.* San Francisco, CA: Jossey-Bass.

Glasgow, J. H., & Adaskin, E. J. (1990). The West Indians. In N. Waxler-Morrison, J. Anderson, & E. Richardson (Eds.), *Cross-cultural caring: A handbook for health professionals* (pp. 214–244). Vancouver, British Columbia, Canada: University of British Columbia Press.

Glass, R. D., & Wallace, K. R. (1996). Challenging race and racism: A framework for educators. In M. P. P. Root (Ed.), *The multiracial experience* (pp. 341–358). Thousand Oaks, CA: Sage.

Gleave, D., & Manes, A. S. (1990). The Central Americans. In N. Waxler-Morrison, J. Anderson, & E. Richardson (Eds.), *Cross-cultural caring: A handbook for health professionals* (pp. 36–67). Vancouver, British Columbia, Canada: University of British Columbia Press.

Goldin, E., & Bordan, T. (1999). The use of humor in counseling: The laughing cure. *Journal of Counseling & Development, 77,* 405–410.

Goldstein, S. (2000). *Cross-cultural explorations: Activities in culture and psychology.* Needham Heights, MA: Allyn & Bacon.

Gonzales, A., & Zimbardo, P. G. (1985, March). Time in perspective. *Psychology Today,* pp. 21–26.

Good, B. J. (1996). Culture and DSM-IV: Diagnosis, knowledge and power. *Culture, Medicine and Psychiatry, 20,* 127–132.

Gopaul-McNicol, S. A. (1993). *Working with West Indian families.* New York: Guilford Press.

Graham, J. (1990). MMPI-2: *Assessing personality and psychopathology.* New York: Oxford University Press.

Greenberg, S., & Motenko, A. K. (1994). Women growing older: Partnerships for change. In M. P. Mirken (Ed.), *Women in context* (pp. 96–117). New York: Guilford Press.

Greene, B. (1994.) Lesbian women of color: Triple jeopardy. In L. Comas-Díaz & B. Greene (Eds.), *Women of color: Integrating ethnic and gender identities in psychotherapy* (pp. 389–427). New York: Guilford Press.

Greene, B. (1997). *Ethnic and cultural diversity among lesbians and gay men.* Thousand Oaks, CA: Sage.

Greene, R. (1986). The functional-age model of intergenerational therapy: A social casework model. In. T. Brink (Ed.), *Clinical gerontology: A guide to assessment and interventions* (pp. 335–346). New York: Haworth Press.

Greene, R. L., Gwin, R., & Staal, M. (1997). Current status of MMPI-2 research: A methodologic overview. *Journal of Personality Assessment, 68,* 20–36.

Greenfield, P. (1997). You can't take it with you: Why ability assessments don't cross cultures. *American Psychologist, 52,* 1115–1124.

Greenwood, S. (2000). International community psychology: Reflections on the anti-racism classroom. *Community Psychologist, 33,* 30–32.

Grier, W., & Cobbs, P. (1968). *Black rage.* New York: Basic Books.

Griffin-Pierce, T. (1997). "When I am lonely the mountains call me": The impact of sacred geography on Navajo psychological well-being. *American Indian and Alaskan Native Mental Health Research, 7,* 1–10.

Gutiérrez, F. J., & Dworkin, S. (1992). Gay, lesbian, and African American: Managing the integration of identities. In S. H. Dworkin & F. J. Gutiérrez (Eds.), *Counseling gay men and lesbians: Journey to the end of the rainbow* (pp. 141–156). Alexandria, VA: American Counseling Association.

Haley, J. (1963). *Strategies of psychotherapy.* New York: Grune & Stratton.

Halila, S. (1984). From Koranic law to civil law: Emancipation of Tunisian women since 1956. *Feminist Issues, 4,* 23–44.

Hall, E. T. (1966). *The hidden dimension.* New York: Doubleday.

Hamilton, D. L. (1981). Some thoughts on the cognitive approach. In D. L. Hamilton (Ed.), *Cognitive processes in stereotyping and intergroup behavior* (pp. 333–353). Hillsdale, NJ: Erlbaum.

Hamilton, D. L., & Trolier, T. K. (1986). In J. F. Dovidio & S. L. Gaertner (Eds.), *Prejudice, discrimination and racism* (pp. 127–163). New York: Academic Press.

Hammond, L. C., & Gantt, L. (1998). Using art in counseling: Ethical considerations. *Journal of Counseling and Development, 76,* 271–276.

Hammond, W. R., & Yung, B. (1993). Minority student recruitment and retention practices among schools of professional psychology: A national survey and analysis. *Professional Psychology: Research and Practice, 24,* 3–12.

Handel, R. W., & Ben-Porath, Y. S. (2000). Multicultural assessment with the MMPI-2: Issues for research and practice. In R. H. Dana (ed.), *Handbook of cross-cultural and multicultural personality assessment* (pp. 229–245). Mahwah, NJ: Lawrence Erlbaum.

Hanh, T. N. (1992). *Touching peace: Practicing the art of mindful living.* Berkeley, CA: Parallax Press.

Hanser, S. B. (1999). Using music therapy in treating psychological problems of older adults. In M. Duffy (Ed.), *Handbook of counseling and psychotherapy with older adults* (pp. 197–213). New York: John Wiley & Sons.

Hays, P. A. (1987). *Modernization, stress, and psychopathology in Tunisian women.* Unpublished doctoral dissertation, University of Hawaii, Honolulu (University Microfilms International No. 8722387).

Hays, P. A. (1995). Multicultural applications of cognitive behavior therapy. *Professional Psychology: Research & Practice, 26,* 309–315.

Hays, P. A. (1996a). Addressing the complexities of culture and gender in counseling. *Journal of Counseling & Development, 74,* 332–338.

Hays, P. A. (1996b). Cultural considerations in couples therapy. *Women and Therapy, 19,* 13–23.

Hays, P. A. (1996c). Culturally responsive assessment with diverse older clients. *Professional Psychology: Research & Practice, 27,* 188–193.

Hays, P. A., & Zouari, J. (1995). Stress, coping, and mental health among rural, village, and urban women in Tunisia. *International Journal of Psychology, 30,* 69–90.

Helms, J. E. (1995). An update of Helms's white and people of color racial identity models. In J. Ponterotto, J. M. Casas, L. A. Suzuki, & C.

M. Alexander (Eds.), *Handbook of multicultural counseling* (pp. 181–198). Thousand Oaks, CA: Sage.

Henley, N. M. (1995). Ethnicity and gender issues in language. In H. Landrine (Ed.), *Bringing cultural diversity to feminist psychology* (pp. 361–396). Washington, DC: American Psychological Association.

Heppner, M. J., & O'Brien, K. M. (1994). Multicultural counselor training: Students' perceptions of helpful and hindering events. *Counselor Education and Supervision, 34,* 4–18.

Herman, J. (1997). *Trauma and recovery.* New York: Basic Books.

Hermans, H. J. M., & Kempen, H. J. G. (1998). Moving cultures: The perilous problem of cultural dichotomies in a globalizing society. *American Psychologist, 53,* 1111–1120.

Hernandez, M. (1996). Central American families. In M. McGoldrick, J. Giordano, & J. K. Pearce (Eds.), *Ethnicity and family therapy* (pp. 214–224). New York: Guilford Press.

Herring, R. (1999). *Counseling with Native American Indians and Alaskan Natives.* Thousand Oaks, CA: Sage.

Hertzberg, J. F. (1990). Feminist psychotherapy and diversity: Treatment considerations from a self psychology perspective. In L. S. Brown & M. P. P. Root (Eds.), *Diversity and complexity in feminist therapy* (pp. 275–298). Binghamton, NY: Haworth Press.

Hinrichsen, G. A. (1991). Adjustment of caregivers to depressed older adults. *Psychology and Aging, 6,* 631–639.

His Holiness the Dalai Lama, & Cutler, H. C. (1999). *The art of happiness: A handbook for living.* New York: Riverhead Books.

Hiscox, A. (1995). The art of West Indian clients: Art therapy as a nonverbal modality. *Art Therapy, 12,* 129–131.

Hiscox, A. R., & Calish, A. C. (Eds.). (1998). *Tapestry of cultural issues in art therapy.* Philadelphia: Jessica Kingly.

Ho, C. K. (1990). An analysis of domestic violence in Asian American communities: A multicultural approach to counseling. In L. S. Brown, & M. P. P. Root (Eds.), *Diversity and complexity in feminist therapy* (pp. 129–150). Binghamton, NY: Haworth Press.

Ho, M. K. (1987). *Family therapy with ethnic minorities.* Newbury Park, CA: Sage.

Hogan, J. D. (1995). International psychology in the next century: Comment and speculation from a U.S. perspective. *World Psychology, 1,* 9–25.

Holiman, M., & Lauver, P. J. (1987). The counselor culture and client-centered practice. *Counselor Education and Supervision, 26,* 184–191.

Hong, G. K. (1988). A general family practitioner approach for Asian American mental health services. *Professional Psychology: Research and Practice, 19,* 600–605.

Hooks, B. (1998). Feminism: A transformational politic. In P. S. Rothenberg (Ed.), *Race, class, and gender in the United States* (pp. 579–586). New York: St. Martin's Press.

Hopson, R. E. (1996). The 12-step program. In E. P. Shafranske (Ed.), *Religion and the clinical practice of psychology* (pp. 533–558). Washington, DC: American Psychological Association.

Hoshino, J. (in press). Multicultural art therapy with families. In C. Malchiodi (Ed.), *Clinical handbook of art therapy.* New York: Guilford Press.

Hughes, C. C. (1998). The glossary of "culture-bound syndromes" in DSM-IV: A critique. *Transcultural Psychiatry, 35*, 413–421.

Hulnick, M. R., & Hulnick, H. R. (1989). Life's challenges: Curse or opportunity? Counseling families of persons with disabilities. *Journal of Counseling and Development, 68*, 166–170.

Hussian, R. A. (1981). *Geriatric psychology: A behavioral perspective*. New York: Van Nostrand Reinhold.

Hussian, R. A. (1985). *Responsive care: Behavioral interventions with elderly persons*. Champaign, IL: Research Press.

Iijima Hall, C. C. (1997). Cultural malpractice: The growing obsolescence of psychology with the changing U.S. population. *American Psychologist, 52*, 642–651.

Irish, D. P., Lundquist, K. F., & Nelsen, V. J. (1993). *Ethnic variations in dying, death, and grief: Diversity in universality*. Washington, D.C.: Taylor & Francis.

Itai, G., & McRae, C. (1994). Counseling older Japanese American clients: An overview and observations. *Journal of Counseling and Development, 72*, 373377.

Ivey, A. E., Ivey, M. B., & Simek-Morgan, L. (1993). *Counseling and psychotherapy: A multicultural perspective*. Needham Heights, MA: Simon & Schuster.

Iwamasa, G. (1997). Behavior therapy and a culturally diverse society: Forging an alliance. *Behavior Therapy, 28*, 347–358.

Iwamasa, G., & Smith, S. K. (1996). Ethnic diversity and behavioral psychology: A review of the literature. *Behavior Modification, 20*, 45–59.

Jensen, J. P., & Bergin, A. E. (1988). Mental health values of professional therapists: A national interdisciplinary survey. *Professional Psychology: Research and Practice, 19*, 290–297.

Jewell, D. A. (1989). Cultural and ethnic issues. In S. Wetzler & M. M. Katz (Eds.), *Contemporary approaches to psychological assessment* (pp. 299–309). New York: Brunner/Mazel.

Jilek, W. G. (1994). Traditional healing in the prevention and treatment of alcohol and drug abuse. *Transcultural Psychiatric Research Review, 31*, 219–258.

Johnson, S. D. (1990). Toward clarifying culture, race, and ethnicity in the context of multicultural counseling. *Journal of Multicultural Counseling and Development, 18*, 41–50.

Johnson, W. B., & Ridley, C. R. (1992). Brief Christian and non-Christian rational-emotive therapy with depressed Christian clients: An exploratory study. *Counseling and Values, 36*, 220–229.

Johnson-Powell, G. (1997). The culturologic interview: Cultural, social, and linguistic issues in the assessment and treatment of children. In G. Johnson-Powell & J. Yamamoto (Eds.), *Transcultural child development: Psychological assessment and treatment* (pp. 349–364). New York: John Wiley & Sons.

Johnson-Powell, G., & Yamamoto, J. (Eds.). (1997). *Transcultural child development: Psychological assessment and treatment*. New York: John Wiley & Sons.

Jones, E. (1974). Social class and psychotherapy: A critical review of research. *Psychiatry, 37*, 307–320.

Jones, E. E. (1987). Psychotherapy and counseling with Black clients. In P. Pedersen (Ed.), *Handbook of cross-cultural counseling and psychotherapy* (pp. 173–179). New York: Praeger.

Jones, R. L. (Ed.). (1996). *Handbook of tests and measurements for Black populations.* Hampton, VA: Cobb & Henry.

Kahn, R. L., Goldfarb, A., Pollack, M., & Peck, A. (1960). Brief objective measures for the determination of mental status in the aged. *American Journal of Psychiatry, 117,* 326–328.

Kail, R. V., & Cavanaugh, J. C. (2000). *Human development: A lifespan view.* Belmont, CA: Wadsworth.

Kamphaus, R. W., Petoskey, M. D., & Rowe, E. W. (2000). Current trends in psychological testing of children. *Professional Psychology: Research and Practice, 31,* 155–164.

Kantrowitz, R. E., & Ballou, M. (1992). A feminist critique of cognitive-behavioral therapy. In L. S. Brown & M. Ballou (Eds.), *Personality and psychopathology: Feminist appraisals* (pp. 70–87). New York: Guilford Press.

Kanuha, V. (1994). Women of color in battering relationships. In L. Comas-Díaz & B. Greene (Eds.), *Women of color: Integrating ethnic and gender identities in psychotherapy* (pp. 428–454). New York: Guilford Press.

Kaplan, M. (1983). A woman's view of the DSM-III. *American Psychologist, 38,* 786–792.

Kaslow, F. (1993). Relational diagnosis: An idea whose time has come? *Family Process, 32,* 255–259.

Kaufert, J. M., & Shapiro, E. (1996). Cultural, linguistic and contextual factors in validating the mental status questionnaire: The experience of Aboriginal elders in Manitoba. *Transcultural Psychiatric Research Review, 33,* 277–296.

Kelly, E. W., Jr. (1995). *Spirituality and religion in counseling and psychotherapy.* Alexandria, VA: American Counseling Association.

Kelly, E. W., Jr., Aridi, A., & Bakhtiar, L. (1996). Muslims in the United States: An exploratory study of universal and mental health values. *Counseling and Values, 40,* 206–218.

Kemp, N. T., & Mallinckrodt, B. (1996). Impact of professional training on case conceptualization of clients with a disability. *Professional Psychology: Research and Practice, 27,* 378–385.

Kenny, C. B. (1989). *The field of play: A guide for the theory and practice of music therapy.* Atascadero, CA: Ridgeview.

Kidd, R. (1997). *The way we civilise: Aboriginal affairs—the untold story.* St. Lucia, Queensland, Australia: University of Queensland Press.

Kim, B. L. C. (1996). Korean families. In M. McGoldrick, J. Giordano, & J. K. Pearce (Eds.), *Ethnicity and family therapy* (pp. 281–294). New York: Guilford Press.

Kim, B. S. K. (1996). The Korean Americans. In P. B. Pedersen & D. C. Locke (Eds.), *Cultural and diversity issues in counseling* (pp. 47–50). Greensboro, NC: School of Education, University of North Carolina at Greensboro ERIC Counseling and Student Services Clearinghouse, ERIC no. ED400486.

Kim, S. C. (1985). Family therapy for Asian Americans: A strategic structural framework. *Psychotherapy, 22,* 342–348.

Kim, W. J., Kim, L. I., & Rue, D. S. (1997). Korean American children. In G. Johnson-Powell & J. Yamamoto (Eds.), *Transcultural child development: Psychological assessment and treatment* (pp. 182–207). New York: John Wiley & Sons.

Kimmel, M. S., & Messner, M. (Eds.). (1992). *Men's lives.* New York: Macmillan.

Kinzie, J. D., Manson, S. M., Vinh, D. T., Tolan, N. T., Anh, B., & Pho, T. N. (1982). Development and validation of a Vietnamese-language depression rating scale. *American Journal of Psychiatry, 139,* 1276–1281.

Kirmayer, L. J. (1998). Editorial: The fate of culture and DSM-IV. *Transcultural Psychiatry, 35,* 339–342.

Kiselica, M. S. (1998). Preparing Anglos for the challenges and joys of multiculturalism. *Counseling Psychologist, 26,* 5–21.

Kleinman, A. M. (1980). *Patients and healers in the context of culture.* Berkeley: University of California Press.

Kluckhohn, F., & Strodtbeck, F. (1961). *Variations in value orientations.* Evanston, IL: Row, Peterson.

Koss, J. (1980). The therapist-spiritist training project in Puerto Rico: An experiment to relate the traditional healing system to the public health system. *Social Science and Medicine, 14B,* 255–266.

Kroeber, A. L., & Kluckhohn, F. R. (1952). *Culture: Critical review of concepts and definitions* (Vol. 1, No. 1). Cambridge, MA: Peabody Museum.

Krueger, D. (Ed.). (1984). *Rehabilitation psychology: A comprehensive textbook.* Rockville, MD: Aspen Systems.

Kubiszyn, T. W., Meyer, G., J., Finn, S. E., Eyde, L. D., Kay, G. G., Moreland, K. L., Dies, R. R., & Eisman, E. J. (2000). Empirical support for psychological assessment in clinical health care settings. *Professional Psychology: Research and Practice, 31,* 119–130.

Kuehlwein, K. T. (1992). Working with gay men. In A. Freemen & F. M. Dattilio (Eds.), *Comprehensive casebook of cognitive therapy* (pp. 249–255). New York: Plenum Press.

LaFromboise, T. D., Berman, J. S., & Sohi, B. K. (1994). American Indian women. In L. Comas-Díaz & B. Greene (Eds.), *Women of color: Integrating ethnic and gender identities in psychotherapy* (pp. 30–71). New York: Guilford Press.

LaFromboise, T. D., & Rowe, W. (1983). Skills training for bicultural competence: Rationale and application. *Journal of Counseling Psychology, 30,* 589–595.

LaFromboise, T. D., Trimble, J. E., & Mohatt, G. V. (1993). Counseling intervention and American Indian tradition: An integrative approach. In D. R. Atkinson, G. Morten, & D. W. Sue (Eds.), *Counseling American minorities* (pp. 145–170). Dubuque, IA: W.C. Brown.

Lai, M. C., & Yue, K. M. K. (1990). The Chinese. In N. Waxler-Morrison, J. Anderson, & E. Richardson (Eds.), *Cross-cultural caring: A handbook for health professionals* (pp. 68–90). Vancouver, British Columbia, Canada: University of British Columbia Press.

Laing, R. D. (1965). *The divided self: An existential study in sanity and madness.* Baltimore: Penguin.

Lamott, A. (1994). *Bird by bird.* New York: Doubleday.

Landau, J. (1982). Therapy with families in cultural transition. In M. McGoldrick, J. K. Pearce, & J. Giordano (Eds.), *Ethnicity and family therapy* (pp. 552–572). New York: Guilford Press.

Langness, L. (1976). Hysterical psychoses and possessions. In W. P. Lebra (Ed.), *Mental health research in Asia and South Pacific: Vol. 4. Culture-bound syndromes, ethnopsychiatry, and alternate therapies,* (pp. 56–67). Honolulu: University Press of Hawaii.

Lazarus, A. A. (1985). *Casebook of multimodal therapy.* New York: Guilford Press.

Lazarus, A. A. (1997). *Brief but comprehensive psychotherapy the multimodal way.* New York: Springer.

Lazarus, A. A., & Beutler, L. E. (1993). On technical eclecticism. *Journal of Counseling & Development, 71,* 381–385.

Lebra, W. P. (Ed.). (1976). *Mental health research in Asia and South Pacific: Vol. 4. Culture-bound syndromes, ethnopsychiatry, and alternate therapies.* Honolulu: University Press of Hawaii.

Lee, C. (1997). *Multicultural issues and counseling: New approaches to diversity.* Alexandria, VA: American Counseling Association.

Lee, E. (Ed.). (1997). *Working with Asian Americans: A guide for clinicians.* New York: Guilford Press.

Lee, H. B., & Gong, Y. (1996). Clinical psychological services in China: Professional issues and cultural considerations. *World Psychology, 2,* 153–175.

Leigh, I. W., Corbett, C. A., Gutman, V., & Morere, D. A. (1996). Providing psychological services to deaf individuals: A response to new perceptions of diversity. *Professional Psychology: Research and Practice, 27,* 364–371.

Lemma, A. (2000). *Humour on the couch.* Philadelphia: Whurr.

LeVine, E. S., & Padilla, A. M. (1980). *Crossing cultures in therapy: Pluralistic counseling for the Hispanic.* Monterey, CA: Brooks/Cole.

Levine, M. (1998). Prevention and community. *American Journal of Community Psychology, 26,* 189–206.

Lewinsohn, P. M., Teri, L. & Hautzinger, M. (1984). Training clinical psychologists for work with older adults: A working model. *Professional Psychology: Research and Practice, 15,* 187–202.

Lewis, J. A., Dana, R. Q., & Blevins, G. A. (1994). *Substance abuse counseling: An individualized approach.* Pacific Grove, CA: Brooks/Cole.

Lewis, M. I., & Butler, R. N. (1974). Life review therapy: Putting memories to work in individual and group psychotherapy. *Geriatrics, 29,* 165–169.

Lewis-Fernández, R. (1996). Cultural formulation of psychiatric diagnosis. *Culture, Medicine and Psychiatry, 20,* 133–144.

Lezak, M. (1995). *Neuropsychological assessment.* New York: Oxford University Press.

Lin, K., Poland, R., Chang, S., & Chang, W. (1995). Psychopharmacology for the Chinese: Cross-ethnic perspectives. In T. Lin, W. Tseng, & E. Yeh (Eds.), *Chinese societies and mental health* (pp. 308–314). Hong Kong: Oxford University Press

Lin, K., Poland, R., & Nakasaki, G. (Eds.). (1993). *Psychopharmacology and psychobiology of ethnicity.* Washington, DC: American Psychiatric Association.

Lindsey, M. L. (1998). Culturally competent assessment of African American clients. *Journal of Personality Assessment, 70,* 43–53.

Locke, D. C., & Kiselica, M. S. (1999). Pedagogy of possibilities: Teaching about racism in multicultural counseling courses. *Journal of Counseling and Development, 77,* 80–86.

López, S. R., Grover, K. P., Holland, D., Johnson, M. J., Kain, C. D., Kanel, K., Mellins, C. A., & Rhyne, M. C. (1989). Development of culturally sensitive psychotherapists. *Professional Psychology: Research and Practice, 20,* 369–376.

Louw, D. A. (1995). Psychology in South Africa: Old problems and new challenges. *World Psychology, 1,* 69–82.

Lovinger, R. (1984). *Working with religious issues in therapy.* Northvale, NJ: Jason Aronson.

Lovinger, R. (1996). Considering the religious dimension in assessment and treatment. In E. P. Shafranske (Ed.), *Religion and the clinical practice of psychology* (pp. 327–364). Washington, DC: American Psychological Association.

Mahrer, A. R., & Gervaise, P. A. (1994). What strong laughter in psychotherapy is and how it works. In H. Strean (Ed.), *The use of humor in psychotherapy* (pp. 209–222). Northvale, NJ: Jason Aronson.

Maki, D. R., & Riggar, T. F. (Eds.). (1997a). *Rehabilitation counseling.* New York: Springer.

Maki, D. R., & Riggar, T. F. (1997b). Rehabilitation counseling: Concepts and paradigms. In D. R. Maki & T. F. Riggar (Eds.), *Rehabilitation counseling* (pp. 3–31). New York: Springer.

Manson, S., & Kleinman, A. (1998). DSM-IV, culture and mood disorders: A critical reflection on recent practice. *Transcultural Psychiatry, 35,* 377–386.

Mapes, L. V. (1998, August 2). Fruit pickers' summer of squalor: Migrant workers in Washington. *Seattle Times,* pp. A1, A14, A15.

Maracle, B. (1994). *Crazywater: Native voices on addiction and recovery.* Toronto, Canada: Penguin.

Marsella, A. J. (1980). Depressive affect and disorder across cultures. In H. Triandis & J. Draguns (Eds.), *Handbook of cross-cultural psychology* (Vol. 5, pp. 237–289). Boston: Allyn & Bacon.

Marsella, A. J. (1998). Toward a "global-community psychology." *American Psychologist, 53,* 1282–1291.

Marsella, A. J., Bornemann, T., Ekblad, S., & Orley J. (1994). *Amidst peril and pain: The mental health and well-being of the world's refugees.* Washington, DC: American Psychological Association.

Marsella, A. J., Kaplan, A., & Suárez, E. (in press). Cultural considerations for understanding, assessing, and treating depressive experience and disorder. In M. Reinecke & B. Cohler (Eds.), *Comparative treatments of depression.* New York: Springer.

Marsella, A. J., & Yamada, A. M. (2000). Culture and mental health: An introduction and overview of foundations, concepts, and issues. In I. Cuéllar & F. Paniagua (Eds.), *The handbook of multicultural mental health: Assessment and treatment of diverse populations* (pp. 3–24). New York: Academic Press.

Martin, A. (1982). Some issues in the treatment of gay and lesbian patients. *Psychotherapy Theory, Research, and Practice, 19,* 341–348.

Martínez, E. A. (1999). Mexican American/Chicano families. In H. P. McAdoo (Ed.), *Family ethnicity* (pp. 121–134). Thousand Oaks, CA: Sage.

Matheson, L. (1986). If you are not an Indian, how do you treat an Indian? In H. P. Lefley, & P. Pedersen (Eds.), *Cross-cultural training for mental health professionals* (pp. 115–130). Springfield, IL: Charles C. Thomas.

Maton, K. (2000). Making a difference: The social ecology of social transformation (1999 Division 27 presidential address). *American Journal of Community Psychology, 28,* 25–57.

Matsui, W. T. (1996). Japanese families. In M. McGoldrick, J. Giordano, & J. K. Pearce (Eds.), *Ethnicity and family therapy* (pp. 268–280). New York: Guilford Press.

McAdoo, H. P. (1978). Factors related to stability in upwardly mobile Black families. *Journal of Marriage and the Family, 40,* 761–776.

McAdoo, H. P. (Ed.). (1999). *Family ethnicity.* Thousand Oaks, CA: Sage.

McCarn, S. R., & Fassinger, R. E. (1996). Revising sexual minority identity formation: A new model of lesbian identity and its implications for counseling and research. *Counseling Psychologist, 24,* 508–534.

McClanahan, A. J. (1986). *Our stories, our lives.* Anchorage, AK: Cook Inlet Region, Inc.

McGoldrick, M. (1998). Introduction. In M. McGoldrick (Ed.), *Re-visioning family therapy: Race, culture, and gender in clinical practice* (pp. 3–19). New York: Guilford Press.

McGoldrick, M., Anderson, C. M., & Walsh, F. (Eds.). (1989). *Women in families: A framework for family therapy.* New York: Norton.

McGoldrick, M., & Gerson, R. (1985). *Genograms in family assessment.* New York: Norton.

McGoldrick, M., & Giordano, J. (1996). Overview: Ethnicity and family therapy. In M. McGoldrick, J. Giordano, & J. K. Pearce (Eds.), *Ethnicity and family therapy* (pp. 1–30). New York: Guilford Press.

McGoldrick, M., Giordano, J. & Pearce, J. K. (Eds.). (1996). *Ethnicity and family therapy.* New York: Guilford Press.

McGoldrick, M., & García-Preto, N. G. (1984). Ethnic intermarriage: Implications for therapy. *Family Process, 23,* 347–364.

McGuire, P. A. (1999). Therapists see new sense in use of humor. *APA Monitor, 30*(3), 1.

McIntosh, P. (1998). White privilege and male privilege: A personal account of coming to see correspondence through work in women's studies. In M. L. Anderson & P. H. Collins (Eds.), *Race,* *class and gender: An anthology* (pp. 94–105). New York: Wadsworth.

McNiff, S. (1986). *Educating the creative arts therapist.* Springfield, IL: Charles C. Thomas.

Merriam-Webster. (1983). *Webster's ninth new collegiate dictionary.* Springfield, MA: Author.

Miller, W. R. (Ed.). (1999). *Integrating spirituality into treatment: Resources for practitioners.* Washington, DC: American Psychological Association.

Minton, B. A., & Soule, S. (1990). Two Eskimo villages assess mental health strengths and needs. *American Indian and Alaska Native Mental Health Research, 4,* 7–24.

Minuchin, S. (1974). *Family and family therapy.* Cambridge, MA: Harvard University Press.

Mio, J. (1989). Experiential involvement as an adjunct to teaching cultural sensitivity. *Journal of Multicultural Counseling and Development, 17,* 38–47.

Moghaddam, F. M. (1990). Modulative and generative orientations in psychology: Implications for psychology in the three worlds. *Journal of Social Issues, 46,* 21–41.

Moore Hines, P., & Boyd-Franklin, N. (1996). African American families. In M. McGoldrick, J. Giordano, & J. K. Pearce (Eds.), *Ethnicity and family therapy* (pp. 66–84). New York: Guilford Press.

Morales, E. S. (1992). Counseling Latino gays and Latina lesbians. In S. H. Dworkin & F. J. Gutiérrez (Eds.), *Counseling gay men and lesbians: Journey to the end of the rainbow* (pp. 125–140). Alexandria, VA: American Counseling Association.

Morales, P. (1999). The impact of cultural differences in psychotherapy with older clients: Sensitive issues and strategies. In M. Duffy (Ed.), *Handbook of counseling and psychotherapy with older adults* (pp. 132–153). New York: John Wiley & Sons.

Morgan, L. (Ed.). (1979). *Alaska's Native people*. Anchorage: Alaska Geographic Society.

Morris, E. (2000). Assessment practices with African Americans: Combining standard assessment measures within an Africentric orientation. In R. H. Dana (Ed.), *Handbook of cross-cultural and multicultural personality assessment* (pp. 573–604). Mahwah, NJ: Erlbaum.

Muecke, M. (1983a). Caring for Southeast Asian refugee patients in the USA. *American Journal of Public Health, 73*, 431–437.

Muecke, M. (1983b). In search of healers—Southeast Asian refugees in the American health care system. *Western Journal of Medicine: Cross-Cultural Medicine, 139*, 835–840.

Murgatroyd, W. (1996). Counseling Buddhist clients. In P. B. Pedersen & D. C. Locke (Eds.), *Cultural and diversity issues in counseling* (pp. 69–72). Greensboro, NC: School of Education, University of North Carolina at Greensboro (ERIC Counseling and Student Services Clearinghouse, ERIC no. ED400486).

Murray, H. A. (1943). *The Thematic Apperception Test*. Cambridge, MA: Harvard University Press.

Myers, L. J., Speight, S. L., Highlen, P. S., Cox, C. I., Reynolds, A. L., Adams, E. M., & Hanley, C. P. (1991). Identity development and worldview: Toward an optimal conceptualization. *Journal of Counseling in Development, 70*, 54–63.

National Institute of Health Consensus Development Panel on Depression in Late Life. (1992). Diagnosis and treatment of depression in late life. *Journal of the American Medical Association, 268*, 1018–1024.

Newman, B. M., & Newman, P. R. (1999). *Development through life: A psychosocial approach*. Belmont, CA: Wadsworth.

Newton, N. A., & Jacobowitz, J. (1999). Transferential and countertransferential processes in therapy with older adults. In M. Duffy (Ed.), *Handbook of counseling and psychotherapy with older adults* (pp. 21–40). New York: John Wiley & Sons.

Nichols, D. S., Padilla, J., & Gomez-Macqueo, E. L. (2000). Issues in the cross-cultural adaptation and use of the MMPI-2. In R. H. Dana (Ed.), *Handbook of cross-cultural and multicultural personality assessment* (pp. 247–266). Mahwah, NJ: Earlbaum.

Nordhus, I. H., VandenBos, G. R., Berg, S., & Fromholt, P. (1998). *Clinical geropsychology*. Washington, DC: American Psychological Association.

Novas, H. (1994). *Everything you need to know about Latino history*. New York: Plume/Penguin.

Okazaki, S. (1998). Psychological assessment of Asian Americans: Research agenda for cultural competency. *Journal of Personality Assessment, 70*, 54–70.

Okazaki, S., & Sue, S. (1995). Cultural considerations in psychological assessment of Asian Americans. In J. N. Butcher (Ed.), *Clinical personality assessment: Practical approaches* (pp. 107–119). New York: Oxford University Press.

Olkin, R. (1999). *What psychotherapists should know about disability*. New York: Guilford Press.

Olson, H. A. (1994). The use of humor in psychotherapy. In H. Strean (Ed.),

The use of humor in psychotherapy (pp. 195–198). Northvale, NJ: Jason Aronson.

Pack-Brown, S. P. (1999). Racism and white counselor training: Influence of white racial identity theory and research. *Journal of Counseling and Development, 77,* 87–92.

Paniagua, F. A. (1998). *Assessing and treating culturally diverse clients.* Thousand Oaks, CA: Sage.

Pargament, K. (1996). Religious methods of coping: Resources for the conservation and transformation of significance. In E. P. Shafranske (Ed.), *Religion and the clinical practice of psychology* (pp. 215–239). Washington, DC: American Psychological Association.

Pauwels, A. (1995). *Cross-cultural communication in the health sciences: Communicating with migrant patients.* Melbourne, Australia: Macmillan Education Australia.

Pearlman, S. F. (1996). Loving across race and class divides: Relational challenges and the interracial lesbian couple. *Women and Therapy: 19,* 25–35.

Pedersen, P. (1987). Ten frequent assumptions of cultural bias in counseling. *Journal of Multicultural Counseling and Development, 15,* 16–24.

Pedersen, P. (1990). The constructs of complexity and balance in multicultural counseling theory and practice. *Journal of Counseling and Development, 68,* 550–554.

Pedersen, P., Fukuyama, M., & Heath, A. (1989). Client, counselor, and contextual variables in multicultural counseling. In P. B. Pedersen, J. G. Draguns, W. J. Lonner, & J. E. Trimble (Eds.), *Counseling across cultures* (pp. 23–52). Honolulu: University of Hawaii Press.

Pérez Foster, R. (1996). What is the multicultural perspective for psychoanalysis? In R. Pérez Foster, M. Moskowitz, & R. A. Javier (Eds.), *Reaching across boundaries of culture and class: Widening the scope of psychotherapy* (pp. 3–20). Northvale, NJ: Jason Aronson.

Phinney, J. S. (1996). When we talk about American ethnic groups, what do we mean? *American Psychologist, 51,* 918–927.

Piercy, F., Soekandar, A., & Limansubroto, C. D. M. (1996). Indonesian families. In M. McGoldrick, J. K. Pearce, & J. Giordano (Eds.), *Ethnicity and family therapy* (pp. 333–346). New York: Guilford Press.

Piotrowski, C., Belter, R. W., & Keller, J. W. (1998). The impact of "managed care" on the practice of psychological testing: Preliminary findings. *Journal of Personality Assessment, 70,* 441–447.

Pires, A. A. (2000). National norms for the Rorschach Normative Study in Portugal. In R. H. Dana (Ed.), *Handbook of cross-cultural and multicultural personality assessment* (pp. 367–392). Mahwah, NJ: Lawrence Erlbaum.

Pollard, R. Q., Jr. (1996). Professional psychology and deaf people. *American Psychologist, 51,* 389–396.

Ponterotto, J. G. (1987). Counseling Mexican Americans: A multimodal approach. *Journal of Counseling and Development, 65,* 308–312.

Ponterotto, J. G., Alexander, C. M., & Hinkston, J. A. (1988). Afro-American preferences for counselor characteristics: A replication and extension. *Journal of Counseling Psychology, 35,* 175–182.

Ponterotto, J. G., & Casas, J. M. (1991). *Handbook of racial/ethnic minority counseling research.* Springfield, IL: Charles C Thomas.

Pope, M. (1995). The "salad bowl" is big enough for us all: An argument for the inclusion of lesbians and gay men in any definition of multiculturalism. *Journal of Counseling and Development, 73,* 301–304.

Prerost, F. J. (1994). Humor as an intervention strategy. In H. Strean (Ed.), *The use of humor in psychotherapy* (pp. 139–147). Northvale, NJ: Jason Aronson.

Primedia. (2000). *The world almanac and book of facts 2000.* Mahwah, NJ: Author.

Prochaska, J. O., & Norcross, J. C. (1994). *Systems of psychotherapy: A transtheoretical analysis.* Pacific Grove, CA: Brooks/Cole.

Pukui, M. K., Haertig, E. W., & Lee, C. A. (1972). *Nana I Ke Kumu (Look to the source)* (Vol. 1). Honolulu, HI: Queen Lili'uokalani Children's Center.

Pullar, G. L. (1996). Indigenous identity on Kodiak Island. In P. Rennick (Ed.), *Native cultures in Alaska* (p. 31). Anchorage: Alaska Geographic Society.

Rao, K. R. (1988). Psychology of transcendence: A study in early Buddhistic psychology. In A. C. Paranjpe, D. Y. F. Ho, & R. W. Rieber (Eds.), *Asian contributions to psychology* (pp. 123–148). New York: Praeger.

Rastogi, M., & Wampler, K. S. (1998). Couples and family therapy with Indian families: Some structural and intergenerational considerations. In U. P. Gielen & A. L. Comunian (Eds.), *The family and family therapy in international perspective* (pp. 257–274). Italy: Edizioni Lint Trieste.

Raven, J. C. (1960). *Guide to the Standard Progressive Matrices.* London: H. K. Lewis.

Reddy, P., Knowles, A., & Reddy, S. (1995). Language issues in cross-cultural testing. *Australian Psychologist, 30,* 27–29.

Rennick, P. (1996). *Native cultures in Alaska.* Anchorage, AK: The Alaska Geographic Society.

Reynolds, A. L., & Pope, R. L. (1991). The complexities of diversity: Exploring multiple oppressions. *Journal of Counseling and Development, 70,* 174–180.

Reynolds, D. K. (1980). *The quiet therapies: Japanese pathways to personal growth.* Honolulu, HI: University of Hawaii Press.

Rezentes, W. C., III. (1996). *Ka Lama Kukui Hawaiian psychology: An introduction.* Honolulu, HI: 'A'ali'i Books.

Richardson, E. (1990). The Cambodians and Laotians. In N. Waxler-Morrison, J. Anderson, & E. Richardson (Eds.), *Cross-cultural caring: A handbook for health professionals* (pp. 11–35). Vancouver, British Columbia, Canada: University of British Columbia Press.

Richmond, J. (1999). Psychotherapy with the suicidal elderly: A family-oriented approach. In M. Duffy (Ed.), *Handbook of counseling and psychotherapy with older adults* (pp. 650–661). New York: John Wiley & Sons.

Robinson, T. L. (1999). The intersections of dominant discourses across race, gender, and other identities. *Journal of Counseling and Development, 77,* 73–79.

Robinson, T. L., & Howard-Hamilton, M. F. (2000). *The convergence of race, ethnicity, and gender: Multiple identities in counseling.* Columbus, OH: Merrill/Prentice-Hall.

Rogler, L. H., Cortes, D. E., & Malgady, R. G. (1991). Acculturation and mental health status among Hispanics. *American Psychologist, 46,* 585–597.

Root, M. P. P. (1996). The multiracial experience: Racial borders as a significant frontier in race relations. In M. P. P. Root (Ed.), *The multiracial experience: Racial borders as the new frontier* (pp. xiii–xxviii). Thousand Oaks, CA: Sage.

Rosenfelt, S., & Estes, L. (Producers), & Eyre, C. (Director). (1998). *Smoke Signals* [Film]. (Available from Miramax, 375 Greenwich St., Fl3, New York, NY 10013). [Release date, July 3, 1998.]

Rosenweig, M. R. (1999). Continuity and change in the development of psychology around the world. *American Psychologist, 54,* 252–259.

Ross, C. E., & Mirowski, J. (1984). Socially-desirable response and acquiescence in a cross-cultural survey of mental health. *Journal of Health and Social Behavior, 25,* 189–197.

Royce-Davis, J. (2000). The influence of spirituality on community participation and belonging: Christina's story. *Counseling and Values, 44,* 135–142.

Ruiz, R. A., & Padilla, A. M. (1979). Counseling Latinos. In D. R. Atkinson, G. Morton, & D. W. Sue (Eds.), *Counseling American minorities: A cross-cultural perspective.* Dubuque, IA: W. Brown.

Rumbaut, R. G. (1985). Mental health and the refugee experience: A comparative study of Southeast Asian refugees. In T. C. Owan (Ed.), *Southeast Asian mental health: Treatment, prevention, services, training, and research* (pp. 433–486). Rockville, MD: National Institute of Mental Health.

Rungta, S. A., Margolis, R. L., & Westwood, M. J. (1993). Training counselors to work with diverse populations: An integrated approach. *Canadian Journal of Counselling/Revue Canadienne de Counseling, 27,* 50–64.

Salameh, W. A. (1983). Humor in psychotherapy: Past outlooks, present status, and future frontiers. In P. E. McGhee, & J. H. Goldstein (Eds.), *Handbook of humor research* (Vol. 2) (pp. 61–88). New York: Springer-Verlag.

Samuda, R. J. (1998). *Psychological testing of American minorities: Issues and consequences.* Thousand Oaks, CA: Sage.

Sanders, K., Brockway, J. A., Ellis, B., Cotton, E. M., & Bredin, J. (1999). Enhancing mental health climates in hospitals and nursing homes: Collaboration strategies for medical and mental health staff. In M. Duffy (Ed.), *Handbook of counseling and psychotherapy with older adults* (pp. 335–349). New York: John Wiley & Sons.

Sang, B. E. (1992). Counseling and psychotherapy with midlife and older lesbians. In S. H. Dworkin & F. J. Gutiérrez (Eds.), *Counseling gay men and lesbians: Journey to the end of the rainbow* (pp. 35–48). Alexandria, VA: American Counseling Association.

Saravanabhavan, R. C., & Marshall, C. A. (1994). The older Native American with disabilities: Implications for providers of health care and human services. *Journal of Multicultural Counseling and Development, 22,* 182–194.

Sarwono, S. W. (1996). Psychology in Indonesia. *World Psychology, 2,* 177–196.

Schank, J. A., & Skovholt, T. M. (1997). Dual-relationship dilemmas of rural and small-community psychologists. *Professional Psychology: Research and Practice, 28,* 44–49.

Schoonmaker, C. (1993). Aging lesbians: Bearing the burden of triple shame. *Women and Therapy, 14,* 21–31.

Scogin, F. R. (1994). Assessment of depression in older adults: A guide for practitioners. In M. Storandt & G. R. VandenBos (Eds.), *Neuropsychological assessment of dementia and depression in older adults: A clinician's guide* (pp. 61–80). Washington, DC: American Psychological Association.

Shafranske, E. P. (Ed.). (1996). *Religion and the clinical practice of psychology.* Washington, DC: American Psychological Association.

Shapiro, E. R. (1995). Grief in family and cultural context: Learning from Latino families. *Cultural Diversity and Mental Health, 1,* 159–176.

Shapiro, M. B. (1970). Intensive assessment of the single case: An inductive-deductive approach. In P. Mittler (Ed.), *The psychological assessment of mental and physical handicaps* (pp. 645–666). London: Methuen.

Sims, J. M. (1996). The use of voice for assessment and intervention in couples therapy. *Women and Therapy, 19,* 61–77.

Sleek, S. (1998). Psychology's cultural competence, once 'simplistic,' now broadening. *APA Monitor, 29*(12), 1.

Smart, D. W., & Smart, J. F. (1997). DSM-IV and culturally sensitive diagnosis: Some observations for counselors. *Journal of Counseling and Development, 75,* 392–398.

Smith, A. (1997). Cultural diversity and the coming-out process. In B. Greene (Ed.), *Ethnic and cultural diversity among lesbian and gay men* (pp. 279–300). Thousand Oaks, CA: Sage.

Smith, D. S. (1995). Exploring the religious-spiritual needs of the dying. In M. T. Burke & J. G. Miranti (Eds.), *Counseling: The spiritual dimension* (pp. 177-182). Alexandria, VA: American Counseling Association.

Smith, H. (1991). *The world's religions.* New York: Harper Collins.

Smith, P. B., & Bond, M. H. (1999). *Social psychology across cultures.* Needham Heights, MA: Allyn & Bacon.

Snowden, L. R., & Cheung, F. K. (1990). Use of inpatient mental health services by members of ethnic minority groups. *American Psychologist, 45,* 347–355.

Spickard, P. R. (1992). The illogic of American racial categories. In M. P. P. Root (Ed.), *Racially mixed people in America* (pp. 12–23). Newbury Park, CA: Sage.

Spinks, J. A., & Kao, H. S. R. (1995). Hong Kong: A review of psychological research, education, and professional issues. *World Psychology, 1,* 71–105.

Stephan, W. G. (1989). A cognitive approach to stereotyping. In D. Bartal & C. Graumann (Eds.), *Stereotyping and prejudice* (pp. 37–57). New York: Springer-Verlag.

Sternberg, R. J., Wagner, R. K., & Okagaki, L. (1993). Practical intelligence: The nature and role of tacit knowledge in work and at school. In H. Reese & J. Puckett (Eds.), *Advances in life span development* (pp. 205–227). Hillsdale, NJ: Erlbaum.

Sternberg, R. J., Wagner, R. K., Williams, W. M., & Horvath, J. A. (1995). Testing common sense. *American Psychologist, 50,* 912–927.

Stevenson, H. C., & Renard, G. (1993). Trusting ole' wise owls: Therapeutic use of cultural strengths in African American families. *Professional Psychology: Research and Practice, 24,* 433–442.

Storandt, M., & VandenBos, G. R. (1994). *Neuropsychological assessment of dementia and depression in older adults: A clinician's guide.* Washington, DC: American Psychological Association.

Struwe, G. (1994). Training health and medical professionals to care for refugees: Issues and methods. In A. J. Marsella, T. Bornemann, S. Ekblad, & J. Orley (Eds.), *Amidst peril and pain: The mental health and well-being of the world's refugees* (pp. 311–326). Washington, DC: American Psychological Association.

Suárez, Z. E. (1999). Cuban-Americans in exile: Myths and reality. In H. P. McAdoo (Ed.), *Family ethnicity* (pp. 135–152). Thousand Oaks, CA: Sage.

Sue, D. W. (1993). Confronting ourselves: The white and racial/ethnic-minority researcher. *Counseling Psychologist, 21,* 244–249.

Sue, D. W., Arrendondo, P., & McDavis, R. J. (1992). Multicultural counseling competencies and standards: A call to the profession. *Journal of Counseling and Development, 70,* 477–486.

Sue, D. W., Ivey, A. E., & Pedersen, P. B. (1996). *A theory of multicultural counseling and therapy.* Pacific Grove, CA: Brooks/Cole.

Sue, D. W., & Sue, D. (1999). *Counseling the culturally different.* New York: John Wiley & Sons.

Sue, S. (1998). In search of cultural competence in psychotherapy and counseling. *American Psychologist, 53,* 440–448.

Sue, S., Fujino, D. C., Hu, L., Takeuchi, D. T., & Zane, N. (1991). Community mental health services for ethnic minority groups: A test of the cultural responsiveness hypothesis. *Journal of Consulting and Clinical Psychology, 59,* 533–540.

Sun, K. (1993). Two types of prejudice and their causes. (Letter to the editor). *American Psychologist, 48,* 1152–1153.

Sunar, D. (1996). An interview with Cigdem Kagitcibasi. *World Psychology, 2,* 139–152.

Sundberg, N. D., & Sue, D. (1989). Research and research hypotheses about effectiveness in intercultural counseling. In P. B. Pedersen, J. G. Draguns, W. J. Lonner, & J. E. Trimble (Eds.), *Counseling across cultures* (pp. 355–370). Honolulu: University of Hawaii Press.

Sussman, N. M., & Rosenfeld, H. M. (1982). Influence of culture, language and sex on conversational distance. *Journal of Personality and Social Psychology, 42,* 66–74.

Sutton, C. T., & Broken Nose, M. A. (1996). American Indian families: An overview. In M. McGoldrick, J. K. Pearce, & J. Giordano (Eds.), *Ethnicity and family therapy* (pp. 31–44). New York: Guilford Press.

Suzuki, L. A., & Kugler, J. F. (1995). Intelligence and personality assessment. In J. G. Ponterotto, J. M. Casas, L. A. Suzuki, & C. M. Alexander (Eds.), *Handbook of multicultural counseling* (pp. 493–515). Thousand Oaks, CA: Sage.

Suzuki, L. A., & Valencia, R. R. (1997). Race-ethnicity and measured intelligence: Educational implications. *American Psychologist, 52,* 1103–1114.

Swan Reimer, C. (1999). *Counseling the Inupiat Eskimo.* Westport, CT: Greenwood Press.

Swinomish Tribal Community. (1991). A gathering of wisdoms: *Tribal mental health: A cultural perspective.* LaConnor, WA: Author.

Szaz, T. S. (1961). *The myth of mental illness: Foundations of a theory of personal conduct.* New York: Dell.

Takaki, R. (1993). *A different mirror: A history of multicultural America.* Boston: Little, Brown.

Taylor, S. E., Kemeny, M. E., Reed, G. M., Bower, J. E., & Gruenewald, T. L.

(2000). Psychological resources, positive allusions, and health. *American Psychologist, 55,* 99–109.

Thomas, A., & Sillen, S. (1972). *Racism and psychiatry.* Toronto, Canada: Citadel Press.

Thornton, M. (1996). Hidden agendas, identity theories, and multiracial people. In M. P. P. Root (Ed.), *The multiracial experience* (pp. 101–120). Thousand Oaks, CA: Sage.

Tix, A. P., & Frazier, P. A. (1998). The use of religious coping during stressful life events: Main effects, moderation, and mediation. *Journal of Consulting and Clinical Psychology, 66,* 411–422.

Toubia, N. (Ed.). (1988). *Women of the Arab world.* London: Zed Press.

Triandis, H. C. (1996). The psychological measurement of cultural syndromes. *American Psychologist, 51,* 407–415.

Trimble, J. E., & Fleming, C. M. (1989). Providing counseling services for Native American Indians: Client, counselor, and community characteristics. In P. B. Pedersen, J. G. Draguns, W. J. Lonner, & J. E. Trimble (Eds.), *Counseling across cultures* (pp. 177–204). Honolulu: University of Hawaii Press.

Troiden, R. R. (1979). Becoming homosexual: A model of gay identity acquisition. *Psychiatry, 42,* 362–373.

Tsemberis, S. J., & Orfanos, S. D. (1996). Greek families. In M. McGoldrick, J. Pearce, & J. K. Giordano (Eds.), *Ethnicity and family therapy* (pp. 517–529). New York: Guilford Press.

Tseng, W. (1999). Culture and psychotherapy: Review and practical guidelines. *Transcultural Psychiatry, 36,* 131–179.

Turner, S. M., & Jones, R. T. (1982). *Behavior modification in Black populations.* New York: Plenum Press.

Uba, L. (1994). *Asian Americans: Personality patterns, identity, and mental health.* New York: Guilford Press.

Vasquez, M. J. T. (1994). Latinas. In L. Comas-Díaz & B. Greene (Eds.), *Women of color: Integrating ethnic and gender identities in psychotherapy* (pp. 114–138). New York: Guilford Press.

Vinet, E. V. (2000). The Rorschach Comprehensive System in Iberoamerica. In R. H. Dana (Ed.), *Handbook of cross-cultural and multicultural personality assessment* (pp.345–366). Mahwah, NJ: Lawrence Erlbaum.

Vontress, C. E., Johnson, J. A., & Epp, L. R. (1999). *Cross-cultural counseling: A casebook.* Alexandria, VA: American Counseling Association.

Wade, J. C. (1998). Male reference group identity dependence: A theory of male of identity. *Counseling Psychologist, 26,* 349–383.

Wadeson, H. (1980). *Art psychotherapy.* New York: John Wiley & Sons.

Walker, L. E. (Action Editor). (1999). International perspectives on domestic violence. *American Psychologist, 54,* 21–65.

Walker, L. E. (1999). Psychology and domestic violence around the world. *American Psychologist, 54,* 21–29.

Walsh, K. (1987). *Neuropsychology: A clinical approach.* New York: Churchill Livingstone.

Watt, S. K. (1999). The story between the lines: A thematic discussion of the experience of racism. *Journal of Counseling and Development, 77,* 54–61.

Waxler-Morrison, N. (1990). Introduction. In N. Waxler-Morrison, J. Anderson, & E. Richardson (Eds.), *Cross-cultural caring: A handbook for health professionals* (pp. 3–10). Vancouver, British Columbia, Canada: University of British Columbia Press.

Waxler-Morrison, N., Anderson, J., & Richardson, E. (Eds.). (1990). *Cross-cultural caring: A handbook for health professionals.* Vancouver, British Columbia, Canada: University of British Columbia Press.

Wechsler, D. (1997). *Wechsler adult intelligence scale—Third Edition.* New York: The Psychological Corp.

Wechsler, D. (1981). *Wechsler adult intelligence scale—Revised.* New York: The Psychological Corp.

Weeber, J. E. (1999). What can I know of racism? *Journal of Counseling and Development, 77,* 20–23.

Weiss, J. C. (1999). The role of art therapy in aiding older clients with life transitions. In M. Duffy (Ed.), *Handbook of counseling and psychotherapy with older adults* (pp. 182–196). New York: John Wiley & Sons.

West, C. (1993). *Race matters.* Boston: Beacon.

Westbrooks, K. (1995). *Functional low-income families.* New York: Vantage Press.

Westermeyer, J. (1987). Cultural factors in clinical assessment. *Journal of Consulting and Clinical Psychology, 55,* 471–478.

Westermeyer, J., & Janca, A. (1997). Language, culture and psychopathology: Conceptual and methodological issues. *Transcultural Psychiatry, 34,* 291–311.

Wilgosh, L., & Gibson, J. T. (1994). Cross-national perspectives on the role of assessment in counselling: A preliminary report. *International Journal for the Advancement of Counselling, 17,* 59–70.

Williams, C. B. (1999a). Claiming a biracial identity: Resisting social constructions of race and culture. *Journal of Counseling and Development, 77,* 32–35.

Williams, C. B. (1999b). *The Color of Fear and Blue-Eyed:* Tools for multicultural counselor training. *Counselor Education and Supervision, 39,* 76–79.

Winddance Twine, F. (1996). Heterosexual alliances: The romantic management of racial identity. In M. P. P. Root (Ed.), *The multiracial experience: Racial borders as the new frontier* (pp. 291–304). Thousand Oaks, CA: Sage.

Wohl, J., & Aponte, J. F. (2000). Common themes and future prospects for the twenty-first century. In J. F. Aponte & J. Wohl (Eds.), *Psychological intervention and cultural diversity* (pp. 286–300). Needham Heights, MA: Allyn & Bacon.

Wolfe, J. L. (1992). Working with gay women. In A. Freeman & F. M. Dattilio (Eds.), *Comprehensive casebook of cognitive therapy* (pp. 249–255). New York: Plenum Press.

Wood, P. S., & Mallinckrodt, B. (1990). Culturally sensitive assertiveness training for ethnic minority clients. *Professional Psychology: Research and Practice, 21,* 5–11.

Wrenn, G. C. (1962). The culturally encapsulated counselor. *Harvard Educational Review, 32,* 444–449.

Yamamoto, J., Silva, J. A., Ferrari, M., & Nukariya, K. (1997). Culture and psychopathology. In G. Johnson-Powell & J. Yamamoto (Eds.), *Transcultural child development: Psychological assessment and treatment* (pp. 34–57). New York: John Wiley & Sons.

Yee, A. H., Fairchild, H. H., Weizmann, F., & Wyatt, G. E. (1993). Addressing psychology's problems with race. *American Psychologist, 48,* 1132–1140.

Young, E. (1995). *Third World in the First: Development and indigenous peoples.* New York: Routledge.

Zarit, S. H., & Knight, B. G. (1996). *A guide to psychotherapy and aging*. Washington, DC: American Psychological Association.

Zinn, H. (1995). *The people's history of the United States: 1492–present*. New York: HarperPerennial.

Author Index

Subject Index

A

AA (Alcoholics Anonymous), 157–158
Aboriginal, 12
Abuse, domestic, 168–169
Acculturation, 99
Adapted therapies, for minority groups, 159–162
Address, form of, 74
ADDRESSING framework, 4–8, 192–194
    as Axis VI of *DSM-IV*, 136, 144–145, 193
    in case examples, 143, 144–145, 146, 181,
       182–183
    in clinician self-assessment, 36–38, 39,
       42–47, 49, 192
    countertransference and, 67–68
    in identity assessment, 61–64
    power differentials and, 169–170
    systems-level interventions and, 164
    within-group diversity and, 75
Affect, in BASIC-ID, 160
African American, 11
Age
    in ADDRESSING framework, 4, 5
    client history and, 94–97
    as cultural influence, 5
    DSM-IV and, 131–132
Alaska Natives, 14–15
Alcoholics Anonymous (AA), 157–158
American Indians
    spirituality, 159
    terms denoting, 12
American Psychological Association
    domestic violence, definition, 169
    ethnic minority data, 191
    standardized testing guidelines, 114
American Sign Language (ASL), 102
APA. *See* American Psychological Association
Art therapy, 162, 163
Asian, 12
ASL (American Sign Language), 102
Assertiveness skills training, 161
Assessment, 89–108
    client histories, 90–103
        acculturation measures, 99
        behavioral observations, 94
        family and others' input, 92–93
        language and interpreters in, 99–102
        medical and psychological input, 97–98

        multiple sources, 90–92, 193
        personal input, 94–97
        professional input, 93
        respect and rapport guidelines, 103
        in standardized testing, 118
    of client self-identity, 58–65
        assumptions in, 60–64
        identity meanings in, 64–65
        questions in, 58–60
    of client strengths, 103–106
    of clinician cultural identity. *See* Clinicians
    formal. *See* Standardized testing
    initial, case example, 178–181
    of unusual client beliefs and behaviors,
       106–108
Assistive devices, 80
Axis I, 137, 193
    in case examples, 144, 181–182
Axis II, 137, 193
    in case example, 144
Axis III, 136–137, 193
    in case examples, 144, 181, 182
Axis IV, 132–133, 136, 193
    in case examples, 144, 181, 182
Axis V, in case examples, 144, 182
Axis VI (proposed), 136, 193
    in case examples, 144–145, 181, 182–183

B

BASIC-ID model, 160
Behavior(s)
    in BASIC-ID, 160
    behavioral assessment, 94
    diagnostic trends, 97
    standardized assessment, 113
    unusual, of client, 106–108
Behavioral assessment, 94
Beliefs of client, unusual, 106–108
Bias
    individual, 22–23
    sociocultural, 23–25
    in standardized tests, 112–114
    in therapy values, 40
Bicultural competence, 160–161
Bicultural heritage, 56–58
Bisexual(s), 14, 55–56
Black, 11

About the Author

Pamela Hays completed a BA in Psychology and French at New Mexico State University, an MS in Counseling Psychology at the University of Alaska, a PhD in Clinical Psychology at the University of Hawaii, and an NIMH postdoctoral fellowship in geropsychology at the University of Rochester. Her research has included a study in North Africa of the impact of rapid social changes on Arab women's mental health and an investigation of the mental health needs of Vietnamese, Lao, and Cambodian refugees living in the United States. She is a licensed clinical psychologist who has worked in a variety of inpatient and outpatient settings, in the areas of rehabilitation, geriatrics, domestic violence, substance abuse, and individual and family therapy. Her articles on cognitive behavior therapy, couples therapy, older adults, and multicultural and feminist issues have appeared in *Professional Psychology: Research and Practice*, the *Journal of Counseling and Development*, the *International Journal of Psychology*, and *Women and Therapy*. From 1989 to 2000, she was a core faculty member of the graduate psychology program at Antioch University, Seattle. She is currently a psychologist at Central Peninsula Counseling Services in Kenai, Alaska, and continues to teach as an adjunct faculty at Antioch.